Walleye Tactics,
Tips & Tales

Walleye Tactics, Tips & Tales

Complete Angler's Library ®
North American Fishing Club
Minneapolis, Minnesota

Walleye Tactics, Tips & Tales

Copyright © 1990, North American Fishing Club

Library of Congress Catalog Card Number 90-60123
ISBN 0-914697-28-5

Printed in U.S.A.
                  15 16 17 18 19

Contents

Acknowledgments

Walleye Tactics, Tips & Tales will vault you years ahead of average walleye anglers. It contains the latest fish-catching tips from the nation's top walleye fishermen, with background information from leading biologists and boat rigging experts. It's the best walleye book on the market today.

The author would like to thank:

His wife Jeanne, who believed him when he said he could make a living without a regular job, and who picks him up when the hours get long and frustrating.

His mom and dad, who both fish a lot and who got him started.

Dan Nelson, a great walleye fisherman who always shares ideas, and who took tons of time to go over the outline and manuscript.

His sister Lynn, who drove countless miles and put up with unending minor adjustments while taking the photos.

Rick Wood, an inquisitive angler who fired questions and helped keep the operation going smoothly.

Terry Strand (no relation), who helped immeasurably during a long fact-finding and photo-shooting trip to the Dakota reservoirs.

Tolly, Byron and Kelly Holton of Indian Hills Resort on Lake Sakakawea. They did everything including catching fish, modeling for photographs, and offering valuable insights into the lake.

The greatest walleye researchers in the world, including Dr. Richard Ryder, Dennis Schupp, Don Pereira and Dr. Dwight Burkhardt.

The sharpest "technical" equipment experts in their fields, Jim Wentworth (electronics and boat rigging) and Ken and DeeAnn Persson (trailers).

The broadest collection of walleye fishing stars ever brought together; an all-star cast in every sense of the word (in alphabetical order, of course, because there's no way to place degrees of importance on their contributions): Jerry Anderson, Daryl Christensen, Dave Genz, Dave "Hot Tip" Jenson, Keith Kavajecz, Mike McClelland, Alan Meline, Tom Neustrom, Don Palmer, Gary Parsons, Bob Propst, Jim Randash, Gary Roach and Mick Thill.

Dick Sternberg, a brilliant fisheries researcher, for giving the author his first real look at the scientific side of walleye fishing. Dick originally pointed him to many of the research scientists he went back to for this book.

Thanks, also, to the NAFC staff members for their behind-the-scenes work: Publisher Mark LaBarbera, Managing Editor Steve Pennaz, Associate Editor Kurt Beckstrom, Senior Editorial Assistant Amy Mattson, Layout Artist Dean Peters, Vice President of Products Marketing Mike Vail, Marketing Manager Linda Kalinowski, and Marketing Project Coordinator Laura Resnik.

Jay Michael Strangis
Managing Editor
Complete Angler's Library

Photo Credits

Most of the photos in this book were provided by the author, with a few from Steve Pennaz. A special thanks goes to Mark Kayser with the South Dakota Department of Tourism for supplying a number of photos, and NAFC staff Layout Artist Dean Peters, who did the inside art.

About The Author

Mark Strand loves walleyes and spends much of his time chasing them in one fashion or another. As a sportsman, he's fished them in the nation's top walleye lakes, rivers and reservoirs in Michigan, Wisconsin, Minnesota, North and South Dakota, Washington, Missouri, Kansas, New York, Arkansas, Ontario and Manitoba, often sharing a boat with the finest walleye anglers in the world.

When he's not actually fishing for them, Mark loves to talk about walleyes, and through his discussions with biologists, researchers and top anglers, he's gathered insights that can help you better understand this mysterious fish.

Mark is a full-time free-lance writer and photographer with a journalism degree from the University of Minnesota, where he minored in fisheries and wildlife science. He worked for a time as a researcher for the Hunting & Fishing Library, and as a writer/photographer for Babe Winkelman Productions before going out on his own.

Success followed Mark into the free-lance arena, and he quickly became a respected and recognized member of the outdoor writers' fellowship. He holds active memberships in the Outdoor Writers Association of America and the Association of Great Lakes Outdoor Writers. His work has been published in the

Mark Strand

NAFC's official member publication, *North American Fisherman*, as well as *Fishing Facts, In-Fisherman, Walleye, Sports Afield* and *Field & Stream* magazines. He was also named Associate Editor of the new *Walleye In-Sider* publication.

The relatively new, but extremely popular, professional walleye tournament circuits have become Mark's pet interests. He's followed both the Masters Walleye Circuit tournament since it began in 1984, as well as the Cabela's/In-Fisherman Professional Walleye Tournament trail.

While Mark has certainly achieved professional success, he says there is one goal he's yet to attain as a walleye fisherman—bagging his first 10-pounder. Well, maybe now that this book is done...

Dedication

Even though this is a fishing book, I want to dedicate it with love, respect and admiration to my hunting partner, a black lab named Buddy. At only $5^1/_2$ years old, he died of a fungal infection while I was working on the manuscript. Sandy, our friend who happens to be his vet, did everything she could to save him. In such a short time, he became a part of everything my wife Jeanne and I did. He made us laugh, took us for long walks and led me to many, many birds. Now, as the finishing touches are put on this book, the cool breezes of a coming fall put an ache in my heart at the thought of an empty bird season. We'll miss you, Buddy.

Foreword

S cientists have for a long time recognized that people like or-der to their lives; in fact, they crave it. We want to put every-thing into a category and "sum it up."

We want rules to follow, road maps, recipes. It's no different with walleye fishing. We want a "pattern" or formula for catching more fish, faster—and the bigger the better.

So, we ask, where do walleyes go after they get done spawning? What's the best color for walleyes? Is it true that walleyes bite best at night? What's the best way to catch them?

The good walleye anglers, until recently, were mainly local or regional experts. As a result, there were many separate sets of ad-vice on how walleyes behaved, where they went, what it took to catch them.

Touring walleye professionals and the pressure of tournament competition have changed that. The Masters Walleye Circuit (MWC), formed in 1984, was the first tournament circuit de voted to walleye fishing. Its teams travel North America to many tournament sites, bringing with them an impressive variety of technique and experience. Even these anglers develop special-ties and biases. But when you put them all on the same body of water under identical conditions, rules get tossed aside. We learn that, on any given body of water, the traditional way of fishing isn't always best. Sometimes, but not always.

Like tournament golf professionals assaulting the local record at any course on the globe, walleye pros bring their versatility and refinements to every whistle stop. At the Detroit River in Michigan, for instance, conventional wisdom said you couldn't catch walleyes with anything lighter than a 1-ounce jig. In a matter of a few days, however, MWC fishermen were showing the locals how to slow the drift of a boat with motor control, and how to "chase their lines" to keep a vertical presentation with a $1/8$-ounce jig. Result? Impressive catches, by any local angler's standards.

If you were a mayfly hopping from boat to boat during the practice days for a walleye tournament, you might see:

• Gary Roach slowly working the 15- to 22-foot depths along mud flats with Roach (slip-sinker) rigs.

• Jerry Anderson working slip-bobbers in two to three feet of water along rocky structure.

• Gary Parsons and Keith Kavajecz "precision trolling" along the deep, featureless lake basin, with planer boards and crankbaits or live bait.

• Mike McClelland and Bob Propst working their way along scattered sand flats with bottom bouncers and nightcrawlers.

• Daryl Christensen pitching light jigs into five feet of water, letting waves wash the bait toward waiting walleyes.

Chances are, there would be only one common thread: Each entrant would catch at least a few walleyes. Granted, one of these "patterns" would hold the key to winning the tournament. Many anglers will fish several to give themselves options on the actual tournament days.

But what should these real-life, on-the-water experiences tell us, the average walleye anglers of the world? For one thing, you can count on fewer rules—even guidelines—about walleye movements and behavior. Some of the old sayings have merit, especially in the areas they were spawned. But we clearly need to keep our eyes open to other ways—even when faithful systems are producing fish.

"If you fish all day, or two full days, in the spots where walleyes are 'supposed' to be and you don't catch any, they're not there," says Daryl Christensen, the Montello, Wisconsin, native who is one of the rising stars of the MWC circuit. "Then, and this might sound weird, but you go looking where they aren't supposed to be, and it's amazing where you find them."

Let's toss out the "rules" about walleyes and walleye fishing. Let the fish come from where they are at the moment, on the lure or bait that makes them open their mouth. That's the purpose of this book—to open your eyes to the many ways you can catch walleyes.

Steve Pennaz
Executive Director
North American Fishing Club

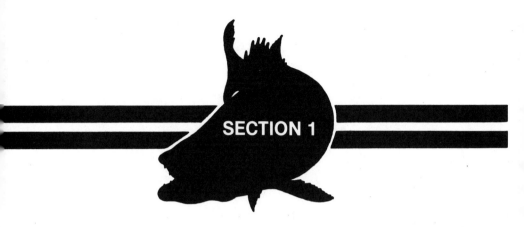

SECTION 1

Understanding Walleyes

1

Walleyes: What's The Appeal?

Arush of wind builds from nothing and draws our attention to the left, far down the open part of the lake. A single angler's silvery boat bobs in the early morning sun in rhythm with the little waves.

The lone angler shifts course with his electric motor, all the while staring at his depthfinder. He lifts and drops a small jig, feeling for the bottom. A barely perceptible tick on the line causes him to rear back and set the hook. From off the bottom, a stubborn weight resists being lifted from its holding spot. For a long time we watch him fight this fish. Finally, a golden shine flashes a circular swath in the darkness below and we see the white tip of a tail. It's a walleye!

Walleye fishing is undergoing radical changes. Yet much of what it takes to become a good walleye angler hasn't changed at all for years.

You probably picked this book up because you want to catch more walleyes. Can it help you achieve that goal? You bet! It contains the words of wisdom for today's finest walleye anglers; the tactics and tips you need to be *consistently* successful.

But stuffing this valuable information into your brain can only take you so far. With it, you can sound like a world champion on a bar stool, but experience is only gained on the water. Knowledge and experience are the keys to success.

"I've been fishing practically every day since I was five years old," says Jerry Anderson, who with partner Bruce Samson, won

Chunky walleyes can be difficult to locate consistently. They use a variety of cover at different depths. Diversity in fishing strategies is the key to finding them. This book will help you develop these strategies.

Masters Walleye Circuit (MWC) Team-of-the-Year honors. "In a lot of ways, fishing ability can be a time thing. You do need some athletic ability, like what we call 'soft hands' for detecting bites. But experience has been my key to success many times.

"I remember one river tournament where we had only mediocre fish going. As we started the second day of the three-day tournament, we were in about 50th place, just about out of it. So when we left the dock, I figured we would go along and hopefully something would develop," Anderson continued.

"Well, we hadn't gone a half mile out of the starting area and I was working a break when I found a turn and a point composed of clam beds that came up out of 30 feet of water. I was catching little pieces of clam shells on my jig so I turned around and told Bruce that this was the spot.

"We hadn't caught a fish, and I hadn't seen any on the locator yet, but we slayed 'em in there and that spot brought us all the way up to third place by the end of the day. Recognizing that spot for what it was, was nothing but learned ability."

Yes, with *small* matters like job and family biting into your fishing time, you probably can't shake loose 200 days a year to be

Nothing beats experience when it comes to boating trophy walleyes. The lessons learned while out on the water make all the difference.

on the water. Yet, this book will help you past a lot of the futility and trial–and–error methods most guys go through.

This book can vault you years into the future—if you use what is being presented. It will help you develop a mind–set that will make you as dangerous as Gary Roach or Bob Propst, even on unfamiliar waters.

Why Walleyes?

The appeal of many fish species is obvious. Largemouth bass are spectacular surface strikers that jump and tie your heart in knots. Salmon peel line from your reel faster than seems possible. Ditto for many saltwater fish.

But walleyes?

For many years, we've debated that one. They *are* glorious on the dinner table, no disputing that. Essays have been written about how good they are to eat. But as Hall of Fame angler Spence Petros says, so is pizza, and it's a lot easier to find.

In this humorous comment is hidden the essence of the appeal: Walleyes are hard to find, at least consistently. It's a game, accumulating little gadgets that make us better at playing them.

As anglers we have at our disposal an arsenal of products, if we could only afford them all! These products will help us find and catch walleyes, assuming we know how to use them. But alone, they are useless. We can spend our lifetime reading about walleyes, attending seminars by top walleye anglers, watching videos and practicing on the water. But we still don't feel like much of a match for this fish. There are so many ways to catch them.

"With walleyes, if what you're doing ain't working, you better try something else," says Dan Nelson, a tournament angler and writer who is at the forefront of all that is new and exciting about this fish. We have to find walleyes to catch them. As Mike McClelland, perhaps today's finest tournament walleye fisherman and theoretician, says, "You can't catch a fish that isn't there."

The weather strongly affects where walleyes go from day to day and season to season, and whether they bite well. And with that hypersensitive eye that causes them to shun bright light, they can see better at night than most other fish. So you can catch a lot of them on a night so dark you're afraid you'll fall out of the boat if you stand up. However, it's a puzzle that so many of today's best

Jerry Anderson has the experience to consistently catch walleyes in a wide variety of waters.

walleye fishermen catch most of their fish, at midday no less, from shallow water.

They're shallow. They're deep. They're in between, in the weeds, on the rocks, over the mud. We've learned so much, even in just the last few years. It's the whole chase thing, knowing something about walleyes, finding them, getting them to bite and guessing why they hit. Do we ever really know? If we catch some today, can we duplicate the feat tomorrow?

The pursuit of perfection is what drives so many of us. Achieving perfection in walleye fishing is always one more pattern or method away.

"The amount of thinking it takes to catch walleyes makes fishing for them a real mind-burner for me," says McClelland. "You don't have as many shallow-water visual aids for most walleye fishing as you do for some other species. You don't have the brush pile as with crappie fishing, you don't have the weeds or the boat docks like you do for largemouth bass. It takes a tremendous amount of thinking, assuming and creating the structure and the situations in your mind with your electronics. You just compute, relate back and assume what you are doing is right.

"I make constant assumptions when I'm walleye fishing," McClelland continues, "because we don't know the answers for sure. For instance, you see marks on a flasher or a graph and you assume they are walleyes, and a lot of times you don't even know for sure why you think they're walleyes."

There are subconscious reasons collected from past experiences that lead top walleye anglers to more walleyes. "The most important question walleye anglers have to ask themselves after they catch a fish is why," says McClelland. "Why did I catch it? Is there something different here? Did the bottom change? Was the fish relating to baitfish? Why was it there?"

That one question will keep you busy your entire walleye fishing life. "You think you have 'em figured out," says Nelson, "but they can go finicky on you so fast. There's no 'usual' way to catch them, and you have to do the little things right unless they're really snapping."

That, in large part, is the appeal of the walleye.

2

The New Walleye Angler

The original techniques and stories surrounding walleye fishing came from Canada and the north-central to northeastern United States, the original range of the walleye. It is estimated that 75 percent or more of all North American walleye waters are in Canada and that of these, 90 percent are on the Precambrian Shield. The Canadian Shield and walleye thinking are inextricably linked in the minds of many.

But the traditional rules of walleye behavior—what type of bottom they like to be on, how deep they go, the best method for catching them have to be stretched now to include a much wider variety of environments.

A group of travelling tournament walleye fishermen pointed this out to us. Walleyes have spread far beyond their native range, thanks to successful stocking programs. Particularly in the western and southern United States, the fish swims in places it didn't exist just a few years ago. In these areas all the traditional rules about walleye fishing that were developed in "traditional" waters didn't necessarily yield consistent results. There is an old saying that "a walleye is a walleye, no matter where it's found." That may be true. But any creature has to make do with what it's dealt, and transplanted walleyes feed on the food that's available to them, where and when they can find it.

The expansion of the walleye outside its native waters gave anglers in new areas a shot at them. Anglers went at them with no

Almost 68 percent of all North American walleye waters are found on the rocky Canadian shield, where much of our early knowledge—and techniques—came from. However, tournament fishermen have expanded that knowledge and developed new techniques.

preconceived notions about how to do it and came up with some rigs and techniques that the old hard cores from the traditional areas laughed at—in the beginning. But when these people— MikeMcClelland, Bob Propst, Dan Nelson, Jim Randash and Dave Jenson, to name a few—started catching fish in the native range of the walleye with their off-the-wall tactics, the fishing world took notice. Now, together with top anglers from the old guard, including people like Tom Neustrom, Gary Roach, Jerry Anderson, Daryl Christensen and many others, they have rewritten the rule book to the benefit of walleye anglers everywhere.

Walleye tournaments, like 'em or not, are the most efficient way to accelerate our learning curve. When 150 or more boats float out on a lake with two good walleye fishermen in each who need to catch fish to win money or build or preserve reputations, things get figured out in a hurry. If the old way doesn't prove successful in a reasonable amount of time, these folks try anything. An amazing variety of methods work, and that's how the walleye rule book has been revised so quickly.

Whether you realize it or not, tournaments have changed the equipment you use. Today's boats can take heavy waves and still

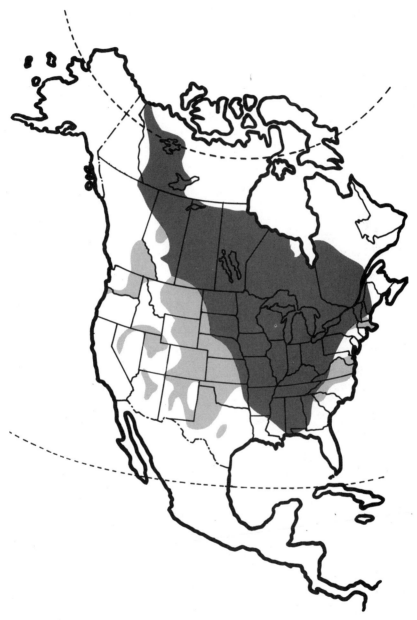

This is a walleye range map done in 1973 for the classic work "Freshwater Fishes of Canada" by W.B. Scott and E.J. Crossman. Since this map was made, the walleye range has expanded south and west, and the fish has been stocked into more waters within its native range. The new areas are indicated by the lighter screen.

allow you to effectively present a bait. Splash guards—little "walls" bolted to the back of the boat that allow you to troll backwards into waves—are much more refined and standard issue in many areas. Outboard motors with a lot of horsepower and slow trolling speeds are a reality. Better sonar, better rod and reel designs, new tackle for improving presentations, getting deeper and going into heavy cover are just part of the list. Much of this innovation is a direct result of manufacturers listening to the needs of people who fish for a living.

The number of walleye anglers, like the overall number of anglers, is growing. According to figures compiled by the American Fishing Tackle Manufacturer's Association and the Sport Fishing Institute, recreational fishing has the following impact on the American economy:

• Generates more than $70 billion per year.
• Accounts for 1.2 million U.S. jobs.
• Creates close to $1 billion in federal income tax revenue and about $400 million in state revenues.
• Nearly $14 billion is spent on fishing equipment, boats, motors and related items.

Parade of boats? No, it's a flight of tournament competitors filing in to weigh their catch. Competitive walleye fishing is disdained by some, but it has quickly improved our methods and equipment.

The outdoor media has a way of inflating our perception of the average-sized walleye. If you only catch "small" fish, don't despair because most anglers do. To catch trophy fish you may have to change tactics, or fish new areas.

A 1989 Gallup poll on American leisure activity showed that 41 percent of all men and 17 percent of all women in the United States are anglers, making it the most popular outdoor activity among men and second most popular among women.

As for walleye fishing specifically, here are some numbers from the U.S. Fish and Wildlife Service's 1985 study:

• In freshwater except the Great Lakes, 4.1 million anglers spent 79.5 million days chasing walleyes in 1985.

• That same year, 1.2 million did the same on the Great Lakes, spending 17 million additional days on the water chasing walleyes.

The numbers have probably gone up since then. They may be hard to picture, but they are significant even when compared to other species.

What If I Only Catch Small Fish?

After absorbing all this walleye knowledge, what should you expect? Lord knows that a heavy woman can get desperate thumbing through fashion magazines; the world seems full of perfectly sculpted competition.

Outdoor communicators are as guilty of leaving this same impression on gawking weekend anglers. Television fishing personalities haul in nothing but trophy walleyes, one after another, cast after cast. In eight minutes of air time they can leave the average person with a lifetime high-water mark to shoot for. How can that be? Don't they ever catch small fish? Don't the guys in the magazine articles ever get skunked?

Of course they do. But this boring footage doesn't get a lot of air play. Television stars don't want to spend their half-hour of time teaching you how to get skunked, so they show you the highlights of many hours of filming.

What should you reasonably expect to catch? How do you know if you are having "success?" The average size walleye, even the ultimate size you can hope for if the sun happens to be shining on you, varies drastically from lake to lake, region to region, even by season. Certain systems only give up big fish at very specific times, under specific conditions. Without naming lakes, the size of fish that will likely win just about every tournament is common knowledge among tournament fishermen. In some tournaments, a one-pounder brings high fives and big money.

As you become a better walleye angler, you'll feel a certain confidence and control over the fish. With it, hopefully, comes respect for the resource.

So, before you consider selling your boat because all you can catch are those 2-pounders consider the very real possibility that 2-pounders are the best your water has to offer. Or it may be that your approach is all wrong; to consistently take trophy walleyes, you do have to fish for them. (We'll get into that in detail in chapter 27.) However, I have seen good fishermen pull numbers of huge walleyes from the same spots where others are taking "cigars." That makes me realize there are things to know and try that can make a big difference.

Once, on South Dakota's Lake Oahe, Dan Nelson and I trolled up a bunch of walleyes in the 5- to 9-pound range. We kept a couple to shoot photos with (thereby perpetuating the myth we just talked about) and released the rest. When we brought them into the landing, we were treated like foreign diplomats. There were literally hundreds of walleyes on the public fish-cleaning tables, none of which were bigger than about 3 pounds.

I've seen Eldon Bailey do the same thing on Southern impoundments. When others around him are catching nothing or dinks, he takes numbers of big fish. Babe Winkelman has done the same on Canadian lakes. It can look like magic.

So what is a good walleye angler today? To take a stab at a definition, a good modern walleye angler:

• Has studied the quarry. They know something about the fish, how it lives, where it lives, what is unique about it.

• Knows something about the kinds of waters walleyes live in, and how those different environments affect them. They know how variables—presence or absence of different types of structure, weather conditions like wind and cold fronts, location of prey, fishing pressure, and time of day, to name a few—can affect the walleye's feeding and location *tendencies*, and they have a reason for the things they try when searching for fish.

• Knows something about the basic seasonal movements walleyes make on the waters they fish.

• Knows how to use sonar.

• Is versatile, fishes a variety of presentations and is in *control* of at least most of them.

• Consistently catches walleyes, can repeat success often and even predict at the beginning of the day what the pattern will be. They are not too proud to admit they were wrong, and change tactics if the conditions demand it.

• Has embraced (and this may take some getting used to) the idea that walleyes should be a catch-and-release fish in many instances and practices catch-and-release even if the law doesn't require it.

Most people will spend their fishing lives aiming to become this good. The experts who provide the following information *are* this good, every one of them. Listen to their hard-won knowledge, and take it out on the water with you.

3

Walleye Fishing's "Great" Lakes

W alleyes are hot. Not so many years ago, the walleye's appeal was limited to a handful of Midwestern states and the provinces of Canada. Today,
more than 5 million anglers pursue walleyes in 41
states. The walleye has become our fastest-growing freshwater
species, both in angler interest and domain.

Heading into the 1990s, walleyes ranked in the top five in angler preference in 11 states. Those numbers are expected to jump
by 10 to 30 percent by the end of the decade. For the first time,
major manufacturers are developing walleye tackle, walleye rods
and reels and walleye boats. There are big-money walleye tournaments and derbies from coast to coast. Publications that for generations ignored walleyes now routinely devote articles and photos to the species. Walleyes are not only popular in the upper
Midwest, but also in the East, Pacific Northwest and South. In
short, the walleye has come of age.

All of this comes as no surprise to long-time addicts, who for
years have recognized the walleye's qualifications as a gamefish.
But if the fish's growing appeal could be summed up in one word, it
would be availability.

Availability, more than anything, determines a fish's popularity. The number of anglers who pursue any given species is directly
proportional to the number of fish at their disposal, and there are a
lot of walleyes out there.

Credit for the walleye's remarkable growth belongs to sports-

Two South Dakota walleye fishermen display their catch from Lake Oahe. Big walleyes may be caught year-round on this Missouri River reservoir.

Complete Angler's Library

men, fisheries managers, and the federal government, which unwittingly contributed to the explosion. In hindsight, the walleye was an unexpected beneficiary of a series of seemingly unrelated and, in some cases, unintended events.

When Congress authorized construction of a series of hydroelectric dams on the upper Missouri River, recreation was little more than an afterthought; flood control, irrigation, navigation and electrical power generation were the primary purposes of these U.S. Army Corps of Engineers projects. Millions of acres of water were backed up behind six earthen dams, initially providing ideal habitat for pike, sauger and bass. But when the maturation process was complete, it was the walleye that best fit into the newly created niche.

Efforts to improve water quality also contributed greatly to the walleye's growth. On Lake Erie, concerned sportsmen worked diligently to clean up their lake and create a hospitable environment for sportfish populations. Those same sportsmen lobbied for restrictions on commercial fishing, which for generations had been an inhibiting factor in population expansion.

All these factors, combined with an increased awareness among fisheries managers of the walleye's potential, resulted in burgeoning walleye populations across the country. That awareness has its roots in the first of walleye fishing's "great" lakes.

North Dakota's Garrison Dam was completed in 1953, the second of six mainstem reservoirs slated for construction on the Missouri River. Initially, anglers enjoyed outstanding pike and sauger fishing. Then, as the system matured, the forage base was depleted and all fish species began to suffer. Rising waters scrubbed the shoreline, removing topsoil and vegetation, leaving a rock/rubble base ideal for walleye reproduction. But without spawning and rearing habitat, most baitfish species vanished.

Convinced the deep, clear waters of the Garrison Reservoir would provide ideal salmonid habitat, then-fisheries chief Dale Henegar of the North Dakota Game and Fish Department stocked rainbow smelt—after considering the objections of those who thought the smelt would eat walleye fry. In 1971, 7,000 gravid (with eggs) rainbow smelt were released into Lake Sakakawea.

The smelt paved the way for a chinook salmon program, but more importantly the prolific forage had a surprisingly positive impact on walleyes, sauger, smallmouth bass and pike. By the late '70s, walleyes were so abundant on the Missouri that Sakakawea and South Dakota's Lake Oahe were claiming the titles of "Walleye Capitals of the World."

About this same time sportsmen's efforts to clean up Lake Erie were yielding benefits. Before long, Erie boasted an estimated population of 44 million walleyes, and the lake's Western Basin was being heralded as the new Walleye Capital.

The Columbia River of the western United States is another unusual success story. How walleyes made their way into the Columbia is a mystery. History will record that one day late in the 1970s an angler carried a large, google-eyed fish into the offices of Wally Pease, a Washington outdoor writer with Minnesota roots, asking Wally to identify the creature. Pease knew what it was, all right—a walleye, and a big one. He contacted Nick Adams of Lindy-Little Joe Tackle Company, requesting that Adams send a field pro from the Brainerd, Minnesota, base to fish the waters.

Adams assigned the job to Gary Roach, an old-time walleye guide and promotional fisherman for Lindy. What Roach discovered on his initial visit to Washington and Oregon in 1982 was one of the finest untapped trophy walleye systems in the world. It sounds like a fish story, but Roach caught so many big walleyes in four days that he went home with tennis elbow. Another of walleye fishing's "great" lakes was born, as well as another contender for the Walleye Capital crown.

That same year, charter captains Sam and Ed Concilla of Erie, Pennsylvania, decided to investigate mysterious marks on their graph recorders, hooks too shallow to have been made by salmon but big enough to arouse their curiosity. Using off-the-wall techniques such as trolling nightcrawler-tipped spinner rigs on downriggers, Ed discovered a massive population of suspended walleyes. Some of the schools were several miles long and nearly a mile wide. Three years later, when the Concillas were finally able to convince local fishermen and biologists that walleyes existed on that end of the lake, the Eastern Basin of Lake Erie hauled out its Walleye Capital banner, and anglers in Pennsylvania and New York had a new playground.

Sportsmen in Michigan's Saginaw Bay area off Lake Huron undertook stocking programs that many say will earn that body of water the title of Walleye Capital. But they'll get a strong argu-

Gary Roach, "Mr. Walleye" himself, with a heaping stringer of Columbia River walleyes taken on that historic first exploratory visit.

Walleye Fishing's "Great" Lakes

ment from the folks up at Bay de Noc and Sturgeon Bay on Lake Michigan.

Did we forget to mention Lake of the Woods on the U.S.-Canadian border, Minnesota's Mille Lacs, Michigan's Lake St. Clair and North Dakota's Devils Lake? How about the St. Clair River that feeds Lake St. Clair from Lake Huron or the Detroit River that flows out the other end into Lake Erie? In spring and fall when walleyes are migrating, Detroit anglers are treated to some of the finest walleye fishing on the continent.

Montana biologists beefed up the forage base in Fort Peck, the first and uppermost Missouri River impoundment, creating another great fishery. There's every reason to suspect that Lake Ontario and Lake Superior will soon be discovered as walleye holdouts. And let's not overlook Canada. With so many fish available stateside, a lot of anglers have stayed closer to home, but Canada has its share of "great" lakes as well.

Intrigued by success stories from the North, biologists in other states undertook experimental walleye stocking programs. Today, walleyes are available in places like Kansas, Missouri, Colorado, Arkansas and even New Mexico, Nevada and Texas. What will be the eventual permanent boundaries of the walleye's range? Who knows.

One thing seems certain: The big, diversified, nutrient-rich waters of man-made reservoirs hold the greatest potential for development of walleye fisheries. The smaller natural lakes that traditionally attracted most walleye fishermen still produce their share of action, but day in and day out the "great" lakes offer superior fishing throughout the open-water period.

Across much of the walleye's natural range, a pair of 7-pound walleyes caught during the Fourth of July weekend will put you in the local papers. On Lake Sakakawea, Dan Nelson and I barely rated a second glance when we showed up at the cleaning table with a two-man limit *averaging* 7 pounds. The Concillas routinely return to port with a box of Lake Erie walleyes that average 6 or 7 pounds.

In many places, a 3- or 4-pound walleye is considered an excellent fish. Out on the Columbia, where 10-pounders are common, newcomers to walleye fishing might not even recognize a walleye that small. Most visitors to Canada would be thrilled by a bunch of 2-pounders for the skillet. But there have been fishing tourna-

NAFC member Joseph Kalo of Elyria, Ohio, caught this 10¹/₂-pound walleye in the Central Basin of Lake Erie out of Vermilion, Ohio.

ments on Lake Oahe where limits of 2-pounders wouldn't even put a team in the top 25.

There are sound biological reasons that big waters produce more and bigger walleyes. The biomass (total pounds of fish per acre a system can support) can be as much as six times greater on reservoirs than on natural lakes. On smaller natural lakes, the biomass can easily be filled by panfish and rough fish, limiting the number of gamefish the lake can sustain. Prolific forage fish like the smelt, alewives, shad and sculpin found in the "great" lakes are more conducive to walleye growth and development.

Larger bodies of water naturally have more spawning habitat, resulting in better reproduction. On a good year, more fish will be produced than the limited number of anglers can possibly catch. Fishing pressure is another factor. In areas where the walleye has only recently been accepted as a gamefish, angling pressure is still insignificant. The smaller, less productive lakes in Minnesota's and Wisconsin's popular resort country, on the other hand, receive intense fishing pressure for the size of the water, and the bulk of a year class can be harvested before it reaches sexual maturity.

Still, there are ongoing threats to walleye populations even on

Walleyes, indeed, are hot. Towns and regions haul out banners and build monuments in honor of this popular sportfish.

the larger systems. Fluctuating water levels on reservoirs reduce spawning potential, often wiping out entire year classes of fish. Inconsistent weather during the spawn results in diminished reproduction. Water quality continues to be a problem in many areas of the country. Gillnetting is an ever-present problem as is Indian spearing. New and improved fishing tactics result in increased creels, sometimes exceeding what the systems can tolerate.

Then there's BC plankton, a European plankton that made its way to the Great Lakes on the hulls of ocean-going freighters. Since its arrival, BC plankton has paved the way for sensational walleye fishing. Because it remains relatively close to the surface during the warm-water period, the plankton pulls smelt out of deeper water and the walleyes follow. As a result, many Great Lakes anglers have replaced downriggers with planer boards and crankbaits.

Only time will tell what impact BC plankton ultimately will have on the Great Lakes. Some fear it will multiply and eventually eradicate all other forms of plankton in the environment, destroying the food chain and upsetting the entire ecosystem.

What effect will low water have on the drought-plagued upper

Many major reservoirs are truly excellent walleye fisheries, and yet they still receive relatively light fishing pressure.

Walleye Fishing's "Great" Lakes

Midwest? In the late 1980s, many of the best walleye reservoirs saw reduced reproduction when low water levels left most spawning habitat high and dry. With less water at their disposal, fish were concentrated and easily caught by anglers, resulting in unprecedented harvests. Some forage populations have been reduced dramatically as well.

On the Columbia, gill nets threaten the future of walleye fishing.

There are many biological, environmental and political issues that need to be addressed.

Walleye populations may continue to thrive or they may succumb to unchecked harvest, environmental threats and political indifference. For now, however, one thing is certain; on many of North America's "great" lakes, the good old days for walleye fishing are right now.

4

Walleye: The Fish

W alleyes, like everything else around us, have not always existed. Where did they come from? It was through the miraculous natural selection process we call evolution that the North American walleye, or *Stizostedion vitreum*, was made. The walleye that swims today in Lake of the Woods on the border of Ontario and Minnesota, the Missouri River system, lakes Erie, Michigan, Huron and Superior, the Columbia River or Old Hickory Lake in Tennessee—home of the current world record—had to descend from somewhere, from something.

Scientists say that all *percoid* fishes (a large suborder including the perches, sunfishes, groupers and grunts) evolved from a common ocean-run *progenitor*, or direct ancestor. So walleyes most likely have saltwater roots, which is not surprising, considering that 99.99 percent of the world's water is marine!

Our walleye is in the family Percidae (or perches, as we commonly call them), which has about 163 species. The Percidae, biologists say, originated from this common European ancestor during the Cenozoic period (the latest era of geologic time, during which mammals, birds, plants and modern continents evolved). It is believed that the percoid fishes spread to North America during at least two "invasions."

But when the fish arrived in North American waters, only three large species evolved: the walleye, the yellow perch (*Perca flavescens*) and the sauger (*Stizostedion canadense*). Why? The most often-given theory is that the already-present Centrar-chidae species (bass and panfish to you and me) competed strongly for their developed niches, leaving relatively few openings in the food chain.

What do we know about this European ancestor, this distant patriarch of our modern walleye? It was probably anadromous, a fish that migrated from the sea into freshwater rivers to spawn. (This lure of flowing water still calls many walleyes during the spring spawning ritual!)

Compared with saltwater fishes, most freshwater species are considered relatively primitive in development. Often, they are less advanced in terms of maneuverability, protection against predators, consistent contact between the sexes at spawning time, efficient feeding and the ability to live in deeper water.

Ah, but the walleye would seem to be most advanced for its role in our waters! An efficient predator with several important advantages over its prey under certain conditions; a fish that can and will live both shallow and deep—deeper, in fact, than most other freshwater species.

Relatives Of The Walleye

There were at one time two recognized subspecies of walleyes in North America, the yellow walleye (the fish we know today simply as the walleye), and the blue walleye, or blue pike (*Stizostedion vitreum glaucum*). The only waters the blue walleye inhabited for certain were the Great Lakes. But by the mid-1960s their numbers dropped, ironically, after some record harvests. Experts say that water pollution and intensive commercial fishing, among other possible factors, led to their decline.

By 1971, the blue walleye was considered extinct. Occasionally, there are rumors of a blue walleye being caught, usually from somewhere other than the Great Lakes. But qualified biologists seem to agree that these fish are simply color phases of the yellow walleye, not the fish that once roamed Lake Erie and Lake Ontario.

"Occasionally, people in northwestern Ontario will catch blue-colored walleyes they think are the blue pike," says Dr. Richard Ryder, a distinguished fisheries researcher with the Ontario Ministry of Natural Resources, one of the world's foremost walleye authorities. "But the coloring is simply in the mucous

Along with 162 other species, the walleye is a member of the Percidae family and evolved, over millions of years, from a common saltwater ancestor. Scientists theorize this ancestor was anadromous (migrated into freshwater to spawn).

coating of the fish. They're just yellow walleyes that have a blue pigment. You can tell the difference between these and the true blue pike, because when you wrap these fish in newspaper, the slime comes off and the newspaper turns blue."

The closest relative is the sauger (*Stizostedion canadense*), a fish often mistaken for the walleye. Once you've examined a few specimens of each side by side, it is fairly easy to tell them apart. Saugers have a blackish or grayish overall body color, often noticeably darker than a walleye from the same body of water. On the fleshy part of the dorsal fins, the sauger has dark blotches that the walleye does not have. The sauger also lacks the white tip on the lower part of the tail, a walleye trademark. Saugers don't get as big as walleyes; a 3-pound sauger is a major-league catch.

The sauger usually spawns later than the walleye, but many times in the same locations. The result can be a hybrid called the saugeye, which shows intermediate characteristics.

Knowing a saugeye when you see one is as difficult as it sounds, according to Jim Riis of the South Dakota Game, Fish and Parks Department, who sees a lot of them from Missouri River reservoirs. "Anytime two things hybridize," he says, "the results will be

The walleye's closest relative, the sauger, is often caught in the same waters. The sauger tends to be slimmer, has telltale dark blotches on the dorsal fin, and an overall "blotchy" appearance. It tastes just as good as the walleye, though!

Complete Angler's Library

variable. In the case of the saugeye, characteristics of each parent will be present or absent in various individual offspring, in varying degrees. On some (saugeyes), you might even see that white spot on the tip of the tail, at least faintly."

Positive identification on the water is virtually impossible, biologists say (darker-colored walleyes are sometimes mistaken for saugeyes). You can have a strong hunch, though, because a saugeye's body shape tends to be more like a sauger than a walleye from the same water: relatively long and thin.

The walleye is also related to the Eurasian and American yellow perches and the darters. There are 95 darter species in North America, a fish that is generally very small (one to three inches long). Darters do not have a swim bladder, so they spend most of their time resting on the bottom.

The Zander: Coming To America

The European zander, a distant relative of the walleye, is attracting an increasing amount of attention on the North American front. It looks almost identical to our walleye and grows to amazing sizes (the European record is about 44 pounds).

There are some important differences between the zander and the walleye, however. The zander is a nest-builder at spawning time and gives at least some parental care to the eggs, while walleyes randomly broadcast their eggs and offer no care to them. The zander can tolerate warmer temperatures than the walleye and can successfully spawn in areas where walleye eggs would suffocate.

For those reasons, several fisheries officials in North Dakota have led an embryonic program to transplant the zander to North American waters. North Dakota, under the leadership of now-retired Game and Fish Commissioner Dale Henegar, weathered a lengthy three-year ordeal that included importing several batches of eggs and fry that had to be destroyed because they may have come to this country diseased. Finally in June 1989 a load of about 180,000 zander fry was sent swimming into its first North American home, shallow, plankton-rich East Spiritwood Lake.

When it comes to opening our waters to it, the zander has ardent proponents and opponents. Environmental conditions—water temperatures, growing seasons, forage base and competition from other species, among others—are never the same from one

This walleye (left) and sauger were taken from the same waters at midday.

Complete Angler's Library

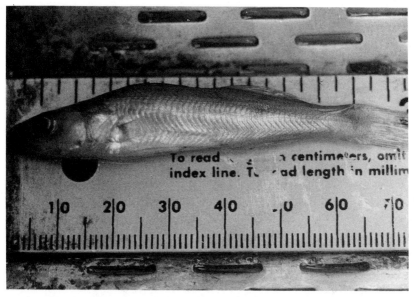

To read ... centimeters, omit
index line. T... ad length in millim

Zander are now swimming into North American waters for the first time. Will this European relative be good for our fisheries? Time will tell, but many are worried they could be another "exotic disaster" like the carp.

lake to the next, much less from one continent to the next. The zander may not reach its ultimate size here. North Dakota officials estimate a top end of 40 pounds, with good numbers of 15- to 18-pound fish. Tempting, to say the least, to a diehard walleye fanatic who has never landed a 10-pounder.

But the zander could become competition for other staple species beloved by North American anglers, principally the largemouth bass. To let them in or not has become a moot question; the fish are here. Will they be good for us or an "exotic disaster" as some fear (think about carp, starlings, Eurasian milfoil and the new purple loosestrife, which is choking the life out of many of our wetlands)? Will they be stocked, whether by professionals or "midnight stockers" into large river systems, where they will spread into other states, which may or may not want them? History says they surely will.

The zander comes from the same genus as our walleye, meaning it has the same number of chromosomes, making hybridization an inevitable eventuality. Dick Ryder, who has studied the fish in the Netherlands, Finland and Sweden, says spawning times and locations could easily overlap some years, just as walleye and sauger spawning do. "Who knows," Ryder says, "we could end up with some kind of jumbo walleye with hybrid vigor, which would thrill the angler. But it's just hard to say.

"It's not that the zander might not be good," he continues, "but the risk is just too great to take. Nobody can predict what's going to happen, because our knowledge of all the factors isn't quite where it should be to assess these things. We've had so much bad luck with imported species, I'm surprised they're still trying it."

North Dakota biologists cite declining walleye habitat and an open niche as rationale for bringing the zander to their state. Observers—including Ontario researchers who studied the fish for possible import more than 20 years ago, and decided it was a bad idea—feel the North Dakota project is a move that doesn't consider the wishes of neighboring lands. The North American zander chapter is just beginning to be written.

But enough about the relatives. Let's go in tight for a close look at the walleye itself. There are many striking things about the physical makeup of a walleye that impress us at first glance. But to understand them requires going more than skin deep.

5

Walleye Senses

J ust as traveling musicians are guaranteed to have written a song about life on the road, virtually every book or magazine article ever done on the walleye has listed a litany of nicknames for this fish. Forever doomed to life as the "walleyed pike" on restaurant menus, the walleye is, of course, not a pike but a perch.

So what do some people call it? Depending on where you launch your boat, they are sometimes called jack salmon, dore, pike-perch (also a nickname for the zander), yellowpike, jack glasseye, gum pike, susquehanna salmon, bugeyes, pickerel, yellow pickerel, marble eye and okau, whatever that means.

That Eye!

The walleye gets its true name from its prominent eye. The word *walleye* means "an eye in which the cornea is white or opaque." (The word walleyed, by the way, comes from an Old Norse word, vagleygr, meaning to have a film over the eye.) That eye is special and different. You can tell that at first glance.

The glassy, milky-white appearance you see when light hits it directly comes from a reflective membrane called *tapetum lucidum*. It is, in simple terms, a very white light-gathering and reflecting substance that sits behind the fish's retina. It gives walleyes a sight advantage over their prey under low-light conditions: prey fish, including the related yellow perch, lack this pigment.

In essence, this is how it works: When light enters the walleye's eye, it is recorded by the retina, and gets bounced around (reflected) by the tapetum back to the retina, in effect artificially "multiplying" the amount of light the walleye can use to see by.

Saugers, by the way, also have tapetum; in fact, they have more of it than the walleye, and it is more uniformly spread on the eye. Biologists say this accounts for the apparent fact that saugers typically live in deeper water than walleyes.

Think of it. This eye gathers light, bounces it around like a pinball machine and is specially developed for life in dim, even dark, surroundings. But is it a curse in bright light?

This question has been debated for many years. The notion that walleyes "prefer," as fishermen like to say, deep water, only coming shallow under the cover of clouds, twilight, heavy wave action and the like, raises another good one: Does bright light "hurt" their eyes? Is it futile to fish in shallow water in a clear-water lake in the middle of a sunny day?

Scientific study would say yes, to a point. Studies done in Manitoba on second-summer walleyes showed they moved vertically shallower in a tank of water when light levels were turned low, and deeper when light levels were increased. (Variables such as pH, carbon dioxide, oxygen, and so on, were kept as constant as possible.)

Dr. Ryder in Ontario concluded after 15 years (1962-76) of observation, both below and above water, that "light is the principal controlling variable of the environment that determines spatial and temporal dimensions (where they go and when) of feeding and reproduction in the walleye." His daytime underwater observations revealed that walleyes were active in the turbid regions of his study lakes but "rested in contact with the substrate (bottom) in clear-water regions...physical shelter served to shield the eyes of the walleyes from the ambient light."

In this classic study, cited often in popular fishing literature, Ryder also found that walleyes feed most intensively during periods of *rapidly changing* light levels. He learned this by actually fishing the same spot for 24 hours at a time, noting when he caught each fish and what the light intensity was. (Rapidly changing light levels occur naturally at sunrise and sunset, known for generations to be a "hot" time to fish walleyes. They also occur when clouds suddenly cover the sun, a storm comes on quickly, wind disturbs the surface of a calm lake, etc.)

The sun reflects off a walleye's tapetum, a light-gathering pigment in the eye that gives the fish a sight advantage over prey in low-light conditions. The walleye got its name from the distinct appearance of its eye.

So if you really want to torture a walleye, do you take it out of the depths and hit it with a good floodlight? What does that do to him? Dr. Dwight Burkhardt, a professor of psychology at the University of Minnesota, has scientifically studied the walleye's eye. He is best known for identifying those colors to which the walleye eye is most sensitive, and that it has at least the fundamental basis for color vision. But he's also done work on how well the walleye can see in bright light.

Various theories have been offered on this matter. Most seem to say that walleyes are temporarily blinded by bright light. But Burkhardt has done recent work that indicates that, given time, a walleye's eye adjusts to bright surroundings, just like ours do when we go outside after a matinee movie in a dark theater.

The amount of tapetum in the eye, Burkhardt says, varies from walleye to walleye, and in the matter of a few weeks can change in an individual walleye in response to its environment! In other words, at least in theory, walleyes can become acclimated to life in relatively bright conditions if they have to in order to feed, or if some other factor forces them. It may not happen in nature, but it could. (As we talk with some of today's best walleye anglers, you

Holy rapidly changing light levels! When the sun is blocked by an approaching storm, when waves diffuse sunlight, and at sunrise and sunset, intense walleye feeding sprees can be triggered.

will begin to think of walleyes as more of a shallow-water creature than traditional wisdom says.)

"It seems true," Burkhardt says, "that walleyes can still see well even when subjected to very bright light, as long as they don't move too quickly from very dim to very bright waters." How long does adjustment take? Best guess: about 20 minutes.

Traditionally, expert fishermen have thought that walleyes avoid bright light at the expense of all else by 1) swimming to deeper water, 2) swimming to a more turbid or wave-swept portion of the lake, or 3) remaining in shallow water and using physical shelter such as boulders, weeds or downed trees for shade. They undoubtedly do all of these, but they may also be willing to stay in relatively bright light and feed if that's where their food is. Light is no doubt a critical force governing a walleye's lifestyle. But it may

Complete Angler's Library

not dictate it: Witness recent fishing success in very shallow, relatively bright water.

Oh, and a word about Burkhardt's findings regarding the color sensitivity of the walleye's eye, because it reinforced years of hard-won angling theory regarding what color lure to use. Without going into detail about the study, Burkhardt found that the cones—the receptor cells in the eye responsible mainly for daylight vision—are most sensitive to orange and green light. Additionally, Burkhardt found other color-discriminating cells that can distinguish red from green, indicating that the walleye has the basis for at least "fair" color vision.

What does all of this mean? According to Burkhardt, walleyes can probably tell red from green very well but probably can't discriminate blues from yellows. It is also difficult, probably, for walleyes to distinguish blues from blue-greens. But they can sometimes tell the differences between colors by differences in brightness.

It is *probably* true that this means something only for daylight vision. During periods of darkness, rods, the other receptor cell in the eye, take over the primary role in walleye vision, as they do in humans and virtually every other animal. What role the cones play, if any, in nocturnal vision is unknown.

At night when it's extremely dark, even humans have little ability to discern color. The rods in a walleye's eye are most sensitive to green light, even though they probably don't see it as "green" in the way we think of it.

Should that affect what color lure you use at night? Maybe, maybe not. Says Burkhardt: "It could be true, with all other things being equal, that a walleye might be able to see a green lure better than other colors when conditions are very, very dim. But we just don't know how dark it has to be before the walleye is relying solely on its rods for vision. I learned through years of doing vision research how sensitive to even a minute amount of light the human eye is. So you can imagine this walleye's eye, with all the advantages it has, might be able to function using the cones even at night, if there is any light at all, say from the moon."

Burkhardt, despite not being a fisherman, raises another age-old question about this fish when he wonders—even though we know which colors walleyes probably see best—what color of bait or lure will prove to be most effective for catching them?

Heading out to fish the sunset and after-dark periods can pay off. Even though we don't know for sure how a walleye sees at night, we know we can catch them, making night fishing a popular activity in many areas.

"There are certain objective aspects of vision research we can deal with directly," he says. "But what about the subjective side of vision? We know which colors the human eye is most sensitive to, but when you ask a lot of people what their 'favorite' color is, you get a lot of different responses. The same logic might apply to walleyes. We can be fairly certain what colors are most visible to them, but do we always know what color is going to trigger a response from a given fish? It's possible that there could be a variable, something we might call 'color preference' in walleyes, and it could vary from individual to individual.

"It's also known that movement is critical for producing a behavioral response from most animals," Burkhardt says, "and that's certainly got to be true for fish."

Aha! So color is no doubt important; if the walleye can't see your lure, it will have a harder time biting it (although other senses such as hearing, which includes lateral line, and smell, help walleyes zero in on your offering). But action or movement—the *way* you present your lure to the fish—also has a lot to do with triggering a response, or getting the fish to hit your offering.

It is known that many animals have what are called motion-sensitive cells, nerve cells that respond only when an object moves; some even respond only when an object moves in a certain direction! While it is not known for sure that walleyes have such cells, it is likely they do. We will go into even more detail on lure colors and how to trigger fish into striking elsewhere in the book, particularly in Section IV—Catching Walleyes.

There we'll discover why some top fishermen think color selection is important, while others disagree. One top pro buys a dozen or more lures in a single color, claiming precise lure presentation, not color, is the key to success.

Sound Receptors

A walleye sits, resting, at the edge of a weedbed. It has its back to a tiny minnow some distance away, but it knows it is there. The walleye can feel the minnow finning quietly, and the walleye knows how big the minnow is.

A leadhead jig drops at the base of a rock pile even farther away. The walleye hears the jig hit bottom.

Farfetched? No. Walleyes know what's going on around them even when they can't see everything. There are sounds and vibrations underwater, lots of them. Some attract walleyes, some simply catch their attention for a moment before being ignored, and others help them notice and zero in on prey.

It's important that you avoid making the wrong kinds of noises and that your lures and live baits give off the right "vibes" to trigger walleyes into striking or biting. Walleyes use two kinds of sound receptors to help them sense what's going on around them: an ear similar to ours in function, and its lateral lines.

Walleyes can feed efficiently in 50 feet or deeper, even in muddy waters. How do they do it?

Water has been described as an ideal medium for transmission of sound. Vibrations, or sound waves, travel both faster and farther in water than in air.

Walleyes can hear high-frequency sounds (from about 100 to 1,000 hertz, or cycles per second) with their ears, which are connected by something called a Webarian apparatus to their swim bladders. (Fish have ear bones in their skulls but no external ear openings.) The swim bladder resonates the sound, making it easier for the fish to hear, much like the inner chamber of a guitar amplifies the sound made by the strings.

"Fish couldn't hear very well without the swim bladder," says Dr. Greg Bambenek, a Minnesota psychiatrist who has done research in fish sound reception.

But because there is only one swim bladder, centrally located on the walleye's body, it is difficult for the fish to pinpoint where the sound is coming from. Nailing down the exact location of "sounds" underwater is better accomplished by the lateral lines.

Lateral Line

As the name implies, the lateral lines are series of nerve endings running the length of most fish, one on each side. They are extremely sensitive to even the slightest vibration. And, because there is one on each side of the walleye, the fish can tell where a "sound" is coming from, because the sound will hit one lateral line slightly before the other.

The lateral line is used to pick up mainly lower frequencies from about 2 to 100 hertz (this includes sounds like people walking on the shoreline or dropping a tackle box on the boat bottom).

Picking up on vibrations with these hairlike filaments is not exactly hearing as we think of it, says Bambenek. "It's probably a different sensation than we have," he says. "One way I can think of to describe it to people is that it's more of a feeling sense, kind of like listening to loud music. You can feel the beat, particularly the bass beat, vibrating against your pants leg or even the hairs on your leg, if you concentrate. This is pretty much the same sense that deaf people use that allows them to dance; they can feel the beat even though they can't hear it."

This concept of feeling vibrations is called *near-field displacement*. Walleyes can "hear" the swimming motions of other organisms around them, including the vibrations given off by your crankbait, nightcrawler, even the tiniest jig (you probably didn't think a nightcrawler gave off vibrations the walleye could feel, did you?). Rapid turns of baitfish and irregular swimming patterns are telltale signs to a walleye's senses that trigger the predatory instinct.

Do you see why it's important how you present your lures? Do they "feel" and "sound" wounded, like an easy meal, to the walleye? Or do they seem like they are swimming along fine, something the walleye will have to chase to eat?

Some experts believe that every underwater organism gives off

Lure color may be important—even critical at times—but so is the action you put into your presentation. The right movements can trigger a response!

Walleye Senses

The lateral lines along both sides of a walleye's body are extremely sensitive and can detect the slightest vibration in the water. They help a walleye find food when sight feeding is impaired and even allow the fish to distinguish between healthy and wounded prey.

a unique set of vibrations, and that the walleye's lateral line sense is acute enough to distinguish them by instinct. If you can find walleyes but can't catch them, try switching lures. It might be the one you're using is not sending out the right vibes.

The sound receptors, most experts agree, become more important when other senses are diminished. This happens, for instance, in extremely dirty water, at night or in very deep water— essentially situations where vision is impaired.

Smell And Taste

There is virtually nothing scientific that tells us the senses of smell and taste are important in walleye fishing. One expert will scream and yell about things like scent tracks and the importance of scent in turbid water. Another, equally excited, will talk about catching as many walleyes on gasoline-soaked baits as on those enhanced with commercial scent products.

People have long suspected that the walleye's nose isn't "for nothin'." A fish's nostrils are lined with a tissue that is sensitive to odors. Some fish's scent-related feats are impressive: When it comes time to spawn, salmon can find their way from the sea into the same stream in which they were hatched by the odor of the water. There are those who believe walleyes can do the same thing, given that they often return to the same spawning site year after year. Scent is probably important in catching walleyes, given that anglers who believe in commercial scent products swear there are times when walleyes seem to reject any untreated offering.

Whether it be a product that claims to cover unnatural odors, or one that professes to attract fish, often does not matter. Some anglers, in fact, swear that WD-40, a commercial lubricant that contains fish emulsions, is one of the best lure treatments available.

There are many products designed to mask odors or attract fish with sex hormones. But we won't go into specific claims here.

One of the most recent developments relating to a fish's ability to sense odor came from Dr. Bambenek. He created a test to determine a person's "L-serine profile."

L-serine, an amino acid given off by humans, has been shown to repel fish. Humans vary in their L-serine concentrations; typically, males give off more than females, and white people more

Commercial "fishing" soaps claim to remove or mask L-serine, a human amino acid known to repel fish. Washing your hands with one before handling lures, and after gassing up the boat, is probably a good idea.

than blacks. A group of white males, all top fishermen, pro-duced—to the man—profiles showing only trace amounts of L-serine.

There are many products available that claim to wash off or mask L-serine. Again, we'll leave the claims to the manufacturers, but cleaning your hands and lures before baiting up is probably a good idea. Especially if you're after trophy fish, which as you'll see in the next chapter, are relatively rare.

6

Walleye Life Cycle

Walleyes are classified, among other ways, as a cool-water fish. It is a rather loose, intermediate term that places the walleye between cold-water fish like lake trout, and warm-water fish like bass and sunfish. Walleyes have a preferred temperature range of between 65 and 75 degrees in the summer. The walleye will tolerate warmer temperatures, especially to feed, but rarely is found in water much above 80 degrees. Winter water temperatures, of course, get much colder than that in most walleyes' range.

The cool-water label does have some significance, according to Dennis Schupp, a regional fisheries research supervisor for the Minnesota Department of Natural Resources who is respected throughout North America as a walleye authority.

"The key thing, I suppose, about the cool-water definition," Schupp says, "is that the main walleye range tends to be in the northern temperate zones of North America, where summertime water temperatures seldom get much above the low 70s. But one other characteristic that is physiologically important is that we need to have an extended period of cold weather—ice cover, low temperatures—for successful spawning. It's true for many members of the perch family. (Studies on yellow perch have shown that the longer they are exposed to cold water in winter, the more viable their eggs are the following spring.)

"As you get farther south in the United States," continues Schupp, "the cold winter water temperatures aren't there for a

The innate drive to reproduce calls walleyes to spawning grounds each spring. Here, a fisheries biologist milks eggs from a ripe female for a hatchery program. These eggs will soon be fertilized by milt (sperm) from a smaller male.

long time. We don't see good walleye hatches from natural spawning down South like we do in the North. I realize there have been successful introductions in places like Texas, but for the most part you are looking at the northern tier states and southern Canada as the prime walleye range still, and it may be for this reason that they need that long period of cold weather to bring off a good hatch."

Supplemental stocking is an important part of today's North American walleye program, but the staple will always be naturally reproducing wild populations. What does it take to bring off a big year class of walleyes in the wild?

Walleye Spawning

Every spring, at the combined urgings of increasing day length and warming water temperatures, walleyes try to spawn.

Research has demonstrated that they will make do with whatever remotely satisfactory potential spawning sites are available, including flooded grasses. But the ideal environment for natural reproduction of the walleye is a lake, river or reservoir that is large enough to have windswept shores with suitable habitat.

Prime spawning habitat consists of sections of shallow shoreline exposed to wind and strewn with golf ball- to baseball-sized rock, gravel and boulders. Female walleyes randomly broadcast their eggs onto the substrate, after which males deposit sperm over them. If the fertilized eggs drop into crevices between rocks, they have a good chance of escaping egg-eating predators. Wind acts to keep silt and sediment from suffocating the eggs during incubation.

Another classic walleye spawning site is an inflowing river with current washing over rock and gravel areas. At spawning time, large numbers of walleyes will "run" up into the river. It helps if the river has a deep pool or two for the fish to hold in during the day. Otherwise, they typically run up the stream or river at night and return to the main lake during daylight hours.

Walleyes will also spawn over shallow bars and reefs in a lake if they are covered with the "right stuff." In reservoirs, many walleyes spawn along the riprap (crushed rock used to fight bank erosion) linings of the dam and surrounding shorelines.

Spawning takes place at slightly different times each year, depending on whether it is an early or late spring. Water temperatures at the peak of the spawning runs vary from north to south in the walleye's range, essentially from the mid-40s in the north to the mid-50s in the southern United States. (The actual dates of the spawn also correspond to the climates; spawning can peak as early as mid-March in the south and as late as mid-May at the northern end of the range.) Not all fish spawn at the same time; the average run lasts about three weeks, with a peak of activity somewhere in the middle period. Males, typically smaller than females (they grow slower and reach smaller ultimate sizes), are the first to arrive on the spawning sites and the last to leave, often accounting for most angler catches at this time of year.

Murphy's law could have been written by biologists studying the results of walleye spawning efforts. It doesn't always work out well. It is estimated that, about one in five years, walleyes bring off a strong year class of young, about one in five is a complete bust, and the other three years are somewhere in the middle on the scale of success.

So, the number of new walleyes recruited into the system can vary by a factor of 25; in other words, one age group of walleyes can have 25 times more individuals in it than another.

That helps explain why some years are better for walleye fishing than others and why some lakes get hot for a few years, then cool off considerably. (Although fishing pressure can also serve to cool off the number of fish being caught.) It can also help explain why you catch a lot of a certain size walleyes in some lakes and bigger or smaller ones in other lakes—although this, too, is a complex matter involving other variables like forage base.

Aside from the presence or absence of suitable habitat, weather conditions—as we might expect—are the main variable in spawning success. Good hatches have been correlated with late, cold springs when the walleyes spawn later than normal. You might think that "planting their seeds early" would be an advantage, giving the young longer to grow before their first winter. But first things first; the eggs have to hatch into a hospitable environment, one in which a food chain—including food for tiny walleyes—has begun to develop.

Lake Erie data support the notion that an early spring that sees a quick "false" warming of the water, followed by one cold front after another, is a death trap to the eggs and newly hatched fry. A good year class is more likely to come out of a late spring because chances are better there won't be a drawn-out period of wildly fluctuating water temperatures that can kill huge numbers of fry before they are established and begin to grow.

Wind, already discussed as a key to success, can also spoil a spawn. If the winds are too high, they can dislodge and wash away the eggs, making them easy pickings for predators and depositing them onto less suitable bottom areas, where they are less likely to hatch.

Survival Of The Fittest: How Many Live?

Life is a struggle for the walleye before it begins, and things don't get any easier after the egg hatches. A young walleye is born into a world of savage realities where predators line up for a chance to suck it in. Washing about almost helpless for up to two weeks, early survival is simply a numbers game. One study done in Lake Oneida in New York turned up fry mortality of about 95 percent within the first three weeks.

If you knew the odds of any given egg living to become even a marginal keeper in the traditional line of thinking, you would marvel at every 2-pound walleye that chomps down on your bait.

The odds for any of these walleye fry reaching adulthood are infinitely small. It is estimated that about 125 fish, out of 1,000,000 eggs, reach four years of age!

Depending on its location, a walleye's size, in relation to its age, varies considerably. A southern walleye generally grows faster and is heavier than a northern walleye of the same age, but it normally won't live as long.

Complete Angler's Library

The chances of that egg growing into a trophy walleye, say a 10-pounder, would test the capacity of the calculator you use to balance your checkbook.

Each spawning female walleye, depending on size, deposits between about 60,000 and 250,000 eggs. The average has been estimated at about 85,000. Of those, five to 20 percent hatch. It takes almost ideal conditions for 20 percent to hatch, so in most cases, hatching success is probably less than 10 percent.

Wisconsin researcher Steve Serns went to lengths to estimate the total number of eggs deposited in Escanaba Lake for three years from 1979 through 1981. Through another considerable statistical effort, he figured the approximate number of fingerlings that survived into their first fall. During the first two years of the study, it came to less than one-tenth of one percent; in 1981, he came up with about .7 percent.

The fingerlings, as they are now called, will experience mortality rates of about 50 percent—again assuming good feeding and habitat conditions—each year, until reaching catchable size. In most waters, fish of about $1^3/_4$ or 2 pounds are considered keepers. Growth rates vary in different regions and widely even in the same region. (Rules of thumb: Fish grow faster in southern climates where the growing season is longer; they also grow faster where supplies of prime forage are more plentiful.) A very crude average says it takes three or four years for a fish to reach catchable size.

The numbers game enters also into situations where walleyes are stocked artificially to bolster populations or introduce the fish to new waters. A stocking is considered a success when, of the astronomical number of fingerlings put in a system, about five percent are eventually caught by anglers.

But those are abstracts. Let's look at some numbers:

• You can figure to wind up with about 125 keeper fish, four years old, out of 1 million eggs. (Remember, this is variable; some Ontario figures say it takes seven to eight years for a fish to reach 2 pounds!)

• If you have your sights set on a 10-pounder as a trophy, extending our 50-percent mortality rates another eight to 12 years (the time it takes for a walleye, depending on environment, to reach 10 pounds), figure—optimistically—on about two fish that size out of that original million eggs! To look at it another way, it has been estimated roughly that it takes the successful spawn from five or six females to produce one 10-pound walleye!

Now, how do you feel about that 2-pound walleye you just caught? Do you see why experts are becoming concerned that walleyes are not considered a candidate for catch-and-release?

How Fast Do They Grow?

Growth rates, as we have said, vary from North to South. But a complex set of factors—such as balance of walleyes to their forage—can also cause growth to vary significantly within a given region.

But the ultimate size walleyes attain isn't much different from the southern to the northern tip of their range. That is because they live longer in the northern climates. Says Dennis Schupp: "As a rule with fish, it's live fast, die young."

Walleyes in Greer's Ferry reservoir in Arkansas have been known to weigh 15 pounds at age seven or eight. (Remember those Ontario figures? It can take the same length of time for a Canadian fish to reach $1^1/_2$ or 2 pounds!) The primary reason walleyes get big in northern waters is a lack of fishing pressure, although evidence also tells us the colder climates see better survival rates from year to year. But when it takes that long to grow a decent fish, even moderate pressure from sportfishermen can diminish the supply.

How old do walleyes get before dying of natural causes? In the colder northern waters they have been known to reach 20 years of age, while in the South, they rarely live more than about eight.

The accompanying growth chart reflects this. It compares walleye growth rates from various regions. Notice that the lines stop sooner for the southern than for the northern populations.

Community Competition

So far, we have talked about the walleye as though it's the only fish on the face of the earth. In the real world, walleyes swim alongside many other fish species. Some are food sources for them, some are potential predators and some are both at different stages of the walleye's life.

Scientific research has also shown that in the absence of sufficient food stocks, walleyes will eat each other, thereby, it is theorized, naturally controlling their own population numbers during times when other forage is scarce.

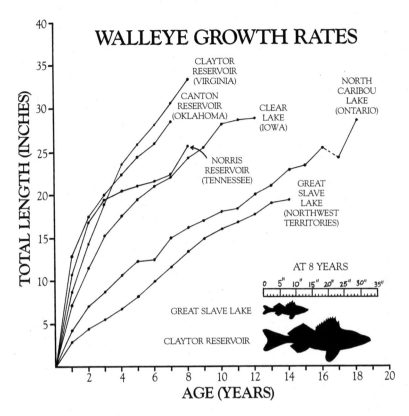

WALLEYE GROWTH RATES

This chart clearly shows the difference in growth rates among various populations of walleyes. The fish from southern waters grow much faster, in general, than their northern counterparts. But southern fish also die younger. (From Synopsis of Biological Data on the Walleye, FAO Fisheries Synopsis No. 119.)

The study of interrelationships among different fish species and the other organisms in their environment is called community relations. There isn't room here to go into the subject in any detail, but as it relates to successful walleye spawning and survival of young walleyes, here are a few tidbits to consider:

• Lakes, rivers and reservoirs tend to have a certain species mix by nature, which is regulated by the system's habitat. A lake tends to be dominated by bass and panfish, for example, for good reason: Conditions are favorable for their reproduction and growth. If young walleyes are put into a lake with a good panfish-bass population, survival can be virtually nil in some cases. They can be wiped out by the voracious "locals."

• Even if young walleyes get to the size where they could turn on the large numbers of panfish, researchers have found that "pan-fish-shaped" prey are not the recipe for sustainable walleye growth. An abundance of longer, thinner prey fish like yellow perch, smelt, shad and the like is better. Putting walleyes into bass/panfish lakes is a low-percentage play.

• If walleyes are forced to compete with large populations of northern pike and other fish that feed on these long, thin prey, there will be a limit to walleye success. Northern pike, for example, have been known to virtually eat yellow perch into extinction in some systems.

So where can and do walleyes live? In what type of waters do walleyes thrive? Does the environment have a strong bearing on the feeding behavior and success of walleyes, or—as some have said—is "a walleye a walleye" no matter where it is found? These are all good questions, and we'll look into them in Section 3, Where To Find Walleyes. But first, Let's look at getting properly equipped for successful walleye fishing.

SECTION 2

Getting Equipped

7

Choosing
A Walleye Boat

I magine this scene in suburban America: A guy named Dick pulls up in the driveway while his wife and kids watch from the kitchen window. They all recognize the car, but there is something attached to the back of it. It's a boat! The kids run outside to gather around Dad, their new hero, who has brought home a lifetime of recreational vistas.

Dick's wife, meanwhile, is tapping the toes of her right foot on the waxless linoleum, arms securely folded, her jaw muscles contracting spasmodically. It's not exactly the kind of boat she had in mind.

The Missus drives directly to the hardware store without stopping to celebrate the latest addition to the family. She buys a series of big black letters, returns home and plasters them on the front of the boat. To this day, the boat bears the label, "DICK'S FOLLY."

My brother's friend Dick wanted a boat badly. He ended up getting a bad boat because he bought the first thing he looked at.

Dick's tragic story, sad to say, is a true one. While Dick's Folly was not a walleye boat, it underscores the most important part of shopping for a walleye boat: think about how you fish, where you fish and what else you want the boat to do.

Walleyes are found in tiny natural lakes, rivers big and small, and massive, sprawling bodies of water like the Great Lakes. Some anglers fish alone or with one good friend most of the time; others take the kids and dog along. So what's the best boat for walleye

The owner of "DICK'S FOLLY" failed to think about what he really needed before buying his boat, breaking an important boat shopping rule. It's important to analyze your needs—and wallet—before buying a boat.

fishing? If you grew up in the heart of the natural walleye range, the answer used to be simple: a 14- to 16-foot aluminum deep-vee fishing boat with a tiller-controlled motor, a depthfinder of some description and perhaps an electric motor in the back. Now the question is almost unanswerable, especially if you are limited to only one boat.

There are certain handling and layout characteristics that tailor a boat to walleye fishing. But many anglers like to fish bass, troll the Great Lakes for salmon and fish crappies, muskies and other species. Some families like to water ski. Buying and equipping a "walleye boat" is a series of compromises, like so many areas of life in a specialized, recreation-conscious world.

What Is A Walleye Boat?

If there is one thing that makes a boat a walleye rig, it's *controllability*. The term *boat control* was born on the windswept waters of the walleye's world. Regardless of how you power your craft, you have to be able to put it where you want it and keep it there.

That's because so many walleye presentations—from live-bait rigging to jigging to trolling—demand that you literally position

Complete Angler's Library

Many pieces of specialized equipment have been developed for walleye fishermen. Splash guards were invented by backtrollers who were tired of getting soaked by waves washing over their transoms.

the bait by moving the boat. If you want to vertically jig, you have to hover your boat in place over the top of the fish, no matter how furiously the wind is blowing. If you want to put a trolled crankbait or a live-bait rig precisely along a jagged course (be it a drop-off, weedline or transition zone between two bottom types), the boat has to steer responsively.

Control carries over into safety as well. Our boats are required to take us to places thought too dangerous until just a few years ago. The hulls of today's walleye boats can handle big water, letting you drift and cast weight-forward spinners on the Western Basin of Lake Erie, backtroll into three- or four-foot waves on Minnesota's sprawling Mille Lacs Lake and troll spinner rigs along a wave-tossed bank on immense Lake Sakakawea in North Dakota.

Walleye tournament anglers are using a growing variety of techniques, including downriggers and planer boards. If you wish to mimic the versatility of these top fishermen, you'll need a lot of storage space on board. That type of space is found only on today's modern, well-designed boats.

The serious tournament angler also relies on speed to win

races to fishing spots. This means that a new generation of big, roomy boats powered by huge outboard motors often rules competitive walleye fishing. Do you need a 120-horse or bigger motor for your walleye trips? Not unless you get into tournaments or are bitten by the speedbug. So, really, a "walleye" boat can be many things, depending on how and where you fish.

Tiller vs. Console: The Raging Debate

Nothing polarizes the walleye angling community more than a discussion of tiller vs. steering wheel boats. Today's top anglers won't argue the notion that there are many ways to catch walleyes, from jigging to rigging to crankbaits, and that walleyes can be found both shallow and deep. But they don't give an inch on their preference for tiller (hand on the throttle) or console (steering wheel) controls.

Speed And Handling

The choice, from a purely fishing perspective, becomes one of a little more speed or a little more precise handling. Console boats can offer more speed, because you can safely handle a bigger motor with the steering wheel.

"The extra speed really helps me," says top tournament angler Keith Kavajecz, who runs a new generation Skeeter console boat with a 135-horsepower outboard. "I figure on most tournament days, I get in 40 minutes or more extra fishing time than the guys running the tillers."

Yet, tillers offer advantages over console boats during the actual fishing process. Typically, it's tough to make an outboard bigger than 50 horsepower that will "troll down" enough to be used as a fishing motor (although manufacturers are making great strides every year; even 75- and 100-horse motors that troll are beginning to appear).

When backtrolling in heavy waves, a powerful tiller is extremely effective. Steering wheel advocates have argued that the turning radius of the bigger tillers is too restrictive to allow precise control. (Turning radius is equally restrictive, or even more so, with a steering wheel, but console users never pretended to use them much for actual fishing.) Traditionally, that has probably been true. Manufacturers have been concerned about the big motors getting away from the operators; it can be tough to handle 60 or more horses in rough water with one hand. But we are seeing wider steering latitude on the new tillers, even up to 75 horsepower.

Backtrolling

Some anglers base their boat decision almost solely on a boat's manageability while backtrolling. *Backtrolling*, the act of running your boat backwards while fishing, was pioneered by famous Minnesota "Nisswa Guide" Harry Van Dorn. It has become a tradition with walleye fishermen for good reason. No matter how skilled you become, you simply can't follow a precise course as well by pushing your boat bow-first as you can by pulling the boat back-end-first.

Now, both tiller and console walleye boats can be fitted with electric trolling motors in the back. Therefore, when the wind is not too heavy, you can backtroll with either boat. But when the wind kicks up you almost have to use a powerful bow-mounted electric in a console boat, because it's more efficient to pull the boat bow-first into the waves.

Top anglers do a good job of controlling their boats in this way. But not as good as equally skilled anglers who simply fire up their big tiller-controlled motor and continue backtrolling. (Although you don't have to look far to get an argument on even this point these days!)

You see, "slop" in the steering wheels doesn't allow quick turns when running backward. (Also, have you ever tried to comfortably hold a fishing rod out the side of the boat while running a steering wheel backward?)

There is a solution, but it will hit you in the pocketbook. A smaller gas-powered "kicker" motor—10-horsepower is the most popular size—can be installed on the transom, giving you the option of firing it up and backtrolling into heavy waves.

"Most of the top guys who are running the steering wheel boats set up a backtrolling station in the back," says Jim Wentworth, a sonar and boat rigging expert whom we will hear from in detail on both subjects. "They'll have an electric back there for sure, and a lot of them put in the gas kicker, too."

Gary Parsons, a member of Team Skeeter, argues that the console boat shouldn't be set up to fish as a console boat.

"We've designed pedestal holes on both sides of the back of

our boats," he says, "one that lets you run the kicker, and one that lets you run the transom electric. We troll a lot of crankbaits, and we don't use the big motor for fishing. With that 10-horse kicker, we have almost a 180-degree turning radius, and it trolls down incredibly slow, so you can fish with it even on relatively calm waters.

"The big motor lets us run at high speeds," Parsons continues, "staying drier and experiencing less fatigue. Yes, it's faster, but once we start fishing, the boat is set up to fish just like a tiller boat. We think it's more of an overall family boat, too, because you can put big enough engines on them to let you do a little waterskiing in the afternoon if you want to."

Some of today's most successful walleye pros say that the trend is turning completely to the steering wheel, because with all the gear pros have to carry, they need a huge boat with lots of room. According to touring pro Mike McClelland it's getting almost ridiculous.

"In order to compete anymore on the variety of waters we fish, you have to fill the boat with more stuff than you even know how to use."

Backtrolling with a transom-mounted electric motor is just one method of presenting a bait by moving the boat. Bow-mounted electrics, smaller "kicker" outboards and big tiller-controlled motors can also do the job.

Complete Angler's Library

Nothing polarizes the walleye fishing community like a good debate over the merits of tiller vs. console boats. Here, Keith Kavajecz maneuvers his console–controlled Skeeter with the front electric.

But realize that the console itself robs the boat of precious interior space. Next time you look at boats in a showroom, visualize the inside of a console boat without the console. It will be a lot roomier.

The debate rages on. In order to compete with the consoles, tournament anglers pressured outboard manufacturers into coming up with 75-horsepower tillers. A diehard tiller fan will change to a console model only to pick up a touch more top-end running speed.

Making Your Choice

So what do you need? Given a choice, most walleye anglers should probably opt for a tiller-controlled motor of about 50 horsepower on a boat about 16 feet long. After all, you probably won't fish tournaments, so taking 10 extra minutes to get to your spots is really no big deal. However, if you plan to fish a lot of big water or do a lot of long-distance running, you might be a good candidate for the steering wheel boat with a big motor.

If you do all your fishing on smaller waters and prefer the ease of handling—not to mention trailering, loading and unloading and storing—go to a smaller rig. There are many fine 14-foot boats on the market that are wider and more stable than those of yesteryear. If you regularly tackle larger, windswept waters, consider an 18-foot or larger craft. Whatever you do, don't make the same mistake our friend Dick did. Think about what you need before you buy or trade up.

8

Rigging Your Walleye Boat

A walleye boat isn't complete without a bit of "candy." The well-equipped walleye angler could consider these "must-have" items: Marine batteries, battery energy gauge, manual battery charger, electric motors in the front and back, splash guards to keep you dry while back-trolling, sonar units, power trim, stainless steel props, rod holders, self-leveling drink holders, bumper, paddle, fire extinguisher, night running lights, personal flotation devices, anchors, rope, spotlight, AM/FM stereo, and anything new that comes along, forever and ever amen.

We'll only discuss a few of these necessities here to help you decide what you need and want for your next boat. Let's get into specifics.

Powering Up: Marine Batteries

Electricity is one of those modern marvels you never notice until something goes wrong. You turn the key and your motor starts. You click on the depthfinder and sonar signals start relaying information back to you. Drop the trolling motor into the water, turn the handle, and presto, your boat quietly moves along.

"Think about what you're most dependent on out on the water," says Wentworth, owner of Fish Lectronics in Nisswa, Minnesota. "Sure, your boat needs to stay together so it doesn't sink. But beyond that, if you don't have any battery power, you're dead on the water. As far as I'm concerned, batteries are by far the

Marine batteries may look identical to their car-powering counterparts, but there are significant internal differences. They are designed to provide hours of continuous power, not just short bursts of energy like those needed to start a car.

most important part of the modern fishing boat."

He's right, and he should know. Wentworth has been rigging and servicing boats in the heart of walleye country since the beginnings of the modern fishing revolution. He has been responsible for thousands of rigs, including those of famous fishermen like Al and Ron Lindner and Babe Winkelman. Your choice of batteries and how you care for them can mean lots of trouble-free outings or a series of ruined weekends.

As you put together your walleye boat, buy top-notch marine batteries. As the name implies, these batteries are made for use on a boat, not in your car or anywhere else. Marine batteries, simply put, are built to take a pounding. Compared with other similar batteries, they have denser plates that are reinforced with special separators to reduce vibration damage and loss of active plate material—stuff that happens quickly to car batteries pressed into service in your boat.

In a deluxe rig, you'll need two different types of batteries: a starting (cranking) battery and a deep-cycle battery. Cranking batteries, because they are made to deliver short bursts of power, are used to start the big motor. Then, assuming the motor is equipped with an alternator, the battery is continually recharged while you run the engine. Deep-cycle batteries are built to provide hours of continuous power and be fully recharged with a battery charger.

Because sonar units draw relatively little power, in most installations they run off the cranking battery. Electric trolling motors and any other juice guzzlers get hooked to the deep-cycle battery. If you have a large boat requiring a 24-volt system to power the electric motors, simply hook two 12-volt deep-cycle batteries together.

Battery Energy Gauge

Nearly as important as the battery itself is a relatively new gadget on the fishing scene: a battery energy gauge.

Strictly speaking, you don't need one. Everything works without it. But putting one on your boat or carrying a portable model takes all the guesswork out of how much battery power you have left, when to charge batteries and for how long.

Marine batteries have amp-hour ratings; the most common sizes are 80 or 105 amps. A battery energy gauge is the only device

This little gauge will tell you at the flick of a switch exactly how much juice your battery or batteries have left. On the author's boat, it's rigged to the starting battery (Batt 1), and the two trolling motor batteries (Batt 2).

that gives you an accurate measure of how much juice (amp hours) you have left, even during use.

Battery gauges have another advantage: They can add to the life of your expensive batteries. The night before you go fishing, you can find out—for sure—how much juice you have. Right before you leave in the morning, it's a simple matter to check again. In the middle of the day, if you need to save electric motor power for the calmer evening hours, you can quickly find out where you sit.

Deep-cycle batteries, Wentworth explains, actually set up a chemical memory if not fully discharged before being recharged. This renders them unable to discharge past a certain point in future use before "acting dead." Think about it; by constantly topping off your charge, you turn your deep-cycle battery into a shallow cycle battery. (Besides, these batteries are only good for about 100 cycles, regardless how far they are run down before being recharged.)

There are devices with indicator lights on them that supposedly show how much battery power remains, but experts say they can be off by as much as 50 to 75 percent. And marine voltmeters only read battery voltage, which stays about the same (around 12 volts) whether your battery is fully charged or nearly dead. Voltmeters tell you whether your alternator is working if you have one, but beyond that they don't offer much practical information.

"You can see what this energy gauge can do for you," Wentworth says. "By measuring the charge before you start fishing and again afterward, you can teach yourself how much juice you use the way you fish. It will be less when it's calm, more when it's windy, for example, with electric motors. You only charge when you need to, and you're never without power unless you're not paying attention.

"Most people never check their starting battery," continues Wentworth, "but if you have a bad wiring setup, you can get a constant energy drain, and when you least want it your motor won't kick over. And an energy gauge can sniff out a bad battery, because it shows if the thing doesn't charge 100 percent."

The gauge alleviates another age-old problem, that of "cooking" the acid out of your batteries by leaving them hooked to a charger too long. It's an excellent way to ruin your battery.

"Even with these so-called trickle chargers," says Wentworth, "there is a constant charge going in as long as they are hooked up. Even if the box says the charger will automatically shut off, it won't. I've seen guys hook their batteries up to these automatic trickle chargers, forget them for a few days and destroy them by literally cooking all the acid out."

Manual Battery Charger

Wentworth recommends a manual battery charger with a timer on it. That way, all you have to do is check the level of charge with the energy gauge. When it gets very low, figure out how many amp hours you need to put back into it, and set the timer for that many hours. (For example: If you have a 105-amp hour battery and it has 20 percent charge left, you have to put 80 percent of the charge back into it. Eighty percent of 105 is 84, so you need to put 84 amp hours of charge into the battery. Your charger will say right on it how many amps it puts in each hour. If you have a 10-amp charger, it will take about $8^1/_2$ hours to fully charge your battery. No guessing. Set it and forget it.)

One thing to remember is that temperature can affect charging time. According to industry officials, as temperature drops below about 60 degrees, both the charger and the battery operate less efficiently. So, the lower the air temperature, the longer it takes to fully charge your battery.

The charger shuts itself off at the end of the time, and you can check it again with the energy gauge to make sure everything is fine. It takes only a few such operations and you can guess how long to set the charger without getting out a calculator. Goodbye guesswork, goodbye dead batteries on the lake! There are only a couple of makers of these gauges. Wentworth suggests the Altus brand made by Altus Tech of Minneapolis, Minnesota.

Electric Motors Fore And Aft

Nothing revolutionized boat control possibilities more than the advent of the electric trolling motor. We now, in fact, take them for granted.

But before you buy and install any electric motors, make sure you buy the right ones. Notice I say motors. It's a real advantage to have two electrics—a transom-mounted "backtrolling" motor and a bow-mounted, foot-controlled partner.

In calmer conditions, you can backtroll with precision using

With the advent of long cords and even remote control, a lone angler can now run both electric motors at the same time, a sophisticated technique that began with the tournament pros and is now being used by knowedgeable weekend anglers as well.

the transom motor alone. Following even complex contours is easy because the boat is extremely responsive when steered backward. When the wind kicks up, you have options:

• Fire up the big gas outboard and steer with it.

• Use the big motor to keep from being blown down the lake and make course corrections with the rear electric.

• Use the front and rear electrics in concert. You can hold in heavy current or wind with the front electric by nosing the bow of the boat into the wind. Then, the extra push you get with the rear electric will usually let you steer with one motor or the other, or both.

• Use the front trolling motor by itself for sneaking up on shallow-water fish or anytime you are casting. Some walleye anglers also like to troll along contours with the front electric.

Whatever you do, don't buy your electric motors before buying your boat! One of the most common mistakes boat owners make is buying an underpowered electric that is too short for their boat. You've seen these people on the water; waves are bobbing their boat up and down, and their electric motor is sucking and shooting water and air every time the boat rides up even a little. In

Make sure the shafts on your trolling motors are long enough to sit deep in the water, no matter how high your boat rides. Inquire before you buy!

Rigging Your Walleye Boat   83

heavy water this is unavoidable, but it should have to get pretty rough before it happens.

There is no equation for "this size boat, this size electric." But it's a good idea to buy more, rather than less, power than you'll probably need. An electric motor that is more than your boat needs in calm conditions will be tested when the wind kicks up. Also, you can run it at slow speeds much of the time, saving on battery power and the life of the motor.

Most boaters will get by fine with a 12-volt system. But for big and/or heavy boats (like the new 18-foot and longer aluminums and many fiberglass models) a 24-volt electric motor can provide the additional power that makes a difference in fishability. You pay an even greater price than having to buy two deep-cycle batteries together to run them, though, says Wentworth:

"With a 24-volt motor there are trade-offs. They're not as efficient. The battery energy-to-pounds-of-thrust efficiency is better on the 12-volters. The 12-volt motors just don't have the top-end push for some of the heavy rigs, though, so in some cases, you have to go to 24 volts."

Here are some tips for maximizing your electric motor rigging and performance:

• It's okay to extend wire length to rig motors a long way from a battery. Use #6 wire for making longer connections. With shorter leads, #10 works fine.

• Be sure to fuse the power line for the trolling motors as you did for the sonar units.

• On your rear backtrolling electric, reverse the head so it can pull your boat in reverse rather than push it, as most motors come from the factory equipped to do.

Splash Guards: Unless You Want To Get Wet

Nothing crashes into your life like a wave that hits flush with the transom and shoots up into your face while you're backtrolling. To avoid this problem consider purchasing quality splash guards.

In the early days, splash guards were crudely crafted from tire rubber and other makeshift materials, often standing too tall to see over. Now we have first-rate, custom-made clear lexan guards with rounded corners and slots for trolling motors. They are such an integral part of walleye fishing that they are becoming standard

As the angler lowers the rear electric into the water, notice that the head has been reversed so that "forward" gear actually pulls the boat strongly in reverse, for backtrolling. A few motors are coming this way from the factory, but most still need to be adapted.

equipment on an increasing number of boats.

If you don't have a set on your rig, put one on. Go ahead, spin back-end first into the wind and let the waves meet you. Not much happens. You feel powerful and in control, the way you should feel on the water.

What you want is a guard that's about eight to 10 inches above the top of the transom. There is no need to build a "wall" like many did in the early days. One thing you might do to the factory-made guards though, is: take some fine sandpaper and work over all the exposed surfaces so they won't cut your line when you're fighting a big fish.

What else is there? For the big motor, power trim and tilt. With really big motors, you don't have a lot of choice; Hulk Hogan would have a hard time lifting them. But trim is nice even on smaller outboards. It's great for running in shallow water and eliminating porpoising and planing problems. Just play a bit with the trim until the problem goes away. The result is more motor efficiency and more top-end speed.

Many anglers prefer stainless steel props to traditional aluminum. The reason behind the development of stainless props is speed, according to Bill Foner, a high-performance boat specialist.

Foner points out that stainless props can be made thinner and more precise, while remaining stronger than aluminum. "If I was running in a lake with a lot of rocks and other hazards," he says, "I think I'd rather have the forgiveness of an aluminum prop. You can always carry a spare. If you bang something with a stainless prop, it might not show any damage, but there's a chance you can mess up the motor gears, and then you're not going anywhere."

Rod holders make precision trolling—or any trolling, for that matter—a lot easier. And if you get a bit less serious as the day goes along, you can put your rods in the holders no matter how you're fishing. That leaves your hands free to hold refreshments.

Add some type of bumper to protect the boat from grinding away against the dock. Store a paddle in the rod locker for those times everything goes wrong or you just want to push off from shallow water without grinding your electric motor prop. A fire extinguisher is mandatory in most states. So are night running lights, which should come standard on better boats. And don't forget PFDs (personal flotation devices).

A good anchor (or two) is a must. Make sure you spend enough money to get at least 100 feet of heavy-duty, smooth-as-silk rope. The person in charge of letting out the line will thank you many times. Buy a spotlight. You'll use it to load and unload, to look for shallow fish at night and to untangle messes.

Oh, and music. An AM/FM stereo is always nice to have.

There you have it—a fairly complete, new-fangled rig. Picture it: just you, Willie Nelson and some big, hungry walleyes.

9

Trailering Your Boat

Trailers, you might say, are kind of a cross between Rodney Dangerfield and a street-corner evangelist: not only do they get no respect, almost nobody pays attention to them.

The excitement surrounding fishing trips doesn't leave much room for disciplined thinking. You carefully pack the boat, make sure you have life jackets along, at the last moment substitute one rod-and-reel for another ("better bring the ultra-light in case the crappies are biting..."). Then you pack the kids or your buddies in the vehicle, brush past the trailer one more time without looking at it and away you go.

"Lunch packed?"

"Check."

"Plenty of gas?"

"Check."

"Extra oil?"

"Check."

"My lucky hat?"

"Check."

"How about the trailer?"

"Still under the boat."

"Okay, we're ready."

For something that performs the critical task of delivering you (and your boat) to and from the water, trailers really do get ignored. Even while shopping for a new boat, trailers rarely enter the conversation, except when you're figuring out which one is cheapest to keep the total package price as low as possible.

There is a science to good trailer design and things to know about fitting them to the boat you own, as well as an art to trailering. We won't dwell on these things. After all, you are anxious to get on the water. But if you don't think about these things a little, you may never get there.

Matching Trailer To Boat

The most critical step in trouble-free trailering is getting the right trailer for your boat. Trailers are given a rating that indicates how much weight they can safely handle. That number is a function of many variables, including the axle, springs, weight of frame, frame materials and tires.

Tires have a surprising influence on the final rating of a trailer. The day of eight-inch tires is long gone, although you still see some on the road, faithfully turning over 200 times for every revolution of a truck's tires. Thirteen- and 14-inch tires are the norm today.

Axle design and strength probably have more to do with how well a trailer performs than anything. Properly built, a trailer axle should have a *positive camber* when the boat is not on it (in other words, it should crown upward in the middle, causing the trailer tires to slightly toe inward). When the boat is loaded, the weight should force the axle to a horizontal position, putting the tires flat on the road.

One of the most common mistakes boat owners make is overloading a trailer. You should have a trailer that's heavy enough to carry *all* weight normally put on it, not just the weight of the boat and motor alone. Think about it; 12 gallons or more of gas weigh a lot, as do marine batteries, anchors, full coolers, tackle boxes and whatever else you normally bring along. An overloaded trailer is easy to spot on the road—the axle is bending downward, and the tires are riding only on the inside tread. This kind of thing is a principal cause of sway. You can get by with it for a while, but usually not forever.

"The springs on a trailer work best when they're stressed to about 75 percent of normal capacity," says DeeAnn Persson of K-Dee Supply, makers of the K-Dee Launcher, considered one of the finest boat trailers on the market. "If the trailer is rated for 1,400

Tackle boxes, gas cans, coolers, it all adds up. Take into account everything you will put into your boat when figuring how much trailer you need. Then buy a trailer that can easily handle everything, not just the cheapest you can find.

pounds, then 1,000 to 1,100 pounds would be ideal."

Most 1,400-pound trailers have axles that can support 2,000 pounds. Tire selection, as stated, often dictates load carrying capacity. Sometimes simply putting on different tires can upgrade the capacity and performance of a trailer.

On a related note, you should also have a vehicle that's matched to the boat, motor and trailer. Common sense will tell you whether your vehicle is overmatched. Still, if your vehicle "doesn't even know the trailer is there" (a sign that you have plenty of control over the rig), driving is not the same. Leave plenty of braking distance between your vehicle and others on the road, don't pull out in front of people like a drag-racer and learn how wide you need to swing on turns. You may not be able to do the drive-through at McDonald's, for example.

Also, if you have a rig approaching 2,000 pounds, consider putting brakes on the trailer, even if they're not required. (Some states have mandatory brake laws for trailers over a certain capacity, usually about 1,500 pounds.)

Driving with a trailer can be scary for people new to it. Occasionally bumpy roads or wind from semis can start the trailer swaying. If this happens, simply grip the wheel firmly and hold it straight. If you try to steer opposite to the direction of the sway, you'll make it worse, and you could lose control. Just hang on and it will straighten itself out. If this happens a lot, there could be several causes. Too much or too little tongue weight and poorly balanced loads (you may have to move gas tanks, tackle boxes and other gear to spread the weight out better) are the most common.

Rollers vs. Bunks

Admittedly, there are two schools of thought on boat trailer construction. Rollers make loading and unloading easier at less-than-ideal landings. Bunks, experts agree, offer more support and protection to the boat while trailering. (It's estimated that up to 75 percent of all weight is in the rear half of most boats, making aftward bunks a real help in supporting the load.)

Today's state-of-the-art trailer has a combination: bunks for solid support and a system that can actually winch the boat up off the bunks and onto a set of rollers, making loading and unloading easy even in shallow water or troublesome ramps.

You can drive a boat directly onto either type of trailer, although bunks should be sprayed with silicone a couple of times per season to "grease the skids," especially if you have an aluminum boat.

If you've never driven a boat onto a trailer, don't panic. Just learn how to line up the nose of the boat with the center of the trailer. Motor up to the trailer—making sure the tow vehicle is securely braked—and bump it; then hit the throttle just enough to skid the boat up as close as you can come to the winch. It gets easy with practice.

Tongue Weight

Tongue weight is the measure of downward pressure on the front (tongue) of the trailer when the boat is on it. Depending on how far forward or backward the boat sits on the trailer (and the balance of the boat's load), the tongue can be extremely heavy, perfectly balanced or actually so light it flies up in the air when you release it from the hitch.

How your rig is balanced determines, to a large extent, how well it rides on the highway. Proper tongue weight, according to Ken Persson of K-Dee Supply, is about five to 10 percent of the

Why involve three people and a set of waders every time you want to put the boat in the water or take it out? If you learn to back the trailer in right, it's a simple matter to drive on with the outboard.

Trailering Your Boat

rig's total weight. It's easy to figure how much your rig weighs. The owner's manuals or boat and accessory catalogs list weights. Add everything up, take a range of five to 10 percent of that, put the tongue or jack stand on a bathroom scale, and you'll know immediately how you're doing. (There are no rules of thumb to guide you, such as "one person should be able to lift the tongue, but with some difficulty" that you sometimes hear. Smaller rigs weigh considerably less than larger ones. A big boat can have 300 pounds or more on the tongue when it is properly balanced.)

On most trailers, U-bolts or a similar arrangement on the winch make it easy to adjust the boat forward or backward to affect the tongue weight. Take the time to get it right.

Using Safety Chains Safely

Some old-time trailer builders and fishermen will tell you not to attach safety chains to your vehicle, that if the trailer comes off the hitch, it should be allowed to roam free. Don't buy into that argument, for a couple of reasons.

Number one, we live in a litigation-happy society. That means, anybody who gets bonked with your roaming trailer will probably sue you and win. Number two, safety chains, if properly used, can turn a potential disaster into nothing more than a quick stop to put the trailer back on the ball.

The secret is to cross the chains, forming a "cradle" that will catch and hold the trailer tongue. The trailer will sway back and forth as the tongue fights the chain arrangement, but you can usually slow to a perfectly safe stop.

Wheel Bearings: The Whole Story

Just about anyone who has traveled a lot to fish has a wheel bearing story to tell.

As you drive, road heat builds up tremendously in the wheel bearings. Then, as you immediately back the trailer into the water, the temperature shock can create a vacuum, allowing water, filled with debris, to seep into the wheel bearing. If the grease seal gives, more water gets inside. Do this a few times and foreign materials build up. In time, the bearings rust, ruining their performance even after they've been cleaned and repacked with grease.

The answer? Regular maintenance, even if you employ a bearing protector. The spring in the protector will take more pressure than the grease seal, but it is still easy to break the seal, causing leakage when you submerge the trailer tires. Load grease into a bearing protector only until the little piston starts to move. If you pump grease in until it forces its way out around the edges, you may have broken the grease seal. Gently apply a moderate amount of grease several times per season, rather than forcing it plumb full once.

Wheel bearings, whether protected with one of these devices or not, should be cleaned and repacked with fresh grease every fall. Any water that finds its way inside should be removed before winter brings a series of freezes and thaws that rust and pit the bearings. Anglers who put on a lot of miles and launch their boat a lot should check bearings frequently.

There may be good news on the horizon for nonmechanical boaters: Traditional bearings could be replaced very soon with a greaseless bearing system. Estimated cost of replacing your old grease-bombs with the new technology? About $75.

Some final thoughts on trailering and trailer care:

• If you can come close to affording it, get a spare trailer tire.

By crossing the safety chains, you provide a cradle for the trailer tongue that could turn a potential disaster into nothing more than an inconvenience.

Make sure changing tools are easy to access. Trailer tires often wear out from sitting in the elements long before the tread wears down. Think about how many years you've had your trailer, not how many miles you've dragged it. Inspect older tires for signs of cracking.

• Many trailers are put together with a lot of bolts. Check them frequently to make sure they're tight.

• Jack stands, the little wheel-and-arm assemblies that swing down to hold the trailer up for easy moving and hitching, are becoming more than a luxury. If you don't have one, think about having one installed.

• At the very least, keep a strap tightened across the back of the boat while trailering. An even better option is a pair of transom tie-downs, available at marine dealers. They attach at angles to the transom, holding the boat steady even on rough roads.

• Trailers with a double-bow support cradle the front of the boat, preventing any upward bouncing on rough roads. They spread the stress of trailering through the trailer and boat hull, giving you a smoother ride and making the miles easier on your investment.

• Mud flaps on the tow vehicle help protect the trailer and boat paint.

Trailering is being talked about more. Chevrolet, for example, has developed a publication on the subject, available at dealers. And, while this may have been more than you wanted to know about the most-ignored piece of equipment in fishing, it could save you a ruined trip somewhere down the line.

10

Sonar: Your Electronic Eyes

To watch a walleye master like Gary Roach at work is to appreciate what the word "pro" stands for. As he pre-fished one morning for a Masters Walleye Circuit (MWC) tournament, his skill with sonar—his ability to instantly interpret every blip across the face of his flasher—carried his boat across the water quickly.

"Okay, here's that big rock flat they were talking about," he said. The boat made graceful arcs left and right, cutting across the water's surface, working out the area. "There's a fish. Ooh, look at that. See that? There's another one. Okay, there's the edge of it. Let's look for a shallow hump."

The boat droned over a large area, occasionally spinning tight corners. "Watch for boats for me, will you?" he asked. He never took his gaze off the flasher dial. "There's another fish. Ooh. Another one. No wonder; there's the edge of a hump. Should we stop and catch a few of these? All right, give me a 'crawler."

Walleye fishing is a mysterious sport. So much of what goes on in the walleye's world is beyond the reach of our senses. We can't see into the water, except in calm, clear, shallow situations.

There is a wonderful machine that allows us to study the shapes and happenings below the surface, no matter how deep or dark. It's called a sonar unit, and it should become your "eyes" for much of your walleye fishing. People like Gary Roach use sonar to get a clear mental picture of structures, transition lines between areas of harder and softer bottom and cover; and to spot baitfish,

"OK, there's the edge of the hump." Gary Roach is at work, eyes glued to the sonar unit, which is mounted in a lockable compartment in his boat. The compartment helps reduce glare, which often makes it difficult to read a sonar unit, and offers security.

larger fish and other details that are missed by most anglers. This is a major reason these guys catch so many fish.

Members of the North American Fishing Club can take a tip from the pros. Coming off the water after a day of fishing, you should be able to draw the outlines of the structures you fished. You should know if there are sharp or slow-tapering breaks in the lake. In fact, you should be able to take soft clay and make a model of the underwater shape of the lake.

Says another top walleye pro, Tom Neustrom, "Always draw a mental picture of the piece of structure in your mind, no matter whether it's a weedbed, sunken island, point, or just the line between mud and sand. Think about what it looks like under there while you fish it. Pay attention to your depthfinder, but use your head to picture what things look like," Neustrom continues. "After you do it a few times it becomes automatic, just one of the things you do. People make way too much out of it; they think it's so much harder than it really is."

Sonar units are getting as common as canoe paddles. Just as common are misconceptions about what they can do for you and what all those signals mean. Can you learn sonar use by reading a

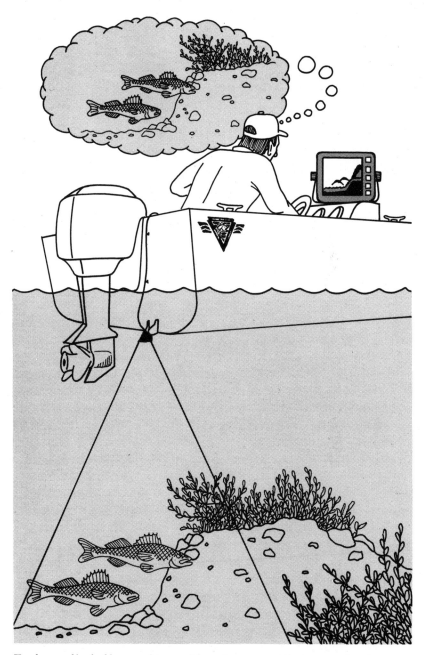

Teach yourself to build a mental image of the underwater world by learning what the various sonar signals represent. When you look at the sonar screen, don't see dots, blips or scratches; try hard to "see" the fish, the weeds and the bottom contours!

Sonar: Your Electronic Eyes

chapter in a book? No, but you can learn what to expect and what certain things look like. It's up to you to learn the rest out on the water.

How Sonar Works

Without going into microelectronic detail, here's how sonar works, and what it can and can't do:

• The sonar unit gathers power from your battery and sends an electrical signal down the cord to the transducer. The transducer converts the electrical impulse into sound waves that can travel through water. The sound waves power their way down, where they bump into the bottom and anything else dense enough to reflect them. The reflected signals bounce back to the transducer where they are received and again changed into electrical impulses. Those impulses—based on how long they took to go down and come back—are displayed on the screen or dial at different "depths."

Believe it or not, one signal is sent down, returns and is displayed before another is released! It happens incredibly fast, about 10 times per second on the average.

The sound waves entering the water take on a certain shape. This is called the area of coverage or *cone angle*, implying that the signal is cone-shaped. It is actually shaped more like a water balloon held vertically. The strongest portion of the signal is in the center of this hypothetical cone, which explains why it is harder to pick up fish and other objects toward the edges of the cone. Different transducers operate at different frequencies, making the cone angle larger or smaller. Most transducers on fishing sonar operate at about 200 kilohertz, which is a good compromise for showing details in structure and finding fish. For getting a wider look at the bottom, and for applications like following downrigger balls, anglers often use wider-angle transducers operating at about 50 kilohertz.

• All modes of sonar—flashers, paper graphs, liquid crystals, videos and digital readouts—work exactly the same. The laws of physics don't change when you go from a flasher to a liquid crystal. (Many units, in fact, can work off the same transducer—one at a time, of course.) *The major difference is in how they display information to you.*

There are some differences in performance, though. Flashers

work *faster* than other types, because the signal goes through less processing before being displayed. You can see this by comparing different types on the water. Almost before your eye can follow the changes, a flasher display moves up and down with the varying lake contours.

Liquid crystal displays, while acceptably fast for most uses, lag behind. The display just can't scroll by as fast as a flasher can "bleep" new information.

Paper graph performance speed is limited by how fast the stylus can scratch display information on specially treated paper. If it is too fast, the display is difficult to read. The picture type display is preferred by many anglers, though, for examining fishing spots in detail.

• For quality performance sonar units need sufficient power and a sensitive receiver. All of today's top units have adjustable power, or *sensitivity*, settings. In shallow water you don't need the sensitivity (sometimes called gain) turned up as high as when you're in deeper water. In fact, you can have the finest sonar unit in the world, but if you don't have the sensitivity turned up high enough, the only thing you may see on the screen is the bottom signal.

That's because the bottom is much denser than other targets, such as weeds, sticks and fish. Many anglers go through their lives using their sonar units only to tell them how deep the water is! It's easy to get a bottom signal. But to see all the "little things," you need to *turn the sensitivity up well beyond what it takes to* get a bottom signal. To a lot of sonar users, the display looks "cluttered" when they have the gain turned up where it should be. Maybe they don't want to see all those fish and all that cover down there!

Constantly adjusting sensitivity to match the changing depths and conditions is more important than words can say. "Being able to see fish on a depthfinder has won a lot of tournaments for me," says Jim Randash of South Dakota, a regular in walleye tournament circles. "The use of the depthfinder is the difference between a good fisherman and one who isn't. Make sure you have the power turned up as high as you possibly can and still be able to make out the various things on the display. That's the only way you'll see fish and baitfish all the time."

Even if your sonar unit is completely automatic, learn how to manually adjust the sensitivity. Take an hour to toy with this critical control. Turn it up until the whole dial lights up or the whole screen is filled with information. Turn it down until everything is gone but the bottom signal. Find the middle ground, but always flirt with too much information. Otherwise, you may miss all the details the unit can show you.

What Sonar Can And Can't Do

Sonar, strictly speaking, is a distance-measuring device that works in water. The sound waves sent and received by the transducer can travel through water but are reflected back by denser things.

The time it takes a signal to go down, hit something and bounce back is recorded by the unit as a display at a certain depth. Sonar signals can't distinguish between animate and inanimate objects or give you anything more than a relative indication of size.

They can't show you the difference between different species of fish. You can guess what a signal is likely to be, based on clues such as time of year, water depth and what you have caught in a given spot before. But anyone who says their unit can show the

Notice that the sensitivity knob is turned up quiet high, giving a bottom reading (26 feet) and a "second echo" at twice that depth. Notice also that there is a fish less than a foot off the bottom, which shows up clearly. If the sensitivity were turned down, the fish might not show up.

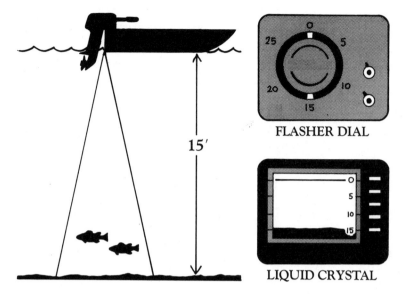

FLASHER DIAL

15′

LIQUID CRYSTAL

Unless you turn sensitivity (sometimes called gain) high enough, a sonar unit won't return signals from anything but the bottom. All the "little things" like fish, baitfish, weeds and other cover won't show up on your display. Turn it up!

difference between walleyes and bass has been out in the sun too long.

Because fish are denser targets than many weeds and other forms of cover, sonar manufacturers have developed units they say will "positively" identify fish, often in a different color than things attached to the bottom. There are even units made with little fish swimming across the screen. These units work well for beginners. But if you are a serious angler and want to improve your skills, buy a top-of-the-line unit that makes no such claims, and learn how to use it.

Flashers and color video units that light up in multiple colors can help if you understand what the colors mean and keep your expectations within the limits of what the unit can deliver. Denser objects show up as brighter colors. Less dense objects show up as paler colors. That's all you can expect.

These same principles apply to units that display in one color. Denser objects and those in the center of the cone show up brighter. Big fish show up as brighter and wider signals than small baitfish. Clouds of baitfish are often mistaken for big fish, but there are ways of at least making a good guess at what they are, and in some cases the differences are obvious once you know what to look for. We'll discuss telling them apart later.

Much of how signals show up is affected by the position in the cone from which the target is marking. Remember, signal strength peaks at the center of the cone and drops off to all sides. If you mark a huge fish on the edge of the cone, it will look smaller than a small fish that swims through the center of the cone! Often, even a huge fish or other dense target will not show up as such—no matter how many colors or shapes the display comes in—if the thing is at the edge of the cone (or if the sensitivity is not turned up high enough).

Where Is That Fish?

Assuming we have this three-dimensional cone of sonar coverage displayed on a one-dimensional screen, how do we know exactly where those fish are that we're marking?

We don't, at least most of the time. For one thing, sonar signals at the edge of the cone travel farther to reach the same "depth" than those in the center. That raises all kinds of interesting possibilities:

• Even if two fish are at the same depth, if one is at the center of our cone and the other at the edge somewhere, the fish directly below us will display as being shallower than the fish at the edge.

• Fish directly on or near the bottom at the edge of the cone can show up as being below the bottom signal! If you know to look for this, you can suspect bottom-hugging fish, say, on a flasher display, and switch to a picture-type unit to see if the signals are indeed fish.

• Fish that start marking at the edge of the cone, pass through the center and exit at the trailing edge of the cone will display relatively deeper, shallower and deeper again. This produces the classic "hooks" or "arches" on a picture display. It is also visible on a flasher, but you have to be experienced and alert to catch it. If you see the hooks, you know the fish were at one point directly below you and now have exited your cone coverage.

Some expert walleye fishermen think that stationary fish displaying as perfect arches are likely to be inactive and tough to catch. These anglers get more excited when they come across worm-like, squiggly fish markings that indicate more active fish.

• With conventional sonar, if a fish is at any edge of the cone

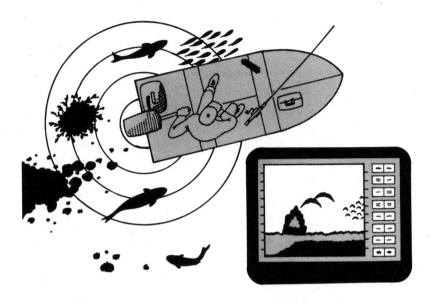

Keep in mind that sonar units show you a one-dimensional display of a three-dimensional world. The "cone" of sonar coverage is gathering signals from a circular swath below you, but showing it on a flat screen or dial. You have to visualize "where" things are under your boat.

coverage, we can't tell in which direction the fish is located. It may be to the front, rear or to either side.

There are now "3D" transducer arrangements that allow you to switch from looking primarily at the right, center or left side of the total cone coverage. That helps pin down which side of your boat the fish is on.

How Much Am I Seeing?

There are a number of different transducers available in various cone angles. The most commonly used is the 20-degree cone angle, but the very narrow 8-degree and the very wide 50-degree cone angles are available.

Wider cones are popular with big-water trollers who want to chart downrigger balls and trolled lures. Some shallow-water anglers also like them for the expanded coverage area they show. (See page 105 for coverage comparisons.)

Narrow-beam transducers with cones of about eight degrees are popular with some anglers, especially those who fish through the ice. The narrow beam allows them to watch for fish that are directly beneath their hole, not 20 or 30 feet away.

Some sonar manufacturers are experimenting with "3D" transducers, which they claim will help anglers pinpoint the location of the fish displayed on the screen.

Suppression: Only At High Speeds

All modern sonar units have one or more "noise-reduction" filters of some kind. Some help you cut down on the amount of microscopic plant and animal matter you display near the surface. These surface clarity controls can be useful, especially in midsummer when huge algae blooms fill the upper layers of water. Other controls help fight electrical or cavitational (caused by air bubbles) interference. These controls, usually called suppression, do exactly what the name implies—suppress, or reduce, unwanted signals.

Simply put, suppression changes the frequency (pulse length) of the signal sent out by the unit. By doing so, it cuts much of the interference out of the display (it does nothing to eliminate the cause). In the bargain, you lose a lot of your unit's precision in discriminating between objects that are close together. Turning up the suppression often blends two fish that may be a few feet or more apart into one big signal. Groups of baitfish and even nearby gamefish can blend into something that looks like it could swallow your boat.

Don't turn the suppression knob up at all unless you need to

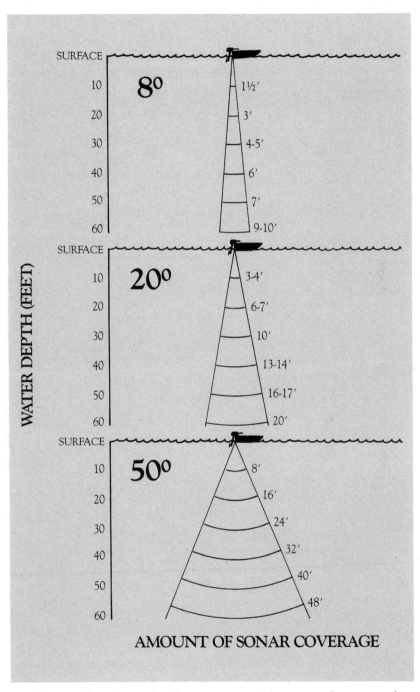

WATER DEPTH (FEET)

8⁰

SURFACE
10 — 1½'
20 — 3'
30 — 4-5'
40 — 6'
50 — 7'
60 — 9-10'

20⁰

SURFACE
10 — 3-4'
20 — 6-7'
30 — 10'
40 — 13-14'
50 — 16-17'
60 — 20'

50⁰

SURFACE
10 — 8'
20 — 16'
30 — 24'
40 — 32'
50 — 40'
60 — 48'

AMOUNT OF SONAR COVERAGE

This illustration shows the amount of bottom coverage with various transducer cone angles.

Sonar: Your Electronic Eyes

while running across the lake at high speed. Even then, use it only to keep your bottom reading visible. When you slow down and start fishing, if you need suppression to keep out unwanted interference, you need to have your electrical system checked.

Knowing how to properly operate today's sonar units and interpret their many signals is vital to becoming a good walleye fisherman. Make sure you study the owners manual of the unit(s) you buy before mounting and using it. That is the best way to insure top performance. And don't be afraid to experiment with your unit. You'll be amazed at the things you'll find when you turn up the sensitivity or override the automatic function. Today sonar can do much more than most anglers ask it to do.

11

Selecting The Right Sonar

hat may at first seem like a dizzying array of sonar styles boils down to only two major choices: flasher or picture-type displays. (There are also digital-only readouts, but they're not for serious fishing applications; you might see them on a boat where the driver is concerned only with water depth.)

So, you have the simplicity of the flasher and a trio of picture-type displays: paper graph, liquid crystal and video. We're not going to get into a lengthy dissertation on the pros and cons of each, but here are a few things to think about:

The Flasher

People have been predicting the demise of the flasher for a long time. It's regarded by some of today's high-tech anglers as crude and hard to use. Crude it's not; in fact, the information displayed on a flasher comes to you faster and is less "processed" than any other unit. Its cheering section comprises the best and most influential anglers in the world.

"There are no big tricks out there," says Jerry Anderson, a top-notch walleye tournament pro. "You don't see seven different screens in front of Gary Roach. He might have three machines in the back, but tell me what he's looking at while he's fishing—a flasher. That's all that's sitting in my boat right now. See what Mike McClelland uses. See what Bob Propst uses. It's no secret."

Nor is it a mystery, according to Jim Wentworth. "If push

When deciding which sonar mode is right for you, realize that there are essentially only two: flashers and picture-type display units like this liquid crystal. While information from a flasher requires a bit more interpretation, many top anglers would not leave the dock without one.

comes to shove," he says, "I guarantee you every pro would be running a flasher. It's pure analog output, with infinite resolution. It's just raw, unprocessed data you can control and interpret yourself. For ease of operation and detail, once you understand the fundamentals of using a flasher, it's the way to go."

Flashers are unsurpassed for running a lake at high speed, looking for structural elements, sections of shallower and deeper water, the presence of fish and areas of differing bottom densities. In fact, this last item, finding areas where rock gives way to mud and the like, may be the flasher's strong suit. The presence or absence of a "double echo" once the sensitivity is set right, and the brightening, widening, dimming or thinning bottom signal say a lot.

There are some situations where the flasher's dial display is a disadvantage. Namely, when your boat is positioned over a steep drop-off, any fish along that break will be lost in the overlapping signal that shows the shallow and deep ends of the break and all the bottom signals in between. (The same thing can happen when fish are holding around big boulders in rocky lakes.) Also, as mentioned earlier, fish sitting tight to the bottom at the edge of the

Complete Angler's Library

cone will display under the bottom reading.

Still, don't dig a grave for the flasher yet. Says Roach: "I hope they never throw it out, personally. Most people seem to want to see fish, so now they've got the little pictures of fish on some (units). This is getting to be like video games or something. I mean, come on, flashers aren't *that* hard to use."

The Picture Displays

It's not exactly like they need equal time. For many (if not most) anglers, the pictorial markings and cross-section of the bottom are the ultimate in a close look at the walleye's world.

Paper Graphs

A good paper graph has the most detailed display of all, about five times the resolution of the best liquid crystal. The drawbacks of the graph are well-documented: Paper is expensive and sometimes hard to get; it's a hassle to load paper when you want to be fishing; and in time the unit collects messy carbon residue. Still, for the serious walleye angler, it remains the ultimate sonar weapon because of its incredible resolution.

Liquid Crystal And Video

There's no question we are in the age of the liquid crystal, because we're in the age of the computer. The heart of the liquid crystal sonar unit is a tiny microprocessor. Customer-wowing bells and whistles can be built in until sonar salespeople sound like carnival barkers. Some have built-in simulators and even video games (do you hear that, Gary Roach?) for those slow days on the water.

Still, liquid crystals are not all glitz. Because of their computer-based circuitry, they can be easily interfaced with Loran-C navigators and any future technological breakthroughs. The screens are getting better all the time, thanks to developing pixel technology. Even top pros are starting to use them, not just putting them on their boats to satisfy sponsor contracts.

Two of the young lions of tournament walleye fishing, in fact, radiate praise for the utility of liquid crystals. Gary Parsons and Keith Kavajecz, recent MWC Team-of-the-Year title winners, use one almost exclusively for their precision presentation tactics.

"We're a little different than the average bear," says Parsons, a

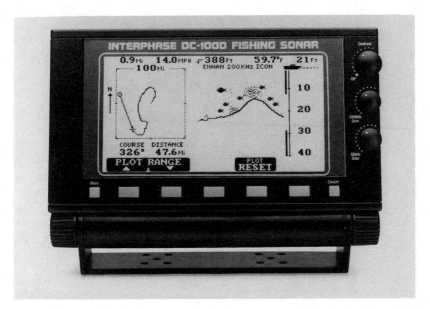

Modern liquid crystal display sonar units, with their improving resolution, give anglers all the information they need. It uses a wide beam to search broad areas and a narrow beam to pick up fine details on the bottom.

part-time dentist from Chilton, Wisconsin. "We actually feel that the liquid crystal or video units help us stay on a contour (follow a breakline) better than a flasher. First off, it gives you a memory of where you were. It also gives you a line to look back at, to see how you're doing. No matter who you are, you can't be looking at the depthfinder all the time; you have to see what the other boats around you are doing."

"It also gives you a digital readout," chimes in Kavajecz, a computer programming wiz for IBM when he's not fishing. "It says 10, 10, 10, and then when it goes to 11 you instantly know you're going too deep. If it flashes 8 or 9 you know you're getting too shallow."

Back to Parsons: "It's the memory that's really nice. We grew up reading flashers, but you take that unit we have now with a 43-degree transducer and I can run structure twice as fast as guys with flashers."

With their liquid crystal or video unit, Parsons and Kavajecz ("P & K" as they're known in the trade) flip the power on in the morning and let it run all day, without worrying about running out of paper like guys who constantly run paper graphs.

"Nobody can tell us that a flasher is just as good," says Kavajecz. "You can tell fish and baitfish on a flasher, sure, but what about when you're on a steep drop-off? That's where walleyes live half the time."

P & K also argue that when inexperienced anglers turn on a flasher, they tend to doubt that the flashes they see are fish or other meaningful displays. "I've fished with a flasher for years," says Parsons, "and when you learn to read them, they're good. But when you start fishing with them you swear something's wrong with them because you think, 'It just flicked at five feet. There, it just flicked at 10 feet. That can't be a fish, it must be a glitch in the unit. What was that?' Stuff goes by anglers so fast they can't interpret it, and they don't believe it.

"The way I learned to read a flasher was by turning one on next to a graph," Parsons continues. "I'd stare at my flasher, see a blip, then quick look over to the graph and sure enough, it was a fish. After a while you can turn the graph off most of the time, but it seems to take a long time to learn to trust a flasher. If you run a flasher for 20 years you're going to trust it, and you'll probably like it better than anything else. But I think I can teach somebody to

Some feel video display sonar units are more fragile than they really are. And although they are reliable and perform very well in the field, their higher price tags have led to inconsistent sales.

run and trust a video or liquid crystal faster."

Video display units make some experts feel that because of the construction of the units—with a cathode ray tube similar to the picture tubes in a television set—they are bound to be fragile. Yet several companies are making video units that stand up to the pounding of big waves. Video sonar makers found a way to mount the tubes in a free-standing state, not connected to the unit's housing; return rates on some brands are among the lowest for any type of sonar. They are expensive, though, and it's a developing, inconsistent market. The allure is there; the displays are often colorful and appealing.

12

Installing Your Sonar

Correctly interpreting the blips and scratchings made by fishing sonar is tough enough without problems caused by poor rigging. Modern sonar units are well-built. Very few units have problems before they are installed on boats. Powerful potential sits in that box. Let's not lose it between there and your boat.

In the next chapter, we'll go into detail on using sonar units. For now, let's concentrate on installing them properly, which means taking the time to read your owner's manual before starting. According to the experts consulted for this book, practically all major installation problems could be prevented if people sat down and studied the manual. In just one evening, many frustrations can be avoided.

End of sermon.

All sonar units have a sending/receiving device called a *transducer*, connected via coaxial cable to the unit itself, which displays the signals on a screen or dial. Paper graph, liquid crystal and video units have a display screen. Flashers use a dial. They all provide information, but in different ways and in varying degrees of detail.

The transducer must be mounted correctly to work properly. In some fiberglass boats, you can install transducers flush with the bottom of the hull in what is called a "shoot-through" mount, but most transducers are mounted externally. If the sonar is installed correctly and working properly, you will get a good reading of what's below the boat even while running at high speeds.

No matter where you mount the transducer, it needs to be running in the "blue water" area. This means it must be mounted away from most of the turbulence being caused by the ribs, or keelsons, or any other irregularities in the boat hull. On aluminum boats, this is almost always smack in the middle between the keelsons. But to be sure, if you can run your boat before installing the transducer, get going about half-throttle and look back at the water flowing away from the hull. (Bring a friend if you own a console boat.) Find the smoothest area and mount the transducer there.

In external bracket mountings, mount the transducer level with the water's surface and at least $1/2$ inch below the water line. With the boat up on the trailer, you can usually eyeball it well enough.

As mentioned, you can install transducers flush with the bottom of the boat and shoot through some fiberglass hulls. (This doesn't work well on aluminum boats because the material blocks out an estimated 40 to 60 percent or more of the signal. Before attempting this or having someone do it for you, find out *exactly*

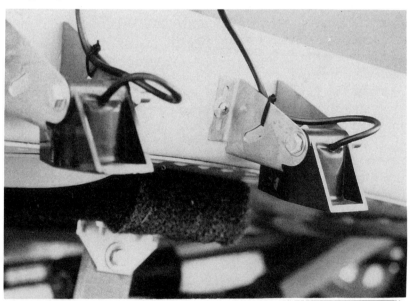

The difference is subtle, but look carefully at the "angle of attack" of these two externally mounted transducers. The flasher's transducer (right) is tipped forward to help with high-speed performance. The graph's transducer (left) is mounted to send signals straight down.

what your hull is made of. Sonar can shoot through fiberglass fairly well, but some fiberglass boats are made with wood or other bracings that can absorb most of the signal. It's an expensive and laborious mistake to put the transducer down and have to move it later.

There are enough advantages to external bracket mounting to make it advisable. If you ever want to troll with downriggers and follow the weights, you can angle the transducer backward to pick them up. You lose that option if the transducer is cemented to the hull. It's also impossible to adjust the transducer angle if it isn't right for either "target marking" or high-speed running. About the only disadvantage in mounting transducers with outside brackets is their vulnerability should you hit something.

In order to correctly mount the transducer for the job you want it to do, there are some things to take into account, according to boat-rigging expert Jim Wentworth.

"With any of the picture-display units—the liquid crystals, paper graphs or videos," he says, "you are looking for those fish to show up as good symmetrical arches when they're right under your boat. In order for this to happen, you have to mount the transducer so it points *straight down* when the boat is in the water. That's why, even when I'm installing a unit in a fiberglass boat where I could do a shoot-through mount, I'll usually suggest we put the transducer on the outside of the hull on an adjustable bracket. That way, if the angle isn't quite right, we can move it until it is."

That's what you want when you have slowed down and are examining an area in detail, but much of the time you will be running at fairly high speed—often half-throttle or more—searching for structure, schools of fish, transition zones between different bottom types and a variety of other things.

For high-speed work, mount the transducer at "a positive angle of attack," Wentworth says. This means that it should be mounted facing forward, so it "looks" slightly ahead of the boat. Again, with an adjustable external bracket, it's easy.

"You can't mount a transducer for both a speed mode and a target mode," Wentworth says. "You have to decide what job you want each of your sonar units to do. I'll guarantee you that every pro uses one unit—usually a flasher—for high-speed running, and a paper graph or good liquid crystal as their target unit."

Rental boats don't have to mean loss of sonar performance. Here, Dave Genz demonstrates use of his "Ice Box" portable rig by Winter Fishing Systems in Minneapolis, Minnesota. It uses a 12-volt motorcycle battery to power the sonar. The box accommodates flashers, liquid crystals and smaller paper graphs, and is an excellent way to take your sonar with you.

If you mount the transducer in a relatively turbulence-free area, you won't have big problems with air bubbles washing across the face of it and causing interference on the display. But there are other sources of potential trouble.

In today's boats, there are many electrical devices that interfere with sonar. Radio frequency interference can be caused by outboard motors, marine radios and anything else that puts out frequencies similar to your sonar. The best way to avoid such problems is to install the transducer wires as far from other lines as possible.

With many boats, however, there is only one internal access area for wiring, leaving you few options. The best you can do, at least initially, is to lay all the wires side by side and see if everything works.

If you get sonar interference, you may have to run the sonar wiring on the other side of the boat, securing it as much as possible.

Interference can also come from your electric motors. This is especially true with bow-mounted electrics, because the only good way—at least for now—to mount the transducer for a front sonar unit is to attach it directly to the housing of the trolling motor. Placing the wires in contact with the motor is inviting interference. And these days, with the advent of pulse-width modulators (called "Maximizer," "Dura Amp" and other trade names) that help you get more out of each battery charge, the interference potential is worse than ever. (Notice the word *potential*; in many cases, there will be no problems.)

The best way to avoid such problems if your motor has a pulse-width modulator is to hook the sonar unit and the electric motor to different batteries. If they are connected to the same battery, Wentworth says, "you will probably have a problem, especially when the sensitivity on the sonar unit is turned up."

When the pulse-width modulators first came on the market, rumors circulated that they could damage or ruin sonar units. A few flashers have been blown, according to Wentworth and other sources, but that problem has basically been corrected. They can cause interference but shouldn't hurt your sonar unit.

Wentworth is experimenting with ways of mounting a transducer to the outside of the hull at the bow. He's developing a system to solve these age-old problems.

While rigging your sonar, make sure you put a fuse in the positive line. It can be an in-line fuse or installed in a fuse panel. Also, consider seriously the addition of quick-connect devices to the power cords. Install them at the unit, so you can easily unplug the current when not fishing. Even though the unit is turned off, there is a drain on the battery that will show up in time and can cause corrosion. If you don't put on quick-connects, at least get in the habit of unscrewing the power connections at the end of each fishing day.

Quick-connects are also used in custom wiring jobs where you will be using different sonar units from the same station. For example, you might want to use a flasher to run at high speed, then switch to a liquid crystal when you slow down to look things over. Even if they use different size power cords, you can simply snap one out and the other in.

There are advancements being made daily in the world of boat rigging. Wentworth has designed custom electrical systems that include:

• Transducer switch boxes that let you choose between transducers of different cone angles (more on this in the next chapter). They can also, at the flip of a switch, let you view the signal coming from the back or the front transducer, to check differences in depth. The change can be dramatic when you're over a sharp-breaking contour.

• A spare battery-in-waiting and emergency jump lines. You can literally jump yourself if your cranking battery fails suddenly or get a jump start from another friendly boater.

• Special recharging lines that allow you to plug in battery chargers without having to get at the battery terminals.

"The future of boat rigging is going to blow people's minds," says Wentworth. "You ain't seen nothin' yet."

Here are a few other tidbits that should help you get the most performance out of your sonar units:

• Don't bend or twist the wires severely, ever. They easily break apart, and you might not see it happen through the sheath.

• Don't change the length of the transducer cord. If it gets cut accidentally and you can splice it without losing more than a foot or so, you should be fine. But the sonar unit is a finely calibrated machine that bases its accuracy on the time it takes the signal to go down and come back. Part of that accuracy is the known

On goes the Loran-C antenna. Like other electronic equipment, it doesn't just go anyplace. Keep it away from your sonar units and other sources of radio frequency, if possible, and mount it high in the boat for better reception.

amount of resistance in the transducer cable. When you change it a lot, you throw off the calibration. (Fortunately, with some brands, transducer cords are interchangeable between units. If you ruin one cable/transducer setup, you can simply buy another and away you go.)

• Whenever possible, install the units on swivel mounts. Being able to change viewing angle makes a huge difference in how well you can see the display, particularly in bright sunlight, and especially with liquid crystals. There are several makes, but you can't go wrong with Johnny Ray brackets.

Mounting Navigational Equipment

It's getting harder to get lost all the time, thanks to modern navigational equipment. Marine compasses let you align lake maps accurately while surveying new waters, and Loran-C units take you back to hard-to-find hotspots with remarkable accuracy. (We'll get into using these tools in chapter 14.)

There's no rocket-science trick to mounting a marine compass. Just get it as far as possible from any potential magnetic fields or large metal areas. All good compasses have magnetic compensators to fight this interference. Install the compass in the boat, then point the boat north (check it against another compass, or do it in a familiar area). Adjust the north-south compensator as needed until the reading is accurate. Now point the boat east or west, and do the same thing with the east-west compensator, and the compass should work well.

If you're entering the high-tech world of Loran-C navigation, mount the module as high as possible in the boat. Try to keep it clear of dense objects that could "blind out" the Loran signal, such as consoles. Also, keep it away from sonar units and other sources of radio frequency, if possible.

You'll need a long whip antenna, so figure out an installation area that will allow you to clamp it down for trailering and "garage time." A variety of lengths and makes of Loran antennas are available. They retail between $30 and $150. It's advisable to get one at least eight feet long, and for general fishing use, figure on spending about $30 to $50. If, however, you plan to navigate on the Great Lakes or other huge, open waters and precision is critical, consider a higher-buck antenna.

13

Using Sonar: Underwater Concepts

When you buy a sonar unit, it comes with an instructional manual that shows most types of signals you're likely to encounter and how to interpret them. Read it. Study it. It's your best guide to operating the unit properly. In other words, getting what you paid for.

Here are just a few basic displays that help illustrate general concepts crucial to sonar success.

Visualizing: The Essence Of Sonar Use

Blinded by the flat surface of the water, hypnotized by the gentle rocking of the waves, most anglers never really get an idea of what's down there underneath it all.

What a mental barrier you have to break down! All your life, you've learned to rely on eyesight for visual information. Now, to become a skilled angler, you have to rely on a sonar machine? It's going to take some faith, understanding and imagination to break down that barrier.

The physical world is not that different above and below water. To train your mind to visualize all the interesting things underwater, it is helpful to observe the structure and contours of dry-land features. Visit an open-pit mine area or a gravel pit. Or just watch carefully as you drive your vehicle down the highway. Land you think of as flat actually has many dips, cuts and points, to borrow a fishing term. You'll see undercut banks, areas of heavy cover, large flat expanses, and deep and shallow areas. If you were

Take as much time as you need to make sense of all those squiggly lines on a contour map. Teach yourself to see the lake bottom in 3D. You can do it!

a fish, where would you go? If you were a minnow trying to get away from a walleye or a walleye looking for a prime feeding spot, where would you go? When it's hot and sunny, where is the shade?

It's not much different underwater. That's one of the first observations a beginning scuba diver makes; other than all the moss and algae collected on everything, a lake bottom could be the field across the road.

Using The Tools We Have

We have two main tools to help us "see" the physical makeup underwater: contour maps and sonar displays. Neither is immediately easy to decipher, much less transfer into a three-dimensional picture. But before you can become a good angler, you have to be able to use both.

Grab a contour map of a lake. You see all those confusing lines, right? Starting now, learn to read it. Take as much time as you need. Start at shore and find the first contour line, which usually represents five or 10 feet, depending on the lake. Don't move to the next line until you have seen the bottom "fall away" in your mind down to five or 10 feet below the shore height. Now move out to the next line and imagine falling deeper into the lake.

This has to become second nature. Glance at the map, see the ups and downs, the hills and valleys, the flat stretches, the vast areas of shallow and deep water. Don't look for lines on a map; make your mind see the depths as if someone has built for you a clay model of that lake bottom.

You have no idea how big a step you just took. Most anglers never get to this point.

Now, go out on the water, map in hand, sonar unit running. Start at shore. Go slowly, watching the display as it drops down to five or 10 feet. You are at the first contour line. Keep going to the next one and the next until you fall off into the basin of the lake. Turn and run back up shallow. Visualize what's under you. Don't just look at the map, and don't just see what's on the sonar display at the moment. Remember in your mind's eye what came before and try to predict what's coming next. Yes, it's a pain in the neck at first, and boating and fishing are supposed to be fun. But give it time to become second nature; then you can start having fun.

The first thing you will discover is that maps are not perfect! They are not made for precise fishing needs; they're made for bio-

The flasher display clearly shows a soft lake bottom. Notice that the sensitivity (right hand) dial is turned up quite high, yet the bottom signal (at 24 feet) is thin, and there is no second echo at 48 to 50 feet, which there would be if the bottom were harder.

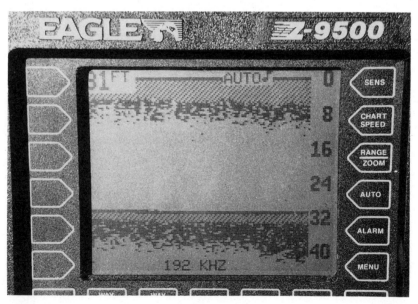

In this photo, we see the same thing on a liquid crystal display. The bottom, in 31 feet, is flat and soft. You can tell this by the thin grayline, or lighter area directly under the thin black bottom signal. With a harder bottom, the grayline is much wider.

Complete Angler's Library

This photo shows a flasher display of a much harder lake bottom. Notice that the sensitivity is turned up to exactly the same level as it was in the upper photo on page 124. But here you see the bottom signal at 26½ feet, a much wider signal than in the upper photo on page 124. Also, a second echo has appeared at twice the bottom depth. The appearance and disappearance of the second echo is the thing to look for when analyzing bottom composition.

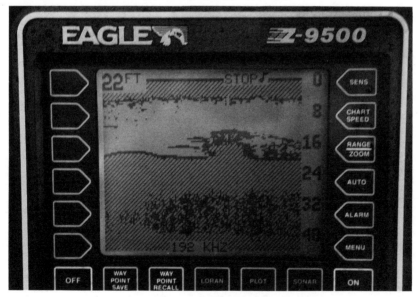

This photo shows a liquid crystal display of a harder bottom. The grayline is much wider than it was in the lower left photo, and you can see a "second echo" of the bottom at 40-plus feet. Notice also the main feature of this display: fish holding all around the hump, which tops off at about 15 feet! Those structure-oriented fish are probably catchable.

Using Sonar: Underwater Concepts

Here's what fish look like on a flasher. The lake bottom is in about 16 feet in this example, and the continuous bottom signal above that indicates a thick mat of weeds. Two fish, the definite lines at 10 and 11 feet, are riding above the tops of the weeds.

However, as this photo shows, weeds can look like fish on a flasher. This shows a nice bed of tall, stringy cabbage weeds that stop growing about six feet from the surface. Fish on a display like this are difficult to pick out.

Complete Angler's Library

logical study, normally by state or federal government agencies. These people don't need maps that have every little point and finger. They just need a rough idea of how much shallow and deep water a lake has, and where the major reefs and bars are. If you can learn to visualize the contour map, you will become very good at reading the sonar display. You'll learn that if you run in a straight line, the display reflects the contours of the lake in that direction. If you run in a zigzag pattern roughly parallel with shore, the display simply shows you the deep and shallow sides of the breakline you are following. Most anglers don't know where on the lake the various readings on their sonar display came from.

Run in a straight line and watch the sonar unit build a display. Look backward. That's where the "history" on the screen was made. Many anglers think the sonar display is like a television screen; they think everything on the left of the display is to their left, things in the middle are directly below them, and the markings just coming into view are off to their right.

"Using your depthfinder is the number one key to walleye fishing," says Gary Roach. "You have to get good at it, and the only way to do it is to practice. Start right on a shoreline break and try to follow it. Try to stay on that depth line as much as you can. Learn the cuts, the little curves in and out. Or go around a whole reef very slowly. You can throw out a crankbait and troll if you want to, but mainly just learn the lay of the land. You'll find little fingers and bars coming off the main reef and little places where inside turns come in toward the main reef.

"And you should learn when you are on hard and soft bottom, too," Roach continues. "Learn what that thing (sonar unit) tells you."

Now, a few technicalities: Boat speed affects the display. When you go fast, everything on the screen is compressed; as you slow down, things spread out, relatively speaking. Also, display speed is usually adjustable. If you are slow trolling or vertical jigging, slow the display down. If you fire up the big motor to run, speed the display up as fast as it will go.

In a way, walleye fishing is a series of skills like any other sport or activity. You don't step into a playoff game the first day you show up for Little League, and you don't perform a concerto the first day of piano lessons. Fishing, because it is unstructured and viewed mainly as mindless recreation, suffers from the idea that all you do is pile into the boat and start catching fish.

You do need practice, but it can be fun. Learn to use lake maps in concert with your sonar, and learn to build a picture in your mind of underwater contours. Those skills should come first, just as you play simple melodies with the right hand before you blend chords in with the left hand. Learn to picture the depths first, and only then worry about looking for fish, bottom surface changes and cover such as weeds and brush. Then the whole thing starts to make sense.

"You need an actual picture under the water all the time," says Mike McClelland. "In other words, I can fish a piece of structure one time, take out a piece of paper and draw it perfectly—the deepest break on it, the little stuff coming off it, everything. I map all of that stuff as I go by building a picture in my mind. I also make a mental note of exactly where the fish are. Are they on the steep break or right up on top? Are they on the shady or the sunny side of the structure's walls? All of that is very important. Then, as I find the edges of the structure, I take land marks (shore triangulation sightings) or punch the thing into my Loran unit.

"If I don't get good shore sightings, I have to do it all over again the next day," McClelland says. "I might come at the structure differently and build it a little differently in my mind, but it usually comes out pretty close.

"Anyway, that's what walleye fishing is all about," he continues; "it's under the water, you know, and making this visual thing in your mind."

14

Loran-C: Finding Your Way

Modern fishing sonar, used to a fraction of its potential, opens a whole new world for the sportfisherman. Things that used to take years or even a lifetime to discover—isolated humps, little rock piles, a deep hole in the corner of a bay—can be tapped in an afternoon.

But once you find that spot, once you catch a few walleyes, can you find it again? What if you only fish that lake once every four years?

If your boat is equipped with a Loran-C unit, you'll have that honey hole nailed down forever. Find the spot, catch a few fish and punch the coordinates into the Loran. When you want to return, recall the waypoint that represents that spot, and the unit tells you how to get there.

Loran, or LOng RAnge Navigation, was originally developed at the Massachusetts Institute of Technology during World War II. It was used by the U.S. Coast Guard during the war and became available for commercial use. That original technology, called Loran-A, has been replaced by a more accurate system, Loran-C.

Loran-C operates off a series of land-based radio towers throughout the world (although there are a number of "dead" areas where transmission is either unreliable or impossible). When you turn your unit on, it locks into a chain of three to five stations, which are up to several hundred miles apart. One is designated as the *master* and the others are *secondary* stations. The towers continually emit pulses at precise time intervals. Signals from the sec-

Land-based radio towers, like this one in northern Minnesota, send precisely timed signals your Loran unit uses to get a fix on your position. Loran-C operates off a series of three to five of these stations, which are often hundreds of miles apart.

ondaries are synchronized with the master, and the Loran unit pinpoints your location by measuring the slight difference—just millionths of a second—in the time it takes for these various signals to reach you.

In Loran lingo, the time difference (TD) gives you your line-of-position (LOP). After finding the intersection of two lines of position, you know your precise location.

Okay, so you know where you are. What if you want to go somewhere else? If you know the coordinates of your new destination, punch them in. Or, as discussed, if you have already saved them as a "waypoint," just recall the waypoint. The unit then tells you the compass heading to take, how far it is to the destination, how fast you're going, how long it will take at that speed, and normally beeps a warning when you get within a specified distance of the destination (not all units display the same information).

There are several modes of Loran display. The traditional screens show a series of numbers, giving you compass headings, distance to go and steering instructions. Newfangled displays, called plotters, actually show your boat, the line of travel you should take and the destination. You watch on the screen, just

Complete Angler's Library

like a video game, as the representation of your boat either sticks to or wanders off course. At any point you can zoom in to follow your progress closely. (Other Loran screens give varying forms of visual steering instructions.)

How close can Loran-C bring you to the recalled way point? Normally within 100 feet, although accuracy is affected by the angles of the various crossing lines of position. Two lines of position crossing at right angles (90 degrees) give the best accuracy, but experts say the angle can become fairly sharp—about 30 degrees—without serious error.

Most of the time—assuming you aren't on the fringes or outside the range of Loran tower reception—it's plenty close for your sonar to take over and put you right on the money. This assumption, though, is based on your unit returning your boat to a waypoint recorded in that unit. If another angler gives you a waypoint he or she found and recorded with a different Loran, you can't expect repeatable accuracy, as it's called, to be as good. Still, it's close enough—much preferred to wandering around sticking a wet index finger up in the air or looking for shore sightings in the fog. Loran-C eliminates these frustrations.

Traditional Loran units use a digital display to denote location and compass headings. Newer models incorporate a video display that shows the boat's position in relation to a selected location.

This brief overview is not intended as anything but a glimpse at long-range navigation. If you decide to put Loran-C on your boat, study various units in some detail, and be sure the one you choose will improve, not jeopardize, your safety and proficiency on the water.

Read the manual that comes with your unit. Another good source of information is a small book put out by the U.S. Coast Guard. It has maps and coordinates of the various Loran-C chains, valuable information on how Loran navigation works, how to care for a Loran unit and a list of other information sources (there is a small charge for it).

Loran-C User's Handbook (CG-462)
Superintendent of Documents
U.S. Government Printing Office
Washington, D.C. 20402
Code #050-012-00171-5, 1980

Loran Use: The Future Ethical Questions

In the not-too-distant future, a satellite-based navigation system, which will probably be called the Global Positioning System (GPS), will supercede Loran-C. It is purported to be even more accurate, able under most circumstances to return you to within 10 feet of the recalled waypoint (although civilian receivers will probably be somewhat degraded). Because of universal satellite coverage, it will work well no matter where you are, experts say. (GPS is in operation today, in fact, but because of a shortage of satellites it can take eight or more hours for your position to be "updated" by the system, too long to wait in fishing applications.)

If you are about to buy your first Loran-C unit, don't fear it will be immediately out of date. The U.S. government has reportedly vowed to support and maintain Loran-C stations at least through the mid-1990s and will undoubtedly continue beyond that because of the number of Loran units in use.

Up to now we've only discussed what these systems can do for you. A big question looms: What does this technology mean for the future of fishing?

We are struggling with ethical questions similar to those raised when sonar became common in the average fishing boat. There's no arguing their safety value in getting us back to shore. But have we gone too far in exploiting its capabilities? Should it be that

Gary Parsons studies the display on his Loran-C unit. Top tournament anglers rely heavily on their Loran-C units to help them return to hotspots or fish they locate during prefishing. Weekend anglers are using them to return to their honey holes as well.

easy, in a Loran-equipped boat, to find an isolated fishing spot?

The biggest moral dilemma, though, goes a step beyond: Whose spots are they, anyway? Probably by the time you read this, maps will be available with Loran coordinates stamped on, identifying hard-to-find hotspots. Even inexperienced anglers will be able to squirrel away little booklets with the best spots on lakes they've never fished. Imagine the resulting fishing pressure on those locations.

For many passionate fishermen, pulling up to a spot and fishing it without knowing where you are and how you got there is not much different from buying fillets at the grocery store.

What appeals to them is the challenge that lies in finding fish through deductive reasoning and trial-and-error, then tricking fish into taking a bait. Locating fish by simply punching numbers on a key pad would take away the recreational value from the sport.

Still others decry widespread use of Loran units for personal reasons. This computer-age device could become the "great equalizer," they say, allowing lazy fishermen to cash in on honey holes painstakingly sought out by more experienced anglers.

"It gets discouraging," says one tournament fisherman. "You work all afternoon to find a spot, catch a couple of fish and up pull two or three boats with those big antennas. You can hear the 'beep, beep, beep' of them punching the spot into their Loran. Just by touching a few buttons, they have your spot. It's sickening."

Like any new technology, Loran use entails ethical responsibility as much as general mastery. How well you use it, in fact, may not be as important as to what extent.

Where To Find Walleyes

15

The Importance Of Environment

"Can you imagine what it must be like to be a fish, having to make all those decisions about where to swim and whom to eat next?"

—Anonymous

To what degree does the environment drive a walleye? Without getting technical about it, a walleye's environment affects the way it lives. First of all, a walleye is born or stocked into a lake, river or reservoir. The fish doesn't choose where it wants to live. If conditions aren't ideal by walleye standards, the fish has no way of knowing that; even if it did, it couldn't do anything about it. A fish simply makes do with the water it is dealt.

Beyond that, seasons change. The water gets colder and warmer as the year unfolds, and the world around the walleye changes dramatically. Food crops get picked over, grow to bigger size, dwindle, then explode again, filling the system with tiny morsels.

There are daily and even hourly changes to contend with. Daylight comes and is followed by the cover of darkness. In the span of a single day, the sun can beat brightly onto the water one minute and clouds darken it the next. The water sometimes sits calm as glass; then wind tosses the surface to a froth, completely changing life in the walleye's world. Or, there might be calm, sunny weather three days in a row.

In some systems, walleyes are the largest predators. In others, there is extreme competition from other terminal predators such as northern pike, muskies, lake trout and bass.

A walleye's life is both complex and simple. The environment changes constantly, and so does the fish in reaction to it. But a fish does what it does for a short list of reasons: Except for the spring spawning season, it has to eat, keep from getting eaten and stay in an acceptable range of oxygen and temperature.

In this chapter, we are going to look at the variety of systems walleyes are found in, and the general effects outside forces—like weather, food and fishing pressure—have on them. Trust me, there will be a lot of practical fishing information. Some of what we talk about will come from researchers, but much will be good old-fashioned tips from the best walleye fishermen in North America, things you can put to use.

Analogies between humans and animals are dangerous, are almost always scoffed at by scientists and rarely make accurate comparisons. Ignoring all that, they do help make a point now and then.

It's easy for us to see that young people growing up in rural Colorado are going to develop different habits, experience different things, and react differently to their surroundings than youngsters born and raised on the streets of Chicago or New York City. At the moment they are born, city and country kids are not "different" when taken as a group. But early on, they learn to adjust to their environment and develop behavior patterns that reflect their lifestyle and surroundings.

Just like humans, fish develop responses and strategies specific to their environment. Walleyes living in a fast-flowing river learn quickly to pounce on anything that even resembles food. They live in a fast-moving world, so they have to react fast or starve.

Walleyes living in a shallow lake that gets relatively warm in summer learn to tuck up in the weeds and ambush prey. The classic notion of walleye life says this isn't ideal, but how do the fish know that? They do what they have to. Walleyes born in a reservoir full of shad, which suspend much of the summer, follow the food to where it is, whether the walleyes prefer to be there or not.

These are just a few examples of the wide variety of walleye environments. Fish simply find a way to get food and stay alive, and you have to take this into account with every piece of walleye fishing advice you get. *Listen to everyone, but always compare the situation other anglers are in to the waters you fish.* The behavior patterns of the walleyes in your lake and the way you should fish for them might be similar to those in other places, or they might be extremely different.

"The trouble is," says Mike McClelland, "that all of our best walleye information has traditionally come out of central Minnesota, and it all applies to central Minnesota lakes. That's great if you only fish in Minnesota. But take your pet methods to Kansas and there's no guarantee they're going to work. Take slip-bobbers to North or South Dakota. Go to your best spot, throw them out and they'll sit there until they deteriorate, but they'll never go down.

"Go find the best piece of rock structure on Lake Erie and wait for the fish to come and they never come," McClelland continues, "because their food is not there. See, when you get into specific walleye information, it's very geographically dictated. Each lake is

For years, the best walleye techniques came out of central Minnesota. Trouble was, these techniques didn't work well in other areas around the country. Tailor your techniques to match the environment you're fishing.

different, and the forage base is the cause. You can't predict how walleyes are going to behave in a given body of water based on how they behave in some other lake, especially if it's in an entirely different region. This especially comes into play when we introduce walleyes into new waters, like southern or western reservoirs."

The point is, environment drives walleye behavior to a large extent. Certainly, there are genetically programmed responses and behavior, too. It's not important to argue what percentage of the time a walleye is working from a genetic control board and when it's responding to what's going on around it. Just keep in mind that the water, weather, food and fishing pressure should be considered when forming your personal walleye fishing strategy.

Are There "Typical" Walleye Waters?

The traditional notion of what makes suitable walleye habitat comes, not surprisingly, from the original walleye range. Natural glacial lakes and flowing rivers in the northern United States and southern Canada have a distinctive flavor and makeup. So when many of us think of walleye waters, this is what comes to mind:

• A good-sized lake that catches a lot of wind. Walleye expert Dennis Schupp says a good rule of thumb is that a natural walleye lake should be at least 1,000 surface acres for winds to assure natural reproduction. There should be clean gravel-, rubble- and boulder-strewn shorelines.

Look for a river or two flowing in, which would sustain a healthy forage base of shad, smelt, yellow perch, suckers, minnows, tullibees, whitefish, ciscoes or various insects.

• A river with good current to keep spawning areas clean and extensive areas of sand, gravel, rubble or even boulders. As with the lake example, a plentiful food supply is a must. Current, whether the natural river current or current manufactured in lakes and reservoirs by wind, has long been associated with active walleyes.

Walleyes have sometimes even been called a "river fish." The implication is that they originally came from rivers—their ancestors were probably anadromous sea fishes, which run from saltwater into freshwater rivers to spawn—and they are most "at home" in rivers.

There is a scientific paper entitled "Percid Habitat: The River

Is there a "typical" walleye lake? Our classic notion is a body of water with rock/rubble shorelines exposed to the wind, where the chance of spawning success is enhanced. This scene is from Minnesota's Mille Lacs Lake, a famous walleye fishery.

Analogy." In it, biologists propose that the habitat we are most likely to find good numbers of walleyes in "may best be identified by conditions analogous to those in temperate rivers."

But the words of those biologists have been misconstrued many times. In fact, they never say that the walleye is a "river fish." They simply say that walleyes tend to reproduce and compete well for available food in a certain type of waters, and those waters are *similar in many respects* to temperate rivers. They say, in a nutshell, that good natural walleye waters tend to have a relatively large amount of fairly shallow water and are found in the temperate regions where cold winter temperatures ensure walleye egg development.

Says Ontario walleye researcher Dr. Richard Ryder: "Many people refer to walleyes as river fish, but it's not really an appropriate term. You could actually say that walleyes are as abundant in lakes as in rivers."

The authors of *River Analogy* go on to say: "Where the area of (shallow) habitat equivalence is large, as in shallow lakes, so are percid (including walleye) populations...Where the area is small in relation to total lake area, as in large, deep lakes, percids represent a lesser component of the total system."

These words simply adhere to the idea that natural walleye waters are probably natural walleye waters for a reason. Very few animal species can thrive anywhere in the world. Those that can are called *circumpolar* (the peregrine falcon is one example, although its numbers are in grave trouble). Walleyes are definitely not circumpolar. Only when the climate and the watery environment are right can they reproduce and maintain a healthy natural population.

But the walleye's range has expanded greatly through introductory stocking. Walleyes are now found in many water types other than those considered ideal. They have been stocked into lakes with little or no suitable spawning habitat, mainly because fishermen have put pressure on state and federal agencies to do so. And walleyes—often big ones—are found in many reservoir systems, including some that seem to stretch the apparent limit of the fish's acceptable range.

Simply put, researchers say that salmonids (salmon, trout and whitefishes) dominate percids in systems of low productivity and cold average water temperatures. These are the cold, infertile waters we call "trout water," whether river or lake, northern or southern climate. Walleyes can be found in such systems, but they won't be a dominant part of the community. In the more fertile, warm-water environments, by comparison, it is widely held that bass and panfish will dominate the system. You can stock walleyes into such a fishery and anglers will catch them, but it's really fighting against Mother Nature to do so.

We catch huge walleyes from southern rivers and impoundments, for example. But that may have more to do with the fact that fish, including walleyes, grow faster in warm southern waters than in colder, northern waters. Walleyes rarely, if ever, are a dominant species in a southern fishery. Fisheries professionals have proposed many possible reasons, including:

• Summer water temperatures may be too hot for walleyes, forcing them into a narrow range of acceptable water temperatures, where they may or may not be able to feed efficiently.

• In the warm, fertile systems typical of the South, there is room in the water for a higher standing crop of fish. In other words, these waters will support more fish per acre than colder, less fertile systems. Southern environmental conditions, while

The natural range of the walleye has been greatly expanded by introductory stockings. Not all of the walleye's new homes are suitable for natural reproduction, but continued stocking can maintain a quality fishery in many instances.

The Importance Of Environment

good for some fish, are not natural for walleyes, so they end up being preyed upon by other high-level predators that are better adapted, such as black bass, white bass, catfish and stripers.

There are many walleye stereotypes. One is that they are deep-water fish. Walleyes are a fish of both deep and shallow water. Yes, there are deep-water walleyes. But as researcher Dennis Schupp says, "Water depth is not so critical for walleyes as it can be for some other fish, such as big northern pike and lake trout. Most of our good walleye lakes, in fact, tend to be quite shallow. Walleyes do inhabit deep lakes, and the deeper portions of many lakes, especially if there is high-quality forage in the depths. So, really, the bottom line is that walleyes will make use of deep water if it's available and it makes sense, but they don't absolutely have to have it."

Walleyes have also been associated with clear water. But Dr. Ryder's research has shown the opposite (which most top walleye anglers know): dirty water is good walleye water.

Ryder found that during daylight hours walleyes in more turbid waters—those with a secchi disk reading of about three to six feet—were generally more active than those in clear waters. (A secchi disk is a round disk painted with white and black triangles that biologists lower over the shaded side of their boat until they can't see it. That depth becomes the secchi reading for that lake on that day.)

Ryder feels that transparency levels of about three feet are optimal for walleyes and that they function best in clarities between three and 12 feet.

This doesn't mean that walleyes won't be found in extremely clear water or water dirtier than three feet transparency. In fact, many good walleye waters fall into both extremes. It's just a rule of thumb to guide your choice of fishing spots.

16

Weather: Friend Or Foe?

Out upon it, I have loved
Three whole days together;
And am like to love three more,
If it prove fair weather.

—Sir John Suckling

Sir John lived in an earlier day, long before fishing guides and weekend anglers began fretting about what "this weather" will do to the walleye bite. But his words have meaning for us. His mind is far from fishing, but think about it: six straight days of stable weather!

When two Englishmen meet, another famous saying goes, the first thing they talk about is the weather. How about two walleye fishermen?

Walleye fishermen love to talk about the weather. Most of the time the topic of conversation is the dreaded cold front. In general, we say, stable weather is good; it puts fish into a predictable pattern of location and feeding. You catch walleyes one afternoon at about 2 o'clock in a certain spot, and you can often return to the scene same time the next day and repeat the performance—if the weather holds. Prevailing wisdom also says that as a storm front approaches, darkening the sky and threatening rain, the fish go on a feeding binge not likely to be repeated for a time.

The storm comes, the sky clears off and the sun shines. This is universally hailed as a bummer walleye day. Some years, you get more storms than others; cold-front alley it's called by discouraged anglers. One front after another is supposed to really knock the fish off their feed, making them almost impossible to catch.

"You can get a system of fronts that come through for two weeks," says Mike McClelland. "There's a thunderstorm every night; the weather goes back and forth from high pressure to low, and nobody is catching anything. Now, the question I have is this: Does this shut the fish off, or does some point during these weather changes present a great feeding opportunity where the walleyes feed immediately and then they're full? We don't know. Even tournament fishermen haven't been able to put anything concrete together about weather. We know the fish don't starve. All you do for sure is get your butt out on the water and start guessing."

It is safe to say that weather has a profound effect on walleye fishing. Some of it is real, some the product of years of mental conditioning; in other words, we tend to get it into our heads that no matter what the weather, walleyes aren't going to bite. That's not the case, says MWC tournament veteran Daryl Christensen of Montello, Wisconsin:

"Tournament fishing all over the country has shown that, cold front or no cold front, somebody always catches fish. So, somewhere on any system, every day, fish are biting.

"We have never seen the case," Christensen says, "no matter how severe the front or other weather change, where we could say across the board that the fish aren't biting. If there were 200 people in a tournament, and all 200 came in with no fish, we might be tempted to say that. But if even one guy comes in with a limit—which always seems to happen—then he found the fish and gave them the right presentation, and we could have done the same thing."

Guides and tournament anglers aren't allowed the option of staying in the cabin and drinking beer if they don't like the looks of the weather. They have to go out, and they have to catch fish. These forced experiments have led Christensen, one of the most consistent producers in MWC history, to some educated guesses about the effects of cold fronts on walleyes.

"I'm not sure that cold fronts turn walleyes off all that much," he says. "My experience has been that on smaller bodies of water

It is generally accepted that walleyes can go on a feeding binge when a storm front approaches. The key to tapping into this golden opportunity is to fish fast and work active fish hard before the storm hits.

Weather: Friend Or Foe?   147

(10,000 acres and less) it does have a profound effect; they do quit biting.

"I think that most of the time in all bodies of water the wall-eyes move deeper after the front passes," Christensen continues. "I believe they're adjusting to the change in barometric pressure. In huge bodies of water, lakes like Winnebago (Wisconsin), Mille Lacs (Minnesota) and especially the Great Lakes, the walleyes still move deeper, but they continue to feed.

"I think the reason for that," Christensen continues, "is that there are so many walleyes in those waters, and the competitive nature of those fish—the way they fight for food—overrides their inactivity. You might think that a small lake with good numbers of walleyes might be the same, but most small lakes don't have the numbers of walleyes I'm talking about. I'm talking schools of 5,000 or more fish in one area."

Christensen, like numerous other tournament pros, has built a reputation for consistency by catching walleyes out of shallow water, usually less than 10 feet. But after a front passes, he says, even reliable shallow-water patterns dry up.

"What you have to do during cold-front days, even if you've got four or five shallow spots you're catching walleyes from," he says, "is realize shallow-water walleyes are pre-cold front fish. When you go back to these spots after the front and don't catch any fish, realize they're not there. They're gone. You can't sit there and assume the fish are there but not biting.

Christensen says he has learned this lesson over and over the hard way. "I still run into times when I believe my fish are still there," he says, "because they've been in my spots all week, and I don't go looking for them. It costs me. Some people never learn about this. They have a pet spot and they stay on it for the rest of their lives. If they don't catch fish, they aren't biting, and they blame the weather. Believe me, they went somewhere else, and they can be caught. Scale down your offerings; go with a smaller leech, half a nightcrawler or a $1/16$-ounce jig instead of a $1/4$-ounce. These fish can be tempted, but they need to be coaxed a lot of times."

McClelland's thoughts closely parallel Christensen's: Weather is one thing you can't do anything about, so if you have plans to go fishing, go. You can always adjust your strategy.

"About the only rule I have," McClelland says, "is that if you

No matter what the weather, pros like Daryl Christensen have no choice: They have to go fishing, and they have to catch fish.

get a cold front, the fish aren't going to be where they were the day before. They'll be out of a strong feeding mode, and they'll be in a comfort zone. You know, all tucked into one spot. Say you were trolling crankbaits up on a flat the day before and killing the walleyes. Well, if a front comes through, they won't be there anymore, but they'll be somewhat close, and you just have to change your presentation to fit with tight, slow-reacting fish. Generally, I would say they go deeper, but there are exceptions to that. But as my foundation (he never uses the word 'rule'), I'd say they are deeper and tighter together.

"Generally, where I'm going to find them is in any corner," McClelland says. "Say you find a long underwater point. Look in the cup, or an elbow, you might say, where the point meets the bank (his terms for inside corner). They usually want to wrap something around them, like the walls on three sides you get with a tight cup. They want a comfort zone with security, and they're together in big groups."

McClelland's key to catching them is to use an in-front-of-their-faces presentation that has a lot of longevity, like a light jig vertically jigged right on top of them or a slip-bobber rig that leaves a live bait dangling in the fish zone.

"You can still catch them," he says, "with patience. All a weather change does is move the fish. You have to find a concentration—and here's where a good sonar unit is invaluable—and just sit on them and wait for a few to go. We don't have any answers for it, but we know the cold front changes the location and the attitude of the fish."

Another widely held belief is that rivers are not as affected by cold fronts as lakes. Possible reasons?

• Current effects might be more dominant than weather changes. River walleyes might be more accustomed to constant change and fluctuating conditions than their lake counterparts.

• The typical walleye river is quite turbid. Increased light penetration or barometric pressure changes are believed to drive fish deep. (Using this logic, we might think that darker-water lakes are less affected by cold fronts than clear-water lakes. This could, indeed, be the case.)

Weather does affect walleye fishing. But in some cases, it seems to affect fishermen more than fish. Pay attention to changing conditions, rejoice in stable weather and fish when a front is

Under the glaring sun of post-front skies, hunt hard for a concentration of fish and choose a "vertical" presentation, such as jigging or slip-bobbering.

approaching. Work hard to find clusters of walleyes after the front passes through, and get off the water when lightning strikes.

These axioms may be the closest we ever come to "rules" concerning weather and walleyes.

Walk The Way The Wind Blows

Wind is the music that calls a real walleye veteran to action. The entire food chain, which can lie dormant in the calm sun, comes alive with the dancing of the waves.

A sustained wind from one direction pushes plankton into an area, which in turn attracts and activates baitfish. The minnows come in to feed, and their frenzied activity stirs walleyes. Waves crash and pound against shore (or any mid-lake shallow structure), cutting light levels and out come the walleyes!

It can mean fantastic fishing action if you have a reliable, safe boat for big water, or can fish from shore. Tom Neustrom has honed his understanding of the wind-walleye connection. He's cashed in on big catches and had wave-soaked skunkings. He knows there's more to it than "see the wind, catch the walleyes."

"Wind is definitely one of the things that activates the bite," Neustrom says, "because it controls the whole food mechanism. But it's not magic. You still have to know what to look for and how to fish it.

"For example, just because the wind is hitting a certain area doesn't mean the fish are going to be biting there. Some people have it in their heads that walleyes are going to travel miles to feed along a windy reef or shoreline or stump field. It doesn't happen; in most cases the fish have to be there in the first place to get activated."

In general, Neustrom says, what you're looking for are potentially or historically good areas that might "turn on" in the wind. How they sit in relation to the wind, though, is the real key. In general, structure (which can mean a million things, depending on the specific lake or reservoir) or parts of structure 15 feet deep and shallower that are open and exposed to the wind are prime candidates to have "wind-affected" fish.

"Wind fish are shallow fish," he says. "They're aggressive biters. They usually set up right on the front face of the structure, not on the back end. If you have a good point leading onto a shallow feeding shelf, a lot of walleyes will be right out on the tip of the point, attacking. That's why it's so important to think about how and where you're going to fish a structure. Just because the fish are active doesn't mean they're easy. You have to think about where you're putting your bait.

"Look for what I call entry points onto shallow structures," Neustrom advises. "Fish those first; then work the whole shallow wind-affected area. Spines or points of rock, the leading edge, anything that funnels fish from the deeper water onto the shallow feeding area should be worked first. A lot of times, there are numbers of biters bunched up in those spots. Then, start covering water if you're dealing with a big expansive flat."

If you know a point, a stretch of shoreline, reef, shallow flat or creek channel—or anything!—that should hold walleyes, fish it when the wind hits it. Check the wind direction and look at your contour map. In a few seconds, you can see the structures that are affected by that particular wind. Spend your time fishing from one to the next, making a milk run, as they say.

Dan Nelson, another veteran of the MWC tournament circuit, feels strongly that walleyes can actually predict the onset of wind. He says that if you've heard the wind is going to be kicking up from a certain direction try the "wind-affected" structures ahead of time.

"I've looked into this quite a bit," Nelson says, "and even the scientists don't fully understand it. But they believe walleyes—most animals, for that matter—can sense minute changes in the weather. I just believe that a walleye can tell when the wind will be blowing, and preparatory to it happening, will be staging in those areas where it's coming."

He has seen it enough times to be convinced. "The first time I really had it sink into me," he remembers, "was on Lake Sakakawea, North Dakota. Dave Jenson and I were fishing south of New Town on an area they call the "river." It was flat calm, and we'd been catching fish fairly deep, about 15 to 18 feet, and then we lost them. This was the middle of the day, clear sky and not a breath of air. We looked deeper and didn't find anything, so we slid up into about nine feet of water and hit 'em. Because this has happened to me enough times before, I said to Dave, 'I bet we're going to get some wind up on this point.'

"Within five minutes, we had a good wind coming directly into that point. In fact, it howled," said Nelson.

Tom Neustrom says wind turns walleyes on. But you won't find aggressive fish just anywhere. Look for areas that have historically produced fish to become more active when the wind blows.

The gentle taper of a sand beach offers minnows a chance to escape prowling walleyes. When searching for likely shallow-water spots, concentrate on banks with a distinct lip or that have underwater ledges that likewise trap forage fish.

He has other stories with similar endings. "It's as if they know the wind is going to come up," he says, "and where it's coming."

Nelson believes that walleyes "make a move" into locations that are going to be wind-affected. It can happen, in his experience, as much as three to four hours or more before the anticipated blow. Keep this possibility in mind for those times you lose track of deeper-water walleyes. Your first instinct in most cases will be to look deeper yet, but that's apparently not always the answer.

Wind makes shallow walleyes come alive and may even draw walleyes into shallow water from nearby deeper areas. Shorelines, says McClelland, are the perfect wind-pounded structure to fish. But not just any shoreline.

"Everything gets washed in against the bank in a heavy wind," he says. "The walleyes move in because they can herd the minnows up against the bank and feed effectively. But think about it: What happens if the shoreline tapers gently right onto dry land, like at a sandy beach? The minnows can just keep running shallower until they escape the walleyes. The bigger fish can only go so shallow. So the walleyes use banks with a slight wall, where they can work minnows just like basketball players looking for a rebound. A lot of times they'll be facing toward shore like they're pigging out against the bank."

Because wind-related shallow walleyes are aggressive fish, use lures designed for the situation. If you're probing a specific, isolated spot such as one of Tom Neustrom's entry points onto a shallow flat, you might want to try a slip-bobber or slow jigging presentation. But for most of this fishing, use something that can cover water, like a crankbait or bottom-bouncer and spinner rig. Fish quickly, because you're looking for fish that are primed to bite. There's no need to dawdle.

"I'd rarely, if ever, throw crankbaits shallow if the wind wasn't blowing," says South Dakotan Jim Randash, another top MWC contender. "But when the wind blows, I put on crankbaits or something else that fishes fast, and work shallow. That's where the active walleyes are."

Shallow and active. Shallow and biting. Shallow and catchable. Does that sound like traditional walleye thinking? It's not. We have been conditioned to think of walleyes as deep, sulking creatures that have to be finessed and teased. Make no mistake—loads of walleyes are found deep. But deep isn't the only direction to look.

17

The Importance
Of Food

Oh, boy. This subject of food and walleyes could easily be a book by itself. In most cases, it's simply the bottom line on walleye location. Where the food goes, the walleyes follow. The only possible exceptions are during the spawn or in the face of extreme environmental conditions; for example, should the water temperature or oxygen content become life-threatening to the walleyes. (Even then, they would no doubt find a comfort zone and begin lining up in the vicinity of food.)

Professional fishermen are an intelligent, opinionated, articulate lot. But fishing strategy, after all, is much more art than science. Hey, these guys go by their experiences, by what works for them, when dishing out information. In many cases, you hear quite disparate advice.

But not when it comes to the food-walleye connection. On this topic, it sounds like they all went to the same school:

Mike McClelland:

"The only thing that moves fish is food. The most important thing to a walleye during a short part of the spring is the spawn. After that, their entire life focuses around food."

Dave "Hot Tip" Jenson:

"If the food isn't there, the walleyes aren't going to be there either."

Jerry Anderson:

"How could anything be more important to walleyes than

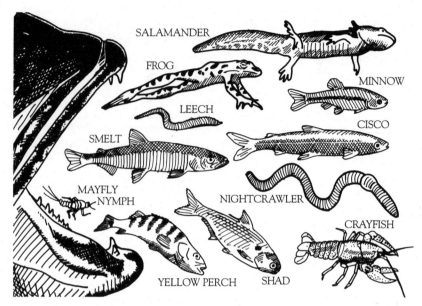

The most common walleye forage includes minnows, smelt, ciscoes, yellow perch and various insects (like mayfly larvae). Knowing the dominant food source, and its favored location in a body of water, will help you locate walleyes year-round.

food? Without it, they don't survive very long."

Daryl Christensen:

"Nothing overrides food for any living creature. When they're hungry they'll be where the food is, or they'll go looking for it and find it."

We could go on, but the point is made: Anything that can bring the professional fishing community into unanimous agreement must be important.

Learn More!

So what does it mean to your fishing? In broad terms, if you can find out what the major forage base is for walleyes in the waters you fish and learn something about the location of that forage throughout the year, that information will help you locate and catch walleyes.

There are ways of getting this information. One of the most under-tapped resources is your local fisheries biologists and managers. They know the waters they work, and they know what the walleyes feed on. In a lot of cases, they have done stomach contents analyses on area waters and have the results available. Just

Complete Angler's Library

ask. It's part of their job as state employees to help you.

Realize that walleyes, when given a choice, usually select soft-rayed fishes (such as shad, smelt, tullibees, ciscoes and minnows) over spiny-rayed fishes like yellow perch or sunfish. Yet, there are plenty of systems, especially in the northern United States and southern Canada, where perch make up the majority of a walleye's diet.

In some cases, walleyes won't prey on certain potential prey species even when they're abundant. Stomach contents analyses on walleyes from Minnesota's famous Mille Lacs Lake, for example, show that the walleyes don't often eat trout perch, even though they are present in great numbers. They have other options they select.

Still, they will eat what they have to when their choices are narrowed. That can mean suckers, bullheads, darters, other walleyes and anything that will fit in their mouths.

There's a lot of information you can gather on your own. Check the stomach contents of walleyes you clean. Make a mental note of where you caught them (remember Mike McClelland's advice about building a mental picture of areas from which you catch fish). Then see what they've been eating. Keep a log book, and it will help you locate walleyes on the same or similar waters years down the road.

Food sources change in a semi-predictable way as the year unfolds. It's a complicated matter, but a simplified picture can help you understand why walleye fishing can be so good in some waters at some times of the year and so slow in others.

In general, as we come out of winter into spring, day length increases, water warms and walleyes become more active. They are preparing for spawning, yes, but they need to feed. The available food in most systems is picked over from last summer, fall and winter, making the walleyes work hard to find a meal. They'll take whatever they can find. Any insect larvae will be gobbled up, as will baitfish or young gamefish they can catch.

Through late spring or even early summer, food can remain relatively scarce, so walleyes have to forage actively all day to find enough to satisfy them. Fishing is usually good or even great at this time of year, and that's normally why. With hungry fish and not enough to eat, the chances are much better your bait will be snarfed up.

Matching your bait to the available prey is often a good idea. In the fall forage has been picked over, leaving only larger prey. Increasing the size of minnows you use can make the difference because the walleye are eating larger prey.

But, as summer really comes alive, most systems experience a boom of available forage. The current year's baitfish crop gets big enough to interest the walleyes, and insect hatches come on in impressive scope. Now, instead of having to search all day for food, walleyes can normally eat their fill in a matter of minutes. The chances are reduced they'll take your bait.

In the fall, for example, when forage is picked over, walleyes seem to prefer larger minnows than they do at other times of the year.

In some cases, lakes experience tremendous explosions of forage, making walleye fishing downright discouraging. In others, there can be a food shortage even in midsummer, giving anglers a dream year.

The strength of walleye populations has even been tied to the state of the forage base. As far back as the 1940s, commercial walleye harvests in the Great Lakes (Saginaw Bay, eastern Lake Michigan, southern Lake Huron, Lake Erie, Bay of Quinte) were shown to rise with the establishment of smelt and fall during heavy smelt die-offs.

A more recent example of forage helping walleye numbers and

general health is found in the Missouri River system, where in the early 1970s rainbow smelt were introduced. The smelt took to the environment and became a good forage base for the struggling walleye population. Skinny, underfed walleyes became football-shaped specimens, and the Missouri River reservoirs became some of the hottest walleye fisheries in North America.

Suspended Walleyes: Follow That Food
It seems safe to say that food drives walleyes. Food in combination with structure and cover almost always spells walleyes. But, as Mike McClelland points out, "Walleyes don't have a chain hooking them to structure. Structure is good because baitfish and other food congregate around it, and the walleyes can operate as ambush predators. But they won't sit on a nice rock pile and starve to death."

When a substantial food source is located in open water, at least some walleyes will follow it. We were long ago introduced to the concept of suspended walleyes by pioneering fishermen on the Great Lakes and other expansive bodies of water.

McClelland has studied the subject of suspension and fished suspended walleyes throughout North America.

"What moves walleyes," he begins, "is a search for food. Any time you get a forage base that suspends—like gizzard shad, tullibees, whitefish, that kind of thing—a certain number of walleyes are going to suspend. In certain cases, like on the Western Basin of Lake Erie, a majority of the fishery is suspended.

"In a lot of cases," McClelland says, "you can find the suspended baitfish on your sonar unit, and the walleyes will be sitting under them, chowing down on the ones that die off or get slashed by other fish. That's why jigging spoons are so effective on these suspended fish; they are used to looking for that fluttering action falling down toward them. It's natural. Walleyes can get below these gizzard shad, like on Lake Erie, and it's like leaves falling constantly.

"Especially when you have other predator fish working the forage, like white bass," says McClelland. "They bust into the baitfish and stun a lot of them, and the walleyes can just pick off the dropping ones. Sure, they'll get right into the baitfish, too, but they don't always have to.

"Their lateral lines can pick up the struggle of a dying baitfish from a long way away," McClelland continues. "Then they just slide over and suck in an easy meal. That's why you can't always catch those walleyes on crankbaits, even when you're at the right depth. They're just not programmed to grab something moving by at two or three miles per hour. That's why guys get over them with jigging spoons and really hammer them.

"We've been watching this happen for 30 years," says McClelland. "Propst grew up with it on McConaughy (a sprawling southwestern Nebraska lake). Propst was using downriggers, lead-core line and jigging spoons in 1955! He was staring at 40-foot water clarity in his lake with deep walleyes and suspended walleyes, and he had to come up with a way to catch them. Bob was using these new 'breakthrough' methods, including planer boards, more than 30 years ago.

"In some fisheries, including a lot of the Southern reservoirs," McClelland says, "most of your summer fishing will be for suspended walleyes. Sure, some fish will be on structure, but the suspended fish will always be there if you can find them. It's not hard; they show up easy on your locator. Then, just drop a jigging spoon down to them. Or, if you troll over them with downriggers, try slowing down and popping the downrigger release when you pass over the school. Sometimes, the action of your crankbait fluttering slowly upward or a spoon fluttering downward will trigger the fish into biting. But generally, they are in with such a bunch of food that they're not easy to catch. Feeding is so easy for them. They wouldn't be in the open water if the food wasn't there, so realize your lure is competing with a lot of other food for the fish's attention.

"I wish I had a 20-page thesis," says McClelland, "on the movements and habits of every major forage fish there is so I could better understand them. I'd like to know when they spawn, when they go to shallow water, when they suspend. That would eliminate even more of the guesswork.

"People are really starting to get on these suspended walleyes in places from the Minnesota side of Lake of the Woods to Lake Erie to down South," McClelland continues. "But they typically don't find them until midsummer, about July and August. We need to look at this thing a lot closer to see whether the suspended fisheries don't set up until midsummer or if they're there at other times and we're just missing them. We have a lot of work to do, but

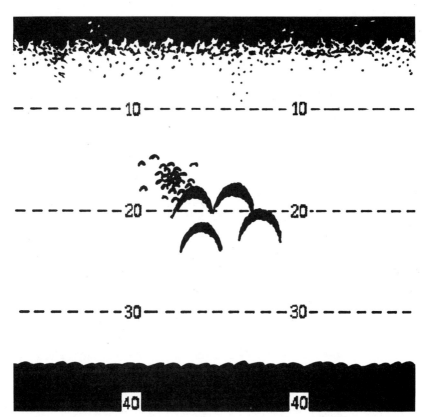

In large, open bodies of water walleyes will often suspend near schools of baitfish, far from any typical structure. Their search for food may take them into waters outside their preferred temperature zone.

it will be interesting. I'm excited about the possibilities.

"You've got to realize that walleyes in different waters are different fish. They go where it's easiest to eat; that's all there is to it. And that's going to vary in different bodies of water. That's why there aren't any good rules about finding walleyes," says McClelland. "You find them where they are at the moment, and they go where they go to find food."

When Walleyes Suspend Off Structure

So far, we've only talked about one kind of suspended walleyes—those in the open, not related to anything but food. But walleyes hugging structure one minute can suspend the next, usually not far from the structure and normally at the same depth as the structure they were using.

Dan Nelson and I were recently jigging along a tapering point on North Dakota's Lake Sakakawea. We were catching fish left and right (believe me, Nelson put us on 'em), which was attracting attention from other boats in the area.

Along comes this inflatable raft with about a 10-horse motor on it, carrying a couple and their little white dog. The guy steers well clear of our point and trolls around the outside over about 80 feet of water. Pow! He catches an $11^1/_2$-pound walleye on a crankbait.

That fish undoubtedly came out of eight feet of water, the same depth from which we were catching ours. That fish was also undoubtedly on our point at one time (the nerve of some fish!), and spooked off when we started catching fish or slid away before we got there. It's not an isolated incident.

NAFC Charter Member and tournament fisherman Gary Kiedrowski has been faced with these suspended fish a number of times, but still doesn't have a sure-fire method of catching these fish. He does, however, do a little experimenting when faced with these "suspended-off-structure" fish and has enjoyed success. He recalls the time a bit of this experimenting paid off during a tournament.

"My partner and I had located a school of walleyes suspended off a mud flat down in 35 feet of water," he says. "The lake was flat calm so we had absolutely no trouble staying right over the fish, but nothing we tried, including vertical jigging and ripping crankbaits, worked and time was running out!

"We finally agreed my partner would rig up a slip bobber and drop a leech into the middle of the school. Incredibly," he continues, "his bobber went right under. I couldn't believe it! The fish that had just moments before rejected a leech on my jig pounced all over his rig. I had a slipped bobber rigged up within seconds. And started catching fish!"

Gary Roach and Randy Amenrud, co-owners of Fishing Pro-Mos, are old hands at catching these suspended-off-structure walleyes.

"It's very common," Roach says. "We see it all the time, especially when there's a lot of fishing pressure."

It doesn't take long to locate these fish. Gary and Randy offer these tips:

• If you're catching walleyes on structure, be it a point, flat or

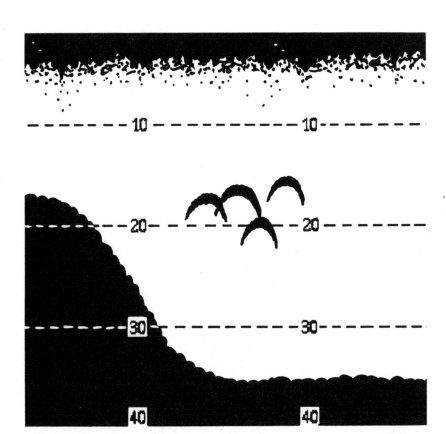

When the walleye bite stops on your favorite rock pile, point or reef, don't automatically assume the fish have moved deeper. Many times they will suspend off the structure, but at the same depth. Be sure to investigate before moving to another location.

sunken island, and they quit biting, take a quick run around the outside of the structure. Keep the same bait on or anything (crankbaits or bottom-bouncer rigs work well) that will run at the depth of the fish. There's no need to run out far—50 to 100 feet off the structure should be enough. Just do circles and see what happens. Then, return to the structure for one more try before moving to a different spot.

• If you mark fish off (but near) structure at a specific depth, that can be the clue you need to find them on the structure! They'll normally be at the same depth. Some walleyes will usually be in both places.

• There is no real formula for predicting when fish will be backed off structure like this. Simply take advantage of it when you notice it.

Fishing suspended walleyes is old hat to many of today's wall-eye anglers. At the same time, it's a new concept or technique to many others, especially those used to "traditional waters." The key is to be aware that these opportunities exist, and employ the tactics we'll discuss in chapters 23, 24 and 25!

18

Seasonal Patterns In Lake Walleyes

alleyes are born or stocked into their environment, and they either learn how to eat or they die. Environment dictates much of what they do, and when. We are the ones who try to attach rules to everything they do, to pin down their seasonal movements so we can predict where they will be when the water temperature hits a magic mark, or when the leaves fall from certain trees.

Except for the spawning season and the influential time around it, walleyes are probably driven mainly by their needs for reproduction, food and safety. Spawn, eat and avoid being eaten. It's all they know.

But top anglers have learned from experience that there are seasonal patterns they can count on. Some secrets of their success are built around observations such as:

• After spawning is completed, walleye fishing often slows. Traditionally, experts have believed the walleyes (females especially) need a recuperation period to restore lost energy from the rigors of spawning. Some mavericks are now suggesting that's not true, that we just aren't looking for them in the right places. Mike McClelland, in particular, is outspoken on this topic:

"Walleyes don't need a recuperation period," he says. Telemetry studies have shown that walleyes travel long distances right after spawning, proving that fish don't need an extended rest.

McClelland and some others believe instead that walleyes— including big females—move directly to haunts fishermen don't

As you venture onto walleye waters, think about seasonal patterns that will narrow your search. Remember that specific situations will dictate the fish's location and activity level, and therefore your tactics.

start checking until much later. "These fish immediately start looking for food," he says. "What we've found out is that they make a beeline. They don't follow current, structure or anything; they go straight to what seems to be a predetermined spot. It might be 20 miles from where they spawned, but they'll be there the next day, eating.

"I think it's the fishermen who go through the 10-day recuperation period," says McClelland. "It takes us that long to start fishing our summer spots. I think we'd catch a lot more walleyes if we started using summer tactics at mid-spawn, because some of the fish will already be done spawning and out there feeding."

• There are some fairly reliable biological "rules" that help predict walleye fishing potential as the year unfolds. For example, as winter gives way to spring and early summer, most of the food in the walleye's world is left over from last year. Food is often bigger than desired for many walleyes, and scarce. The fish feed any time a good chance presents itself, making for good fishing much of the time.

As summer progresses, the current year's baitfish crop explodes, flooding the system with food. Walleyes feed a lot during this time, but it's easy for them to find food. Feeding can be done in short bursts, making it tougher to find a hungry walleye to tempt. As fall comes along, the food crop is again trimmed down, forcing walleyes to forage almost constantly.

• It's virtually impossible to describe seasonal movements of walleyes and cover all the possibilities. That's partly because we don't know the story, really. Even scientific studies contradict each other.

Some call summertime walleyes "homebodies" that don't roam far, and others tab them nomadic wanderers who stop only when they find abundant food, then move on.

The other clue as to how tough it is to neatly classify walleye movements will surface in a long visit with a seasoned pro. Spend about an hour sometime talking with Gary Roach about where walleyes go and when. For every question, you get about 30 specific situations in which he has found walleyes, depending on the lake, river or reservoir type, time of year, weather conditions, current year's forage crop and other factors.

Gary ran out of generalizations long ago about walleye movements and behavior. He is not different from other touring pros.

Perhaps no one alive knows more about catching walleyes in the weeds than Gary Roach. This 7-pounder came from the tip of a weed point.

Complete Angler's Library

The longer you stay at something, the better chance every rule ever made will be broken.

"I don't go by specific rules," says Roach. "I go by what's happening each day out here on the water. I keep looking until I find fish going."

It adds up, in a lot of cases, to confusion and theory.

Despite all the warnings, let's take a brief look at some of the "rules" top fishermen have taught us about walleyes' seasonal movements. Use them to help you decide on which type of spot you might concentrate your efforts at different times of year, in different types of water. But remember that every system is different; the water is deeper or shallower, warmer or cooler, clearer or darker. It's filled with different balances of predator and prey species and is heavily or sparsely structured.

We'll examine first the seasonal patterns that have been observed in lake habitats. In the next chapter we'll explore reservoir and river walleye movements.

Seasonal Movements: Lake Walleyes

Much of the heart and soul of walleye country is dotted with natural lakes. Although we will consider them under this single heading, there are many different types. The usual way of classifying lakes is by fertility, or degree of *eutrophication*. We will discuss three general types of natural lakes:

Oligotrophic, or relatively infertile. This type of water is found mainly on the Precambrian shield of the northern United States and southern Canada. Sometimes thought of as deep, clear lakes, many (most in some regions) are quite shallow, and many have stained water.

Mesotrophic, or of medium fertility. Many of the lakes in this classification fit the bill of classic, natural walleye waters, where strong populations are self-sustaining through spawning.

Eutrophic, or "old," fertile waters. Many are shallow and structureless, "dishpan" lakes as they are known. In many cases, these are not natural walleye waters (they usually lack suitable spawning habitat), having fishable populations built and maintained through stocking.

Oligotrophic Lakes

These are probably the most glamorous of all walleye waters.

We all have visions of spending a week in the only boat on a remote, fly-in lake where hungry fish attack any lure offered. They are also the most fragile lakes, succumbing easily to fishing pressure. Lower fertility lakes hold fewer fish per acre of water, so these lakes may have fragile populations of slow-growing walleyes. But they can kick out impressive numbers of trophy fish, especially if they are in remote locations and receive light fishing pressure. Because many now have roads right to their shores, catch-and-release will become critically important to their future.

Spring And Early-Summer Movements:
Oligotrophic lakes have an abundance of spawning habitat, and yet walleyes are as concentrated as they ever get during spawning time. If there is a spawning river entering the lake, good numbers of walleyes will be grouped on any major flats off the rivermouth for at least two or three weeks. Look also for walleyes spawning on shallow rock or gravel shorelines, and even mid-lake reefs.

Shallow water of any kind is often at a premium in these lakes. Any streams, shallow flats and larger bays—where quicker-warming water brings the area to life—can be good early-season locations. Also, carefully fish any bottleneck areas, places where two islands meet, for example, and form a narrow stretch of often-flowing water. Make long casts here because these shallow fish are extremely spooky, especially if the water is clear.

After the spawn is over until the true summer period begins (as late as mid-July), walleyes can be found in a variety of spots. Always check newly developing weeds in shallow bays, narrows, flats, points and reefs. What surprises many is that any cover, including beaver houses or other fallen trees, can hold a lot of walleyes during this period. Remember, the key now is relatively shallower, warming water that is attracting baitfish or insect hatches of some kind.

Classic walleye structure (points, rocky reefs) can be good, as long as it's located in a relatively shallow portion of the lake. Take a critical look at a contour map of the lake you fish; you'll see general "basins" of deeper and shallower water. At this emerging time of year, concentrate on the shallower sections of the lake.

Oligotrophic lakes, like those found in the northern United States and southern Canada, are the most pristine and least fertile class of lakes. They often give up true trophy fish, but their fragility makes them prime candidates for catch-and-release fishing.

Summer Movements:

There is no timer that dings to announce a major change in walleye location, but generally around the Fourth of July a lot of walleyes will begin working their way into deeper sections of the oligotrophic lake. Still, rule number one is to continue fishing any spots where you caught walleyes during the early part of summer, because some of them will hold fish almost all the time.

Now, those reefs, points and shoreline breaks that drop into deep water can start to see fish holding on them. "Saddles," areas of deeper water between two shallow structures, can be very good at times.

Alan Meline, revered Canadian guide from Nestor Falls, Ontario, has fished all types of these rocky shield lakes.

"The first thing you have to do is divide these lakes into clear-water and dark-water," he says. "Walleye locations are similar, but the timing can be different. In the darker water, things happen earlier in the year, and this pattern holds all through the summer and fall. In the clear-water lakes, you see a lot of the same movements, but they just start later.

"The secret to finding walleyes is knowing where the baitfish go," Meline continues. "It took me years to get this down, and I did it by trial and error. It's not like I didn't catch fish before, and you can, but now that I pretty much know where the minnows are from spring through fall, I have a better idea of where the walleyes are going to move when I lose them."

In late summer on these waters, big walleyes are gaining fame for suspending over deep water to chase free-roaming baitfish like ciscoes, tullibees and whitefish. Downrigger trollers with wide-angle transducers on picture-type sonar find and catch these fish, many in the 10- to 12-pound range, by trolling over sprawling expanses of featureless bottom. Walleyes can also be caught trolling around and near deep reefs and large sunken islands, but be careful with the downrigger balls if the contours are jagged!

Some experts believe that in the darker-water shield lakes that get a midsummer algae bloom (usually about mid-August), many walleyes move back from main-lake structures into sandy or organic-bottomed bays. The fish, they say, tuck up into any type of weed cover that's holding baitfish. This surprising pattern can hold until early fall.

Because the current year's baitfish crop is now in full bloom, walleyes don't have to work as hard to find food. So, feeding periods can be very concentrated, often lasting a half hour or less.

Fall Movements:

As sticky summer nights give way to cooler ones, many fish will come up from deep-water haunts to invade the shallows of oligotrophic waters. Many walleyes are in shallow water all summer, but a significant movement that way can be seen in early fall.

But, when things truly start to cool off in later fall (say about mid-October), many walleyes move into deep water along sharp-breaking structures and shorelines. Even in stained-water shield lakes, good catches of walleyes come from water as deep as 40 or 50 feet at this time of year.

When the water temperature hits about 40 to 42 degrees, ciscoes move into shallow, rocky spawning areas, and many walleyes are right behind. It can make for great late-fall fishing if you can bear the cold weather that often accompanies it.

Again, these are very rough sketches of walleye movements. The only way to nail down the lakes you fish is to fish them. Try everything that looks good, but don't get caught in a rut. If you fish

Bottleneck areas, places where two islands come close together, often create current. If the depth and bottom content are right, walleyes will use these areas. Fish them!

five points and don't catch any walleyes or see much encouragement on the sonar unit, don't keep fishing points. When you do catch a fish, ask yourself why you caught it there. Try to put together pieces of the puzzle of walleye location, and be on the lookout for more than one pattern to be going at once.

Mesotrophic Lakes

This is the bread-and-butter water of most of the natural walleye range of the United States. These lakes may be the toughest to generalize, given that they vary tremendously in average and maximum depth, water clarity, amount of structure and countless other factors.

Before we start, here's another generality to consider: Most experts feel that movement patterns are similar in clear-water and darker-water lakes, although everything happens a few weeks to a month later in clear water. Also, walleyes tend to spend more time in shallower water in dark-water lakes. There is, however, some argument about even this.

Properly managed, mesotrophic lakes can take intense fishing pressure and still maintain reputations as top walleye fisheries, both for numbers and size.

Spring And Early-Summer Movements:

As early as February or March, walleyes begin migrations into the vicinity of spawning grounds in mesotrophic waters—shallow broken rock, rubble or gravel with wind or current moving over them. The percentage of walleyes that spawn in rivers as opposed to wave-swept shorelines or main-lake reefs seems to vary from lake to lake.

Because bottleneck areas—places where an island is close to shore or where two islands are close together—often produce current, they are also good spawning sites if the bottom composition is right.

Telemetry studies have shown that the walleye's homing instinct is powerful. Individual fish usually spawn in the same area year after year. If you find a well-established spawning area, pinpoint it on your lake map. More than likely you'll find fish on or near it each spring.

Some walleyes, especially males, will hang around the spawning sites for up to a few weeks. Also look for them to move to

The classic, natural walleye lake is a "middle–aged," or mesotrophic, lake. This class of lakes features medium fertility, but individual lakes can vary in depth, clarity and structure content. Walleyes can thrive in well-managed mesotrophic lakes.

nearby black-bottomed bays, where it is believed they feed on emerging insect larvae before the current year's baitfish crop is available. The bay doesn't have to be tremendously big or deep, although that helps; but 15 to 20 feet is enough water to hold good numbers of fish at this time of year.

For whatever reason, walleye fishing is slow for a time after spawning is over. Whether we just aren't looking in the right places, as Mike McClelland suggests, or the walleyes are actually going through some sort of recuperation period, history tells us that about 10 days have to pass before the action heats up.

But, boy oh boy, after that "recuperation" period, whatever its significance, the walleyes go on a feeding binge unrivaled during the year! For up to a month, many lakes have scavenging, hungry walleyes of all sizes, fish that can't easily find enough to satisfy their hunger (again, because most of the food in the system is left over from last year, big and elusive and scarce). For the average walleye angler, this is undoubtedly the easiest fishing of the year, at least in this type of lake.

Walleyes feed when the opportunity presents itself, and at this time of year, the chances don't come along often enough. That means a walleye will likely bite your bait if it can find it. In many lakes, weeds are sparse, algae blooms have not begun and the fishing is fast and clean.

Look for walleyes in many spots, but concentrate around the following areas:

• The mouths of spawning rivers and the first breaks out from them.

• Shallow bays with good numbers of baitfish and perhaps newly forming weeds.

• The previous year's bulrushes and weeds.

• Any good-sized shallow flats coming out of deeper water, especially those that could be alternate spawning sites.

• Long, gradually tapering points, especially those with sand and gravel on them. Look them over closely with your sonar unit for baitfish. Says Tom Neustrom, a long-time walleye guide: "At this time of year, the presence of baitfish is everything. I check a lot of points, and if I see minnows on the flasher, I stop and fish. Even if I don't catch walleyes right away, I keep coming back to those spots, because walleyes are going to be there eventually."

• Structures you would normally consider midsummer staples, such as reefs, humps, saddles between them, irregular shoreline breaks and the edges of new weedbeds or any other cover. At this time of year, more walleyes seem to hold on structures that are connected to shore and relatively shallow. What are the attributes of a good piece of structure? Generally, the bigger the better, with as much cover (weeds, brush, boulders), and as many irregularities and "stair-step" ledges going from shallow to deep water as possible.

Summer Movements:

As summer comes into full bloom (dates vary from north to south), walleyes will move out to more offshore structures, although many fish remain in areas they moved to immediately after spawning. The rule probably is this: If they find food there and fishing pressure doesn't move them off, they stay as long as the food holds out.

In some deeper mesotrophic lakes, there are tenuous populations of pelagic (open-water roaming) prey species like ciscoes, tullibees or whitefish. In these systems, or anywhere food is found in open areas, at least some walleyes will leave structure and move out to feed. This could probably happen any time during the year, but has been found most commonly in late summer.

Dense weedbeds become an important walleye location. Even on hot, calm, sunny days, walleyes will hold in thick weeds waiting for prey to come by. Some anglers have had good success rapidly reeling rattling lures across the tops of weedbeds. Walleyes, like largemouth bass, will come out and hammer a lure.

At low-light periods, walleyes often hold on, or even roam along, the outside or inside weed edges. Pay close attention to what the pros call "inside turns" (places where the weedline forms an inward curve with walls on three sides) and weed points, places where the weeds form an outward-jutting arm. They tend to collect groups of walleyes.

In many of these lakes, water temperature layers form distinct thermoclines. In the thermocline, water temperature changes rapidly with a few feet or even inches. In some lakes, only one thermocline forms, but several can. (A well-developed thermocline is easy to see on a sonar unit as almost a "Milky Way" effect somewhere in the middle of the water column.) Often, dissolved oxygen levels below the first thermocline can be too low to support walleyes for long, forcing them to stay in or above it. After the thermocline sets up, assuming oxygen is low beneath it, concentrating on structures at or above that depth is important. Sometimes, deep weedlines form near the same depth as the thermocline, making them a critical midsummer location.

In late summer, suspended walleyes and baitfish can sometimes be found stacked in open water in or on top of the thermocline.

Summertime walleyes will also suspend away from structure, often at the same depth that they use for feeding on the structure. These fish are easy to spot on a sonar unit but are often not actively feeding. Still, they're worth a try, because something as innocuous as hooking a walleye on the structure and drifting out over open water while fighting it can pull the whole school off the structure. (This phenomenon is not restricted to mesotrophic lakes; look for it anywhere.)

Fall Movements:

Similar to walleyes in oligotrophic lakes, many experts agree that fall walleyes in mesotrophic lakes can be found on the same

As the first real warm spell of summer comes on, walleyes often go on a feeding rampage unrivaled at any other time of year. Here, Dave "Hot Tip" Jenson hoists a "hot bite" catch.

Complete Angler's Library

or similar structures as they were all summer but on steeper-breaking sides. Often, hundreds or thousands of walleyes are grouped on structures that quickly go from 10 feet or less down to 40 feet or more.

Weed walleyes, they believe, often move out of the dying weeds to hard-bottomed structure, probably following sources of food. This can happen as early as mid-September in Canada, later in southern climates.

On lakes that form thermoclines, or stratify, surface water cools in fall, becoming denser and sinking toward the bottom, forcing a mixing of temperature layers. This is known as the *turnover period*. As this is happening, fishing is notoriously tough. After it is complete, temperature and oxygen levels are fairly uniform from top to bottom, making deep rock humps and other structures that were off limits to midsummer fish open for business. Those that attract baitfish, or areas that host insect life, also can attract walleyes. But the fish might also be very shallow, where other groups of food can be, often preparing for spawning. Lower water temperatures and reduced light intensity (because the sun is lower in the sky at this time of year) may also draw walleyes to shallow water. So, at this time of year, walleye location can be a "needle in the haystack" proposition.

In late fall, though, the year's food crop has been thinned, making it tougher for walleyes to find a meal. As in spring, they tend to feed when the chance presents itself, making the odds good they will take your bait if they find it.

Eutrophic Lakes

This type of natural lake, you might say, is an unnatural home for walleyes. The nutrient-rich, often bowl-shaped systems found in relatively warm climates are more hospitable to warm-water fish like largemouth bass, various panfish species, and in many cases rough fish like carp and bullheads.

Because the predominantly organic, silty basins usually lack walleye spawning habitat, walleyes are normally present only if they've been stocked. Often, pressure from anglers who want to fish walleyes results in fisheries personnel artificially maintaining a "put-and-take" fishery.

Ironically, these waters can actually harbor more fish life per acre than the previous two, so they can hold some tremendous walleye populations. Many eutrophic lakes are quite shallow, and water temperatures get above the ideal for walleyes, even becoming life-threatening, during the heat of summer. On the other end of the weather spectrum, they are also candidates to freeze out in winter, a condition of dangerously low oxygen levels caused by heavy snow cover that blocks photosynthesis and curtails oxygen production.

General year-round movements summarized: In some eutrophic lakes, there is enough rocky or gravelly shoreline to permit spawning, at least to a limited extent. Walleyes in these systems, following nature's urges, will at least try to spawn on whatever hard bottom is available. Before spawning actually begins they will relate to subtle breaklines near the spawning area. Generally, they will move more in eutrophic lakes than they would in bodies of water that offer more structure.

After the spawn (or spawning attempt) is over, walleyes are likely to be found on anything resembling structure. Weeds grow heartily in these waters, and they come up early. Weed edges become a haven for baitfish, and a shaded feeding location for walleyes and most of the other gamefish present. Reed or bulrush patches can also hold walleyes, as well as any points or other breaks in the shoreline depth.

Wind and wave action are tremendous influences on all fish life in a shallow environment. Look for walleyes to stack up where the wind is blowing into a shoreline, weedbed or other structural element. The chop cuts light intensities, increases oxygen and activates baitfish and walleyes.

To effectively search for walleyes in a bowl-shaped lake, you have to first redefine your notion of structure. If the bottom is practically all uniform, tapering smoothly into a moderately deep basin, a rise of even a foot or so constitutes a major structural element. Look for points jutting out from the natural shoreline breaks. Look for minor "humps" coming off the main-lake basin, or small depressions digging into it.

As you slide away from shore, watch your sonar unit for even a hint of a breakline, where the depth changes quicker than normal for that lake. Likewise, transition zones between areas of harder and softer bottom can collect groups of walleyes. Still, walleyes in these lakes tend to be roamers more so than in other lakes, because the number and quality of holding spots just aren't there.

Abundant weed growth signifies a eutrophic lake. While they are usually not suitable for natural walleye reproduction, these highly fertile lakes may produce large fish if a stocking program has been maintained.

In one classic telemetry study done on Chautauqua Lake in New York, Researcher Don Einhouse found very few walleye movements from out in the main lake in toward shore, or what we might typically call *vertical* movements. He found most summer walleyes living in the outside edge of the weeds, making mainly *horizontal* movements along the weed edge.

Because of the limited location options, walleyes simply tend to stick tighter to weeds as they become more and more dominant through the summer. (It is important to note that in some wind-swept shallow lakes, constant wave action doesn't allow good weed growth to take root.) The traditional method of fishing this lake type is to use a presentation that lets you cover a lot of ground, say quickly live-bait rigging or trolling crankbaits or spinner rigs. Because the fish might be on the move in a constant search for prey, you need to be also, in order to intercept them. Bass tactics, including weedless plastic worms or other snag-resistant presentations, will often yield the most walleyes.

Because shallow lakes rarely develop a thermocline, they can be a good choice for fall walleye fishing during a time when other area lakes are experiencing the turnover and its inconsistent fishing. And in those lakes that do stratify, the effects of fall turnover are much less pronounced. The surface temperature must drop only slightly to initiate the turnover, resulting in more stable conditions than in deep-water lakes.

Regardless of the time of year, if you find a few prime lies, such as key weed areas or dominant structural elements, you have probably found a lake for life.

"There are some general rules that help you find walleyes at certain times of year," says Gary Parsons, a perennial tournament winner.

"But it's nowhere near as fixed as some people would have you believe," Parsons continues. "There are fish living in six feet in the weeds, out on the drop-offs, on deep rocks and mud and right up in very shallow water."

Go out there believing you can find biting walleyes somewhere, and don't write off any possibility until you've fished it. Look in places you'd never dream walleyes would be.

Now you're fishing like a tournament pro!

19

Reservoir And River Walleyes

Aman-made reservoir, simply put, is a river made into a lake. Build a dam and the flow backs up and floods the surrounding countryside. Build a series of dams on a major river and you have a series of lakes.

So the question begs: Are reservoirs lake-like rivers, or river-like lakes? Probably depending on the amount of current flow, they could be either or both at different times.

A reservoir, similar to a river, is a world of constant change. Water levels are manipulated to produce electricity and occasionally to control or prevent flooding. In a reservoir, an underwater point might be 15 or 20 feet deep one year, a prime walleye spot.

The next year that same piece of real estate could be high and dry or under 40 feet of water! Fluctuating water levels on a reservoir also change the strength of current flow and its influence on a walleye's life. In a natural lake, water levels rarely change more than a few feet from year to year.

Rapidly changing water levels and flows tend to keep weed growth to a minimum in many reservoirs. When levels drop, though, vegetation grows well on the exposed earth. After the water level is raised again, this newly flooded vegetation can be a haven for aquatic life of all kinds, including walleyes.

Top reservoir fishermen agree with the basic notion that it's tough to pigeonhole walleye movements. Tournament pros Mike McClelland, Daryl Christensen and Jim Randash all believe that there are only two basic seasonal reservoir movements: when fish

Water levels fluctuate wildly on reservoirs. Normally, alternate high- and low-water periods keep weed growth to a minimum. However, as in this scene, sustained low water allows weeds and brush to catch root. When the water comes back up, walleyes will be there.

are spawning and "the rest of the year."

Their theory holds that walleyes generally move upstream, many all the way to the dam, many within close proximity of other spawning areas (such as inlet streams or suitable stretches of shoreline) during fall staging runs. They move onto spawning sites when conditions become right in spring. After spawning, there is a general movement downstream to a variety of locations. For some walleyes, that means the nearest underwater point, for others shallow shoreline brush, for others a 20-mile swim to an entirely different section of the reservoir.

"There are no rules for this," says McClelland. "I have pinned down many of the movements on Lake Oahe (a reservoir on the Missouri River), but when I tried to apply them to Lake Sharpe, Francis Case and Sakakawea (other Missouri River reservoirs), it was no go; they just aren't the same.

"The forage bases are entirely different for one thing," he says. "I've fished Texas reservoirs and other southern impoundments, and the same thing is true. They are all different, and it comes down to forage dictating walleye locations. You can have the movements down pat on one reservoir, but you still don't have

Low water levels concentrate fish in reservoirs, often simplifying your search. Low water also allows you to pinpoint unique bits of cover that will hold fish when the levels again rise.

Reservoir And River Walleyes

any rules you can live by. At least, I haven't found any."

Still, some general movements are similar on many reservoir types, said Christensen and Randash. Of the walleyes that moved into a river to spawn, some will stay all year if they find food. In fact, some "reservoir" fish will move into a river to spawn and stay two or three years before returning to the main reservoir.

But most walleyes that run up a river to spawn do return to the reservoir right after spawning. Look for hungry, feeding fish in virtually any shallow water: coves (bays), points, flats and backwaters off the main lake. Lots of walleyes will be in the vicinity of the spawning river and alternate spawning sites such as riprap shorelines and the facing of the dam.

Shallow Reservoirs

In shallow reservoirs where there are few, if any, feeder rivers, pre-spawn walleyes tend to hold in deeper water near spawning areas. After spawning they may travel many miles to extensive mud flats that are commonly found in this type of system.

When water over these shallow mud flats warms, hatching insects draw baitfish to the area. The walleyes are not far behind the baitfish.

The main river channel running through the reservoir is also a key to walleye location any time after the spawn.

"I catch most of my reservoir walleyes off long points, close to where the river channel cuts in by the point," says Gary Roach. "It's the same type of area where you would look for smallmouth bass."

The old river channel can act as a highway for some walleyes, funneling them along until it cuts in close to points, humps, timbered flats or any other food shelf. Walleyes stop to feed at these natural breaks.

"A lot of post-spawn walleyes will follow it down the lake," says Christensen. "They don't all blast back and spread all over the place. Chances are, as soon as they hit the lake and get out of that current, they'll start fanning out into shallow bays."

Post-spawn fishing can be good then—even though returning walleyes don't all go to the same place—near known spawning areas.

"During the early part of the season," says Randash, a tournament angler from Rapid City, South Dakota, who has an impres-

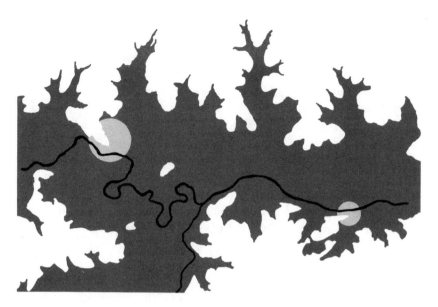

Depth maps can be good tools for locating reservoir walleyes. Look for long, narrow points with deep-water access, feeding flats and other fish-holding structure. Don't be surprised if the maps are off a bit; water levels change.

sive string of wins, "I spend virtually all my time fishing the upper half of the reservoir system."

This same general pattern holds for the Great Lakes as well, notes Christensen:

"Let's call the Great Lakes huge reservoirs, which is what they are, only with a bunch of rivers feeding in. Those fish do the same thing. They come back to the Great Lakes, and the first thing they do is head for the shallow flats and feed. They'll stay there for a long time, until a bunch of boats go in there and spook them out or a major cold front comes in and pushes them a little deeper."

Once walleyes do leave these shallow areas by whatever prodding, they might return (some stay all summer) or they might drift farther out into the main reservoir. A steady downstream migration, in fact, is demonstrable on long reservoir systems like you have on the Missouri River. Fishing gets "hot" for big walleyes a little farther down the system every few weeks through the summer. The retracing of these movements is easy to see in the fall as the fish work their way back up the system.

It's also common in these systems for walleyes to suspend in open water over schools of shad, smelt or other baitfish. Entire methods of fishing in places like Lake Erie, for instance, were developed for these midsummer suspended walleyes.

At this same time, a lot of walleyes can be found in shallow flooded timber or other woody cover. Also, classic walleye structure like that fished in natural lakes—main-lake points, flats, shoreline breaks and sunken islands—can hold good numbers of fish. (Many reservoirs have seemingly endless series of points, though, so you might have to fish a lot of them before finding the ones walleyes are using.) Also, as we have learned, walleyes can be anywhere from 30 or 40 feet deep right on the bottom at the tip of a point, all the way up to a few inches of water alongshore.

Mike McClelland and Bob Propst, arguably the toughest tandem in tournament walleye fishing, have one plan of attack when they see boats catching walleyes on the deep edges of a point.

"We run right up into the shallow part of the same area," McClelland says. "Of course, we run very carefully, making long casts into the shallow water, especially if it's calm. But we know that if there are catchable fish down deep, there are some in shallow committing suicide."

Mud flats, when present, are a key summer location. "It takes a while for the mud to warm up," says Randash, "but after that, it's the heart of the whole reservoir system. Mayflies hatch, other microorganisms live there, and this is what really turns the fish on." Generally, he says, stable weather turns on the flats, but after cold fronts you might not catch a fish.

Another reservoir walleye-holding spot to look for is stair-step ledges, carved out by constant wave action. When water levels drop, crashing waves carve out sharp "steps" in the above-water shoreline area. If water levels rise quickly (so the water doesn't wash away the ledge) a very defined piece of shoreline structure becomes available, which walleyes use to their advantage in feeding. Occasionally two stair-steps form, one deeper than the other. They are easy to find with sonar. Under windy conditions, walleyes will tend to use the shallow step; when it's calmer, the deeper one.

Especially when wind again rolls into these areas, walleyes will be right against shore, facing shore in fact, like hockey players jockeying for rebounds—grabbing minnows that are tossed against the ledge. Eventually, if water levels remain stable, the same wave action that created the steps will eat them away unless

Stair-step ledges, like those in the background of this photo, are excellent places to try when rising waters flood this part of the reservoir again.

Reservoir And River Walleyes

they are covered by five feet of water or more. This leaves you with a straight-dropping shoreline that doesn't attract as many feeding walleyes.

Fall walleye location, experts say, is not radically different from summer, except that you again see a general movement upstream in the direction of next spring's spawning grounds. Also, fewer walleyes seem to come from mud flats and more from steep rocky points and other ledges. As in all systems, the forage crop has been eaten down, so walleyes have to look harder to find a meal. This can be a good time to use bigger baits, like large minnows or crankbaits.

Finding Walleyes In Rivers

Currents can flow in lakes when the wind kicks up. But currents are a fact of life around the clock for walleyes in rivers.

Current, in fact, dictates much of what river walleyes do and where they go. To generalize, they try to hold just out of heavy current and feed on things that wash down to them, like trout or smallmouth bass do in the same environment. Many rivers also have backwater and slack water areas with minimal flow.

Throughout North America there are countless rivers, great and small, that hold walleyes. Many have dams on them, but because they are otherwise closed systems (without numerous smaller rivers or tributary streams flowing in), they are not considered reservoirs. We can also probably generalize that a river has stronger current than a reservoir—although there are lazy rivers and portions of reservoirs with occasionally heavy current. Speed of current and maximum depth vary considerably (think of the Mississippi as opposed to a small backcountry river), but walleye movements are similar in most rivers.

As spawning time approaches, river walleyes do the same thing they do in reservoirs: move generally upstream toward suitable spawning habitat.

While many fishermen concentrate their efforts right below a dam (where legal), good fishing can also be found farther downstream. Numbers of walleyes do not spawn in the tailwaters, choosing rather to deposit their eggs in shallow areas that could be several miles downriver.

Gravel bars, rocky shorelines, and riprap dam facings are prime spawning grounds, but walleyes have been known to lay

Walleyes in a river, whether it's the mighty Mississippi or a small stream like this one, are more aggressive than their lake brethren. They can be easier to catch.

their eggs on flooded vegetation if nothing else is available.

As it is in lakes and reservoirs, female walleyes tend to leave the spawning area earlier than do the males, which can remain for up to two weeks. But, in general many post-spawn walleyes settle into nearby shallow water to rest, if you believe conventional wisdom, and feed. During late spring, the shallows are where warming temperatures and food are found. Some walleyes will be found in deeper holes downstream from spawning areas, but today's pro fisherman seeks out shallow, feeding fish.

Look in back bays, flooded trees or brush, or any shallow food-shelf out of the main current. Crowds of boats will always be around the dam, and so will a certain number of walleyes; don't be afraid to strike off a mile or two downriver looking for potential spots. Away from crowds you'll find just as many fish, and they'll be less pressured. (But shallow walleyes are easily spooked; approach them from deep water and make long casts.)

After the immediate post-spawn period, river walleyes settle into "key fish-holding territories," says Daryl Christensen, who made his mark as a river guide and continues to do well whenever tournaments are held on rivers.

Christensen classifies two groups of key spots:

• Backwater areas—edges of, and right in, shallow-water sloughs, where walleyes can run in, feed and run back out to the main river. Also, any flooded willows, brush or other cover. Walleyes that feed in these areas can often be caught in the slightly deeper areas adjacent to them.

• Traditional summer locations—anywhere current is slowed for any reason. Bends in the river, sandbars, points, fallen trees, undercut banks, bridge pilings, wing dams, piers. Walleyes will hold on the slack side of the current break and dart out to grab food washing by. These areas will remain good spots throughout the summer.

A special note: Don't just fish the downstream side of current breaks. Especially on wing dams, work the front face with a heavy jig. Depending on depth and current flow, it often takes $1/2$ ounce or more to sink through the heavy current and into the slack water along the bottom at the front facing. Once the jig settles to the bottom, slowly work it parallel to the structure, back to the boat. Active walleyes often hold there, first in line to catch food coming by.

River walleyes like to hold near dams—so do fishermen. Don't be afraid to leave the pack and fish downstream. There are just as many fish and they're not pressured.

Reservoir And River Walleyes

Also, there are often more potential spots than walleyes. Look closely for the presence of baitfish on sonar, or for those breaking the surface. They can be the clue as to which areas walleyes are using.

Fluctuating currents can dictate walleye location during summer. "Increased or decreased flow makes these fish move all the time," Christensen says. "When the water starts to drop, they move down current looking for holes to hide in. Begin fishing the upper end of those pools because many times walleyes will lie there waiting for food to wash over the lip.

"If you get a lot of rain and the river rises, you can get an upstream migration of fish toward the dam," Christensen continues. "Any increase in current can stimulate walleyes to move upstream into the flow.

"That can make the dam a great summer spot, because it's a dead-end area that collects fish," he says. "They mill around, find plenty to eat and can provide super fishing for weeks."

As summer wears on and the dog days bring long spells of hot weather, walleyes use deep holes more. Shallow-water spots remain good, but vertically fishing jigs or live-bait rigs in deeper

Wing dams, designed to direct water flow, are excellent holding spots for walleyes. Active fish generally hold in front of the structure, while less active fish hide behind the structure. Fish the front first.

Complete Angler's Library

Keith Kavajecz (right) and Steve Pennaz with a nice bag of river walleyes and sauger. Look deep if you're after sauger; they often hold along the main river channel. Walleyes frequent shallower water; at times you'll find them in a foot or less.

water (which could be 10 feet or 40, depending on the river) can pay off.

River fish, perhaps more than lake fish, pounce on just about any type of bait or lure, especially when they are holding on current breaks.

"A river fish is a more aggressive fish," says Gary Roach. "They can be a lot easier to catch than lake fish because of the current. If food goes by them, they have to grab it quickly or lose out."

As fall comes, walleyes again begin making that time-honored movement upstream toward spawning areas.

"We find in the fall that a lot of times walleyes make what we call a mock spawning run," says Christensen. "Especially if the water levels are not too low, you'll see fish staging in the pre-spawn staging areas, like they are about to go ahead and spawn. It doesn't always happen, but most of the time it does."

Many walleyes will winter in deep holes, especially on smaller rivers. Lots of walleyes will be around the dam, if there is one. But again, if you venture away from the crowds, you'll still find walleyes in a lot of the same places they were all summer. The keys are food and slacker water. River walleyes have to eat, and they don't want to fight the teeth of the current.

Finally, don't forget about the sauger when fishing gets tough. There are times when sauger can save the day if walleyes aren't active. The same techniques that work on walleyes will also take sauger; the difference is the latter are often found deeper than walleyes.

NAFC Charter Member, MWC tournament angler and river rat Gary Kiedrowski regularly fishes the Mississippi, and does extremely well on both walleye and sauger. When after sauger, he'll concentrate his efforts in waters 20-30 feet deep, but has caught fish as deep as 70.

"Saugers don't turn me on as much as walleye," says Kiedrowski, "but they are fun to catch when nothing else will hit. They can be aggressive little buggers, too!"

20

Fishing Edges

Walleyes haven't read many of our rule books; they don't know they are "supposed" to be in a certain place at a certain time. They may be thick in a shallow bay right after spawning every year for four years and then all but disappear on the fifth. Things change; the reason they were there might be gone. A certain rock point or mud flat might be the hotspot of all time. Then nothing more complicated than fishing pressure might drive most of the walleyes away before you know it.

Still, there are many experiences from which we can learn. When top anglers trade notes enough times, you have a set of guidelines to follow.

For instance:

• Walleyes often congregate on structure. The term structure can mean many things, but you'll do OK if you think of it as anything "different" from the immediate surroundings, such as a hump, a point, a weed edge, a sandbar, a downed tree, anything that provides cover for baitfish and thereby gathers walleyes.

Still, experts agree that structure by itself doesn't draw anything. "Walleye aren't going to sit on a nice rock pile and starve to death," says Mike McClelland, a guy who has a saying for everything. "They have to have a reason for being where they are." They do, and most of the time, it's the presence of food.

• Transition lines between different bottom types, even on featureless lake bottoms, are often gathering or holding points for walleyes. Examples: where mud ends and sand or gravel starts; where rock changes to soft, organic bottom. These you can find with a sonar unit once you know what to look for.

• There are many walleyes in shallow water, but proximity to deeper water is an important factor in making shallow areas good fishing spots. Deep is a relative term, different in each body of water you encounter.

• Cover is critical, but it changes as much as anything during the course of the year. Weeds hold tons of walleyes, but again, it's because weeds also hold food. Weeds only grow during certain times of year and come up thicker or thinner on different years.

Examine each system you fish, and analyze what cover is available. In some shallow reservoirs, for example, there might be virtually no weeds or classic "structure." Shallow downed timber, flooded stump fields or anything you can imagine might be the best cover available. If there's food in the cover, there's a good chance walleyes won't be far away. Remember Jerry Anderson's canon: *If it looks good, if it looks like walleyes would use it, fish it.*

• The presence of food dictates walleye location more than any other factor. Where nourishment goes, walleyes follow.

• The presence of fish on the sonar can lead you to deeper-water walleyes in amazing places. When you see fish somewhere, stop and fish them for a few minutes. Don't make a career out of it or "die" on those fish, as tournament anglers say, but fish them. If you catch them and they're carp or you can't get them to bite after giving them a few baits to choose from, move on.

• Everybody who can read a lake map knows about the most obvious structural elements on a body of water, such as the longest point jutting out into the depths. Fish the "best-looking" spots on the map, but be on the lookout for the little, harder-to-find spots. And when you catch a walleye, ask yourself why that fish was there. If you can piece together clues about the spot, you can find other spots on the same lake with similar characteristics and expect to catch fish—at least on that day.

Walleyes On Edges
Food probably controls walleye location more than anything, except at spawning time. We'll explore that idea in depth later in this chapter, but consider for a moment the effect that edges have on the location of everything in nature, including walleyes.

"If it looks good, fish it." Jerry Anderson, long-time guide and tournament fisherman, follows his instincts to walleye success. (This is an early photo in the days before catch-and-release found its way into the walleye ranks.)

Edges are everywhere, and their draw is almost magical.

The edge of a weedbed. The edge where soft bottom changes to harder bottom. The edge where a drop-off is most abrupt. The tip of a point. The edge of a timbered flat.

This is not to say that walleyes won't be found in the middle of a thick weedbed, because at times they will be. They will also be found in the middle of nowhere suspended near schools of baitfish or suspended away from structure, apparently resting.

But a lot of great walleye fishermen believe edges funnel and lead walleyes from place to place and collect them in prime feeding lies. So, finding edges can be the key to finding and catching fish.

Analyze the waters you fish. What sorts of edges are present? If they have very little classical structure such as rock piles, points and the like, there might be no edges except transition lines between bottom types. This is especially true of lakes with bowl-shaped basins, an environment where Gary Parsons shines.

"Even casual fishermen can learn to find these transition lines between soft and hard bottom," he says, "and they can be the key

Fishing Edges

to locating walleyes a lot of days. Once you learn how to distinguish hard from soft bottom on a sonar unit, go out on any lake and find the depth of the transition line in one place.

"Now, the transition will usually be at that same depth all along the shoreline," Parsons continues. "Not always, but most of the time. You're going to have fingers coming out along the shoreline break, but a finger is nothing more than a pile of rocks or other harder bottom. I visualize mud or other soft, featureless bottom as being flat in most cases. The basin of the lake is normally pretty flat and uniform. I visualize structure, then, as anything coming up off that basin.

"So, all the way around that structure, if there is any, you have a fairly equal and uniform depth. It might vary a few feet, but if you find that transition line and it happens to be at 10 feet, or 25 feet, you can follow that depth contour and stay pretty close to the transition line."

Parsons knows that walleyes often sit right on that transition line. He and his partner Keith Kavajecz have made a science out of following it with their liquid crystal sonar, using the precision of the digital depth readouts to pinpoint the depth of walleye locations.

"The digital readouts are great; we love them," says Kavajecz. "Sure, they might not be as fast as the flashers, but they are easy to read and can really help you nail down depths. At the Otter Street MWC tournament one year, for example, we found that 9.6 feet was the right depth to troll. It wasn't 10 and it wasn't 11. Who knows, it could have been partly psychological, but it seemed to work. And it was easy to do with those big numbers to stare at."

Walleyes In The Weeds

Not all walleye waters have weeds, especially reservoirs, where fluctuating water levels make it tough for them to take root. But where they are found, weeds—and weed edges—become a haven for walleyes.

Weeds offer walleyes food, comfort and security. There are plenty of hiding spots from which they can ambush baitfish, and the canopy provides shade, cutting light intensity and cooling the water.

But to a walleye, not all weeds are created equal. If given a choice they prefer the cover of broadleaf weeds, such as cabbage,

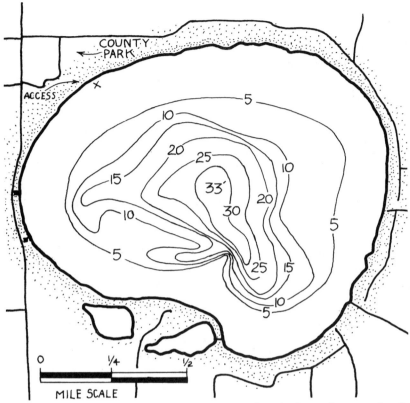

County Park

ACCESS

MILE SCALE

Not all walleye lakes offer classic types of structure like sunken islands or underwater points. In bowl-shaped lakes like this, look for places where the bottom changes from mud to sand, or small breaks along the slope.

over that of narrowleaf weeds, like coontail or milfoil.

Tournament veteran and long-time tackle promoter Gary Roach has fished more weedy lakes and has probably caught more weed walleyes than any man alive. He says that edges in the weeds come in various forms, from distinct outside and inside weedlines to pockets in dense growth.

"Anywhere you have weeds you have edges, and lots of 'em," Roach says. "I hate to harp on this subject all the time, but you need to learn to see weeds on a depthfinder, to find the weedlines (see chapter 13). Just as Parsons says he follows those transition lines and catches walleyes trolling, you need to follow those weed-lines all over the lake, looking for irregularities. You'll find weed points, inside turns and patches where they grow thicker and thinner.

Fishing Edges

"Exploring the weedline is probably the best way there is to find your own spots away from the crowds," Roach says, "because these places never show up on a contour map. Don't be afraid to fish anything that looks good to you. Get a little adventurous and it'll pay off. Walleyes like to relate to those edges, and you'll catch a lot of them by carefully following them along."

Roach also points out a fact well known among tournament pros but often missed by weekend anglers. When most people think of the weedline, or weed edge, they think of the deep edge where the weeds stop growing before the bottom breaks off into deep water. But walleyes also hold on the inside weedline, the shallow-water area between shore and the first thick growth of fish-holding weeds.

"Many times," he says, "the inside weedline is as distinct as the deep weedline. Walleyes don't always hold there, but I make a point of checking it in the late evening, early morning and when the fish have been pressured by a lot of boats and fishermen."

The inside weedline is often visible, especially in clearer-water lakes. And as we'll learn in detail in the next chapter, shallow water holds lots of walleyes, and many big ones. But remember this credo of the pros: When fishing shallow, fish from a distance. Don't expect to motor up to an inside weedline and see fish swimming all over. Stay as far away as possible, making long casts with light baits.

The weedline is deeper in clear water, shallower in dirty water. That's because the sun can't penetrate the dirtier water as well, and the darkness chokes off growth beyond a certain point. The same thing happens in clear waters, but the weedline can be as deep as 25 feet in some cases. In dirty water, weedlines of six to eight feet are common.

So you're ready to attack the water and check out the weedline. One look down the shoreline tells you this could take years! It could, but Roach says there's no need for dragging it out.

"The thing I like to do," he says, "is get among the weeds and run pretty fast. I'm looking for little openings that indicate harder bottom (weeds grow well on organic bottoms and sparsely or not at all on sand or rock). I run in and out, shallower and deeper, with my depthfinder set so I'm just barely not getting a second echo when I'm over the softer bottom. Then, when I hit hard bottom, I instantly get a second echo and I can make a note of where I am.

Complete Angler's Library

"Just run down entire sections of weeds like this," Roach advises. "Sometimes I go fast with the electric motor, backtrolling with a jig or Roach Rig. I move down whole long sections of the weedline, looking for points, inside turns, rock piles, just anything different from what's around it."

This isn't easy on a new lake, because there is a lot of ground to cover. And remember, weedlines aren't the only edges in town. In a lot of waters weeds may not even be present. Check out any kind of edge you find.

Walleyes In The Wood

In many bodies of water, typically rivers and reservoirs, weed growth is limited or even nonexistent. Here, brush and timber may be the only shallow-water cover available, but they offer a food source and shade the same as weeds do.

This type of cover includes submerged stump fields, beaver lodges, flooded timber or brush, fallen trees and even sunken logs. Prime locations are those near deep water. A timbered flat or point near a ledge or creek channel, for example, is much better than one with no deep areas nearby. A tree toppled onto a shallow

Long-line trolling the inside edges of the weeds can be a great way to catch walleyes, especially early in the evening, and early morning before other anglers are out fishing.

flat is less likely to hold walleyes than a tree which has fallen into deep water from a steep bank.

Timber will hold walleyes from spring through fall. However, the fish use flooded brush mainly in the spring as water levels rise.

They will stay in the brush as long as the water rises or remains stable. But to avoid becoming landlocked, they quickly move deeper the moment levels begin to drop.

Just like weeds, the edges of timber are prime locations to fish. More aggressive, but smaller, walleyes will be located there. But don't be afraid to explore the denser cover where larger fish tend to hide.

21

Shallow Walleyes

t the awards stand on the final day of the 1985 Mercury National Walleye Championship on Lake Winnebago, Wisconsin, Mike McClelland stood clutching the first-place trophy and a nice check. The crowd gathered around and asked how he'd done it.

"I told them, too," he remembers. "I said I caught the fish casting alongshore in about a foot of water, sometimes less. They thought, 'He's lying, he has to be lying.' That's only because they had never fished it. Tradition had them fishing other places, other patterns that weren't producing as well."

Sure enough, "Mr. Shallow," as he is sometimes called, returned the following year, using the same tactic: Find prime shallow-water feeding lies, and fish them carefully from a distance. This time, competitors followed to see if he was telling the truth. He was. He repeated as champion. After that, his patterns—like his spots—were no longer his alone.

Walleyes in shallow water is nothing new to a certain inside group of knowledgeable anglers.

"You know," says Daryl Christensen (who fishes almost exclusively in less than 15 feet), "a lot of guys will shine big walleyes in shallow water at night with spotlights, or they'll catch a few in shallow water in the evening or during a big wind, and they say the fish 'moved up' to feed. Well, why should they move up? Why shouldn't they be there to begin with all day long? They are.

"I don't believe for a minute that walleyes avoid bright light,"

Christensen continues, "because I've seen walleyes by the hundreds in crystal clear water a foot deep right in the middle of the day. The only reasons they go deep are if they're uncomfortable, say the water temperature hits 90 degrees, they go down to chase food, or somebody runs over the top of them with their boat."

The reason we don't catch more shallow walleyes, according to McClelland, is that we spook them before our bait gets where they can eat it.

"Shallow fish are there all the time," he says. "Lots of big walleyes, especially, live their whole lives in less than 10 feet of water. Telemetry studies prove that. But they're not stupid. They have highly developed senses for survival, including a lateral line that picks up minute vibrations from a long way away. Can you imagine how much water a 16-foot boat displaces, even when you are 'sneaking' toward a shallow fishing spot with your electric motor? Noise isn't the only thing to worry about. I've sat on shore and watched shallow walleyes move out of the way, up into cover, when a fisherman was coming around the corner from 150 yards away, so I know the fish couldn't see him.

"If you're going to catch shallow walleyes, you have to fish them before you scare them. That means light line, in most cases, and long casts."

OK, so if you accept this crazy notion that walleyes can be had from water you could wade without getting your socks wet, how do you go about finding them? After all, most lakes, rivers and reservoirs have a *lot* of shallow water.

"The first thing I look for, for shallow-water walleyes," says Christensen, "is shallow rock with deep water right next to it. I want that deep water as close as possible, and steep breaks are nice. If you fish such shoreline or mid-lake structure drop-offs, you've probably caught plenty of shallow walleyes without even knowing it.

"A lot of guys will cast up on the shallow shelf and work the jig or whatever down the drop," according to Christensen. "A walleye grabs the bait on the shallow shelf and the first thing he does is run for the deep water to get away from the rest of the fish with his food. It happens all the time to me. So by the time you realize you have a bite, the fish is off the drop, so you think the fish are off the break. A lot of times, they're not.

"Then, as you work your way in closer, what happens?" Chris-

Mike McClelland, known in walleye tournament circles as "Mr. Shallow," has won an impressive number of tournaments with his shallow-water techniques."

tensen asks. "The fish are off the edge because you spooked them out of there. So now you're fishing spooked fish in deep water. But they weren't deep to begin with.

"But that's just one type of spot to look for," Christensen continues. "Weedlines are also great. I can catch walleyes in weeds in a foot of water or 10 feet of water. Shallow is relative. Depending on the depth of the lake and clarity of the water, I would say shallow is anything from one to 10 feet. If the water is stained or dirty, I would not call 10 feet shallow; but if the water is crystal clear, 10 feet becomes shallow. See what I mean?

"Bottom content is not as critical as the presence of food," says Christensen. "I mean, cover is always important to walleyes, so if you have rocks with scattered cabbage weeds, you can't beat that. But if it's not there, that doesn't mean the fish won't be there.

"A lot of real cold-water, deep lakes don't have good shallow cover," Christensen says. "They don't have that shallow weedline. The weeds might not start growing in a lot of lakes until, say, six feet or so. I hate that kind of situation because it means your shallow water is not as good, generally speaking, because the walleyes would have to swim through the weeds, out into the open and get into the shallow water. But why would they? In those lakes, the food is usually buried in the weeds or suspended in the open, so that's where the walleyes are going to be, too.

"On reservoirs, there are plenty of shallow-water areas walleyes will use. Downed trees, timber, stump fields, any kind of cover, especially if it's close to deep water where the fish can slide off in a second if they get spooked. And remember," Christensen warns, "if you want to catch them, it's your job not to spook them."

Another trick to narrow your search is to visit likely shallow-water haunts at night with a strong spotlight. Quietly work along, shining it at intervals, looking for the telltale glow of those eyes. Anywhere walleyes go at night, our experts tell us, they will likely visit during daylight hours. Fish from a distance!

In some instances, shallow walleyes use sight for feeding. But we've already established that wind, which stirs everything up, can generate a feeding spree. Even in shallow water, the world can be basically dark. Especially if the water has some color to begin with, waves crashing in uprooting sediment and filling the area with plankton can all but turn the lights out, even at midday.

"If you say a walleye is a sight feeder," opines McClelland, "you better go back to school. A walleye has a great eye; it gathers a lot of light. But if there's no light to gather, it can't see. Muddy water, in most cases, is caused by suspended particles. A walleye doesn't have X-ray vision, so it can only see a few inches in most turbid, windy situations.

"So why do they prefer dirty water to feed in? The reason is very simple: They can use their lateral line to find prey. Normally, shallow-water minnows are on guard all the time, and they can get away from most walleyes, " McClelland says. "But when the wind tosses up the surface of the water, cutting out a lot of movement that scares them, minnows feel secure, they relax and start eating. That makes them sitting ducks for walleyes, which can easily find them with their lateral line sense. Walleyes can slide up to them, flare their gills, suck in water and the minnow comes right with the flow. An easy meal. Neither one ever sees the other."

Approaching And Fishing Shallow Walleyes

As McClelland points out, the key to catching shallow walleyes is fishing them from a distance. Christensen, who built his

Approach and fish shallow walleyes from a distance. Make long casts and avoid rushing up to a spot with the big motor, which causes waves to rush in and often spook the fish. If that happens, the gig is up.

reputation as a river guide catching big walleyes out of water barely deep enough to cover their backs, agrees. He thinks faith can be the key ingredient to a successful approach.

"I almost never see the walleyes before they strike," Christensen says, "and I'll tell you why. Because I assume they're there. I see a rock reef coming out or a good timbered flat or something, and I assume big walleyes are on top of it. So I stay back and make long casts. I either use a jig with light line, like 6-pound test, or I use a crankbait. If the fish are there, you'll know about it soon enough. You get a real good look at 'em when they're hooked on your line!"

Experts agree that shallow fish, even when their vision is limited, tend to be aggressive biters. You can fish fast, covering a lot of water, just as we discussed in the section on wind.

"You don't have to bother with an ultra-slow presentation," says Christensen, "because those fish are up there to feed."

The exception to this is when the structure dictates a slower presentation. Tom Neustrom suggests going to a slip-bobber or light jig fished slowly when working a specific area, like the tip of a point. The same applies to any shallow-water situation, wind-affected or not.

Finding key lies or feeding stations can take time. At Big Stone Lake on the South Dakota-Minnesota border, McClelland has located more than 100 such spots, often nothing more than one particular rock, that almost always hold walleyes. On Lake Winnebago, the site of his back-to-back Mercury National wins, he only has about 20 spots because, he says, he hasn't fished it as much. Jerry Anderson, a revered guide on Minnesota's Mille Lacs Lake, has countless tiny spots—certain rocks, the very tip of a point—he can pull up on with precision and care and often pluck big walleyes.

It's a principle we normally associate with stream trout fishing, but these pros have made it work with walleyes.

"What I do when I'm fishing new territory," says McClelland, "is painstakingly fish entire long sections of shoreline and entire big offshore structures, using either a spoon (more in a moment on that) or a crankbait. Especially if the shoreline drops off quickly, to eight or 10 feet deep, I'll use a crankbait, something I can crank down, pause, crank down, pause, sort of follow the drop. I'm looking for hot fish. As soon as I catch one, I slow down, usually start fishing a jig and take a real good look at that area. I want to know why.

"I constantly try to build a mental image of what's on the bottom. I'm saying things to myself like, 'OK, there are a few bigger rocks over there. That's mud right there. Now, wait a minute, is that gravel I'm feeling with my jig?' In that way, I build a picture of what that stretch looks like," McClelland continues. "Most guys only think about doing this with their electronics in deep water, and they just blindly fish along in shallow water with no concern about what's really there.

"So you're building this picture in your mind. I've found amazing things in dirty, shallow water, like rows of rocks that run parallel to shore, just a few feet from the shoreline, probably something people used to have in their backyard before the water level rose or something. As soon as I catch a fish, I ask myself why. By doing that, I've put together patterns, such as the one in Winnebago, where shallow shoreline mud, which really got riled up even in a light wind, was the hot ticket. If I wasn't *really* paying attention to what I was doing, I never would have noticed it."

Wind is a big help because it allows you to get closer than normal to shallow walleyes. It lets you make shorter casts with light jigs, a deadly presentation. It lets you cast lightweight minnow plugs, which you can't do at long distances from the fish.

What do you do if you want to go after shallow walleyes under calm conditions, especially in a clear-water lake where walleyes can see more than a mile?

You heard Mike mention it, and it's the obvious choice. Spoons.

Casting Spoons: The Underused Weapon

"Basically, if there's no wind and I'm fishing shallow, I go to spoons."

That statement from Mike McClelland may literally shock walleye fishermen. The last time many of them thought about spoons was during their childhood when they cast from shore with an old red-and-white, hoping for northern pike.

"Bob Propst and I came up with the idea during a team tournament on Lake Winnebago," McClelland remembers. "We knew we had shallow walleyes but couldn't get anywhere near them. We thought about it, and it was obvious. You can cast spoons a

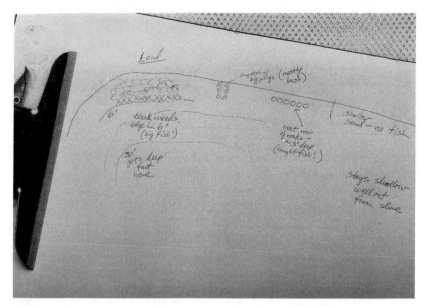

After working a section of shallow shoreline, you should be able to sketch the composition of the bottom and note likely spots. Keep a record of "honey holes;" they will probably hold walleyes year after year.

mile, and you have great depth control. I can cast all the way across a big reef or from a long distance, all the way into shore. Let it sink, start reeling and it comes right up by the surface. Twitch it. Work it fast or work it slow. It's easy and one of the only solutions when you have to stay away from shallow fish and make long-distance casts.

Propst doesn't believe color or type of spoon is a critical factor. "We bought them out of one of those bins in a little bait shop," Propst recalls. "Mike's was sort of faded orange on one side and silver on the other. I was using a Krocodile. We just picked the heaviest spoons we could find for their size and started casting them at those fish. It worked."

It sure did. They won that tournament, too.

"We'd just heave those things out there," McClelland says, "and we'd get three or four strikes on the way in. We were using 6-pound line, so it had so much stretch in it we couldn't set the hook. It was just crazy. But enough fish hooked themselves that it didn't matter."

McClelland and Propst pull out their spoons, which they now carry at all times, every time they encounter shallow walleyes in calm or clear water. Any time casting distance is at a premium, spoons may be the ticket.

Spoons?

Making Your Approach

Normally, with even a minimum of wave action, you can carefully approach shallow walleyes from deep water, sliding into position. But clear water presents the ultimate challenge, the equivalent of stalking feeding trout in a spring creek, or bonefish on a saltwater flat.

Oftentimes, shallow walleyes in clear water can see you long before you're in casting range, even armed with spoons. Daryl Christensen has developed a sneaky boat maneuver that can put you in the money.

"The biggest problem most guys have," he says, "is that they always think about working the deep-water structures and never consider the shallow water nearby. For example, they'll pull onto a deep point and work the outside tip and maybe up both sides. As they motor up, they spook all the shallow fish because they are not thinking in those terms. Think about it; you don't have to worry

Sneak up on walleyes by using an electric motor on your boat. Shallow walleyes are boat-shy. Work them first from a distance, making your approach slowly and quietly. Lighter lines will help you cast farther.

Shallow Walleyes

They may not be a day-to-day staple item, but keep a few casting spoons handy. If you encounter shallow fish that can't be approached with the boat, you might need their long-casting capabilities.

about spooking the deep fish! They aren't going to spook.

"What you want to do is work the shallow water *first*. Get right up against the bank plenty far from where you want to fish, and slowly work toward it, fishing the whole way. Sneak your way to the fish. If it's windy, you can get closer. If it's calm, you have to make longer casts. If you believe the fish are there, they'll prove they are by hitting your bait."

This belief that shallow walleyes exist and the willingness to give them a try are the keys to unlocking a new dimension in your fishing.

"Guys who don't fish shallow for walleyes very often might give it a try, but unless they do it right, they won't catch anything," says Christensen. "As soon as that happens they say, 'Well, that doesn't work.' So they go back to their tried-and-true methods. But it does work.

You don't always catch a boatload of fish, because you stick a 6- or 7-pounder and he tears all over the place and spooks the rest of the fish out. But it's exciting, and you don't always catch a boatload of walleyes fishing deep, either.

"You have to convince yourself that you're going to take a day

Get up against the bank and carefully fish in front of the boat as you approach clear-water shallow walleyes. Start well away from the key area. Here, Lake Sakakawea guide Rod Irion works a section of stair-step ledges that has been flooded by rising water.

Shallow Walleyes

and fish only shallow water for walleyes," Christensen continues. "If you don't, then the only time you're going to do well is when the deep fish are biting. Fishing shallow, you're going to get weeds on your jigs, and you're going to get hung up. You might even lose some crankbaits. But once you get out there and start fishing the shallow stuff, you'll understand, you'll see how incredible that type of fishing can be."

We're talking super-aggressive fish that often hit and run with the line 20 feet before you can set the hook. Shallow walleyes are ready for action, and they come to fight. Do your part and be ready for them.

Catching Walleyes

22

Best Way To Catch Walleyes?

"Anybody who fishes just crankbaits,

or just jigs, or just rigs, or just

anything for walleyes is nuts."

—Dan Nelson

Walleyes in the open. Walleyes on structure. Walleyes shallow; walleyes deep. Aggressive fish, reluctant fish. Walleyes on the weedline. So what's the best way to fish walleyes, anyway? *I got an uncle, see, and he says anything but a floating jig head and a leech is wastin' your time. But my brother and his buddy go out at night and troll Rapalas and they kill 'em. And there's this guy at work who uses Lindy Rigs and nightcrawlers, and nobody catches more than he does.*

Walleyes holding on a classic rocky point on a Canadian lake. Walleyes suspended in the middle of nowhere, chasing ciscoes or gizzard shad. Walleyes lined up on a current break in a river. There is much variety in the walleyes' world, and things can be so different from one system to the next.

So what is the best way to catch walleyes? There is no "best" way, just as there is no "best" way to build a house; so much depends on the environment.

Competitive walleye fishing, no matter what you think about it, has changed your fishing for the better. People kick and scream

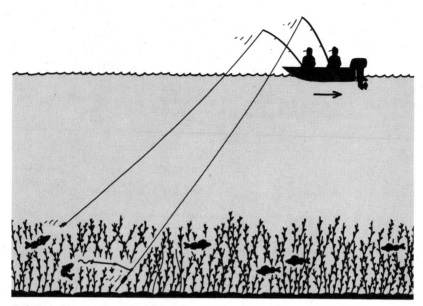

Tailor your presentation to the fish and the type of spot you're fishing, rather than trying to ram your favorite method down their throats. If the walleyes are in shallow water or scattered over a large area, a "horizontal" presentation—crankbaits, spinner rigs, etc.—is the way to go.

about the cost of shooting astronauts into outer space, but they gladly buy digital watches that keep track of appointments and jogging times off the impulse rack at the grocery store. Likewise, weekend anglers gripe about walleye tournaments that take all the fish out of their lake. But they employ the new tackle, equipment and methods that are developed by professional fishermen. Pushing the limits of technology and equipment forces innovation. New products and new ways of doing things, which benefit all walleye fishermen, are the result.

At the same time, wives' tales are severely tested. *You can't catch walleyes in shallow water. Don't even bother fishing for them except during the late evening and early morning. This lake doesn't have anything but small fish.*

Go into a specific region where walleyes behave a specific way, and you'll run into local heroes who can outfish everyone. Usually, they fish one way most of the time. Nothin' wrong with that, but until walleye tournaments gathered the best, most creative anglers on the same waters and moved them from region to region, dogmatic rules about walleyes were the norm, even though they changed according to whose barstool you were leaned up against.

Complete Angler's Library

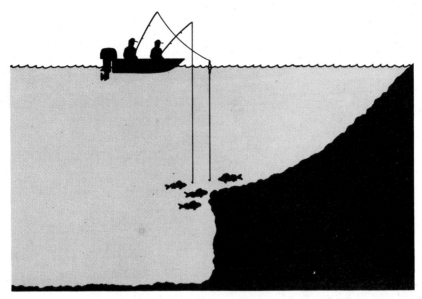

"Vertical" presentations, such as vertical jigging or slip-bobbering, are called for when the walleyes are holding tight on structure or are in a negative mood (after a cold front, for example). This concept is another "secret" of the walleye pros you can try on the waters you fish.

The walleye universe is growing, and new wrinkles on old tactics are exploding on the scene. But thanks to the same touring pros a lot of people curse, the rules have been distilled into two sentences.

It's come to this:

• You can't catch walleyes consistently if you only know how to fish one way.

• The fish's location and mood dictate your presentation.

This is a consensus among top, well-traveled walleye anglers. We can't list every situation, but it means:

• If the fish are aggressive, you can fish quickly and live bait might not be necessary.

• If the fish are finicky, you have to slow down and live bait becomes critical to success.

• Certain situations call for a "horizontal" presentation, such as a crankbait or spinner rig. Examples are shallow water and any time you're trying to cover a large area, searching for fish.

• Other situations call for a "vertical" presentation, such as a jig fished directly below the boat, or a slip-bobber. Vertical presentations are called for when working small, specific spots such as the tip of a point, or an opening in the weeds or when fish are in a "neutral to negative feeding mood" (not biting).

It may sound like common sense, and it is. It's a simple system to apply, regardless where you fish. But many, if not most, anglers tend to hone their skills in one area. Then they try to ram that presentation down the fish's collective throats. Maybe you're a good jig fisherman or good at trolling crankbaits or prefer to drag live bait rigs. The fish don't care what you're good at; they make their feeding decisions based on where they are and what food is available.

You should make your fishing decisions based on the same criteria.

"If the walleyes are scattered on a shallow flat," says Gary Parsons, "you don't go after them by vertically jigging. You'd be there for three years before you caught a limit of fish. You learn to analyze what you're up against, and fish a bait that is suited to that situation. With scattered fish on a shallow flat, for instance, I would probably troll a crankbait or a spinner rig on a bottom bouncer. If it was clear water, I'd probably run my lines off to the

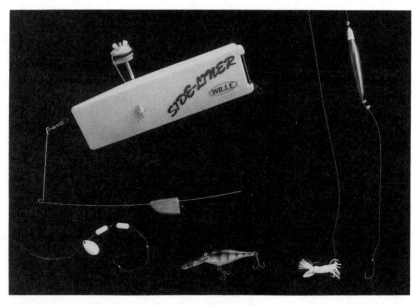

"Horizontal" baits include things like spinner rigs and crankbaits. The Lindy Bottom Cruiser (above spinner rig) helps you keep the bait in the fish zone while covering water quickly. The planer board gets your line out to the side of the boat to avoid spooking fish. "Vertical" baits, at their best when fish are grouped together and/or inactive, include jigs and slip-bobber rigs.

Complete Angler's Library

Count on crankbaits to bring sauger and walleyes to the net when conditions call for a horizontal presentation. This fish was taken on a Countdown Rapala trolled along a rip-rap-line shoreline below a dam.

side of the boat with a planer board to keep from spooking the fish."

Using Parson's logic, it takes just a few seconds to come up with a battle plan. What if the fish are on a fairly small, deep rock pile? It's no use trolling in that situation; you'd spend most of the day turning around and heading back for another shot at them. Camp right on top of them and jig slowly.

If you don't catch any, switch to a lighter jig, another color or a different type of live bait. What should you do if you still can't catch them, and you suspect your boat might be spooking them? Back off and cast a slip-bobber, set to the right depth, and let it soak your bait in front of their faces.

Learn to fish more than one system. If you're a jigger, experiment with live-bait rigs, including bottom bouncers. Learn to cast and troll crankbaits, and rig and fish slip-bobbers. Buy a set of inexpensive planer boards, like Wille's Side-Liners (the best in the business), and practice until you can control them, because getting the bait away from the boat helps in a lot of cases.

Use your "favorite" method when the conditions call for it, but if it doesn't work, try something different. Expand your horizons.

Best Way To Catch Walleyes?   225

It may mean using a new presentation in the same spot or switching tactics on a completely different type of structure. If you are hesitant to change, just keep in mind that there is no "best way" to catch walleyes. The only "way" is the one that works that day, on that body of water.

As you experiment with new techniques, your production may tail off for a while. But don't get discouraged. You'll soon be finding pockets of fish you never dreamed were there, and your confidence will grow as a result.

In walleye fishing, bear in mind that diversity is the key to consistency!

23

The "Little Things"

Before we dig into the variety of methods available to the modern walleye angler, here are just a few words on some of the important little things. You'll literally spend your fishing lifetime polishing them, but I've learned from experience that the right advice from the right people can save a lot of fruitless experiments.

Bite Detection

Fish, including walleyes, bite more often than most of us realize. It's been demonstrated through underwater observation that even top bass pros don't feel a lot of the bites they get on plastic worms. Bass have been seen sucking 8-inch worms completely into their mouths, while the pros patiently work the worm, feeling all the while for the slightest sensation. It's agonizing to think this could happen, and it hammers home how tough it can be to detect subtle strikes.

Think about walleye fishing, where you often slowly, painstakingly, work along, jigging or sliding a finesse bait of some kind. There's no question that most of us get more bites than we feel.

"I get very frustrated," says Canadian walleye guide Alan Meline, who takes parties out on island-studded Lake of the Woods. "You can't believe how many times I can see my clients' line move or their rodtip twitch, and I want to reach over and set the hook for them. Usually, it's too late by the time I say something."

Pro anglers have honed their skills in detecting light-biting walleyes, but even they get fooled sometimes. Less experienced fishermen should set the hook anytime something feels "different." You'd be surprised how many strikes are missed by anglers.

When walleyes bite, they can rip the rod out of your hands or leave you feeling absolutely nothing. They sometimes latch onto your bait and swim along with the boat, an ever-so-slight heaviness the only sign betraying their presence. When they take a bait in, and your line is reasonably (but not too!) tight, you feel a distinct "tick." As Mike McClelland says, "It doesn't get any better than that." It's time to set the hook.

McClelland and several other top pros argue that walleyes always try to take a bait all the way in their mouth. "They don't decide to have half a nightcrawler for lunch," he likes to say. But others argue just as vehemently that walleyes also halfheartedly grab, bump, nudge and otherwise check out baits without actually biting them.

So how hard is it to feel bites, and when should you set the hook? We'll go into detail while discussing each of the major methods of presentation, but here are a few general thoughts from the pros:

First, get a good rod that's balanced to the size bait you're using. Graphite rods are not as expensive as they used to be, and trying to feel light bites without one is crazy. "Balanced" tackle just means the reel should be the right size for the rod, and the bait shouldn't be too light or too heavy. It's common sense.

You'll often hear the advice, "Set the hook anytime you feel anything different." It's sound, especially when you drop a line in the water for the first time. The first time you fish with a good rod, you'll feel every little pebble, rock, log and weed the bait drags over. It's all going to feel like a bite at first, and only time with the rod in your hand is going to teach you what's what. Even after years of fishing, though, pros still get fooled as much as a third of the time.

Get used to your rod or rods, and try to fish with them, rather than constantly switching to try your buddy's. Even top anglers like Daryl Christensen, considered one of the finest jig fishermen on the MWC tournament circuit, admits to feeling lost without his own equipment.

"When I pick up somebody else's rod, it's like I'm learning to fish all over again," he says. "You get used to what everything feels like with your own rods, and that's the only way you can really learn to pick up light biters."

When walleyes are really hitting, you won't need a translator. But those times are few with this fish. Most often, it's not going to feel like much of anything. Sorry, but that's about as close as we can get to a definition.

Some anglers are line watchers. They study the line at the rod-tip, or where it enters the water, and look for the slightest movement, especially when jigging. That can work, if you like it. Others keep a finger on the line all the time and rely partially on a sense of feel. That, too, works. Others rely only on the sensitivity of the rod. Try a few different methods, and find what's most natural for you.

Concentration, without doubt, is a big factor. If you're just out there to enjoy the sunshine and figure out if the seagulls are boys or girls, put up with the fact that you're not going to catch as much as if you're paying attention. There's nothing wrong with getting skunked, as long as you're happy.

A Live Bait Primer

As Dan Nelson said at the beginning of this section, you can't catch walleyes consistently on any one thing. A lot of times, you can't beat the natural, wiggling action, the smell, the attempted

*Daryl Christensen, considered one of the finest jig fishermen in the world, stresses the impor-
tance of getting a good rod and reel, learning the feel of it, and sticking with it.*

escape and everything else that can only come with live bait.

If at all possible, carry with you the three major live baits for walleyes: leeches, minnows and nightcrawlers. On any given day, it's impossible to predict which will trigger more fish.

Make sure the bait is fresh. Take care of it. Most top anglers carry a cooler dedicated to live bait. Nightcrawlers and leeches go in it, along with ice cubes. Keep the lid on so it's cool and dark, and you'll have lively bait even on the hottest days. Keep minnows in some sort of aeration tank, using ice cubes to keep the water cool. Some boats are being built with baitwells specifically for minnows or leeches. Except in the cool of spring and fall, don't drag your minnows alongside the boat in one of those floating buckets. The hot surface water of midsummer is a death trap for them. Keep all bait in water that's free of chlorine such as well or lake water.

Change bait frequently. Don't make it a contest to see how many walleyes you can catch on one leech. Fish any bait only while it's so lively it's hard to handle. (Believe it or not, that is one of the "secrets" of successful walleye anglers.)

The relative size of live baits can be an important factor in success. Often, especially in spring and fall, bigger bait means more fish. That's because walleyes are used to seeing and feeding on holdover forage—baitfish from the year before (spring), or baitfish that made it through the summer, growing in the process (fall).

It's also arguable that bigger baits mean bigger fish, although many big walleyes are caught on tiny baits. To trigger bites from inactive walleyes, you may need to tackle down. When fishing gets tough, don't be afraid to try half a nightcrawler, a smaller leech, a tiny minnow—even a grub or maggot normally considered panfish bait. As Mick Thill, a native American who has won numerous titles in European match-fishing circles, including a gold medal in the World Championships in 1982, says, "Fish snack more than they feast."

You'll hear North American walleye specialists saying the same thing. *Triggering* appeal is a hot topic in walleye-fishing circles these days, a term used when judging how well a given bait or presentation method coaxes halfhearted bites out of reluctant fish. Often, but not always, less is more when you're trying to trigger lockjawed fish.

Keep a good supply of various types of live bait. You're more apt to use fresh bait if it's plentiful. Top fishermen store nightcrawlers and leeches in an ice-filled cooler to keep them fresh and lively.

"As triggers and provokers," Thill says enthusiastically, "maggots are deadly, even on fish as big as walleyes."

Thill serves up this triggering tip, exclusively for North American Fishing Club members, from his match-fishing bag of tricks:

"Often," he says, "I tip a minnow or leech with a colored European maggot." (These are sold under the name Eurolarvae, or Maggies, and are available through Cabela's, Dept. NAF, 812 13th Ave., Sidney, NE 69160, if not at your local bait shop). "It gives you a contrast of colors for one thing. For example, try a white maggot on a leech," says Thill. They also help cover the hook, soften the feel when the fish bites and increase the amino acid released when the fish closes its mouth around your bait.

"When fish taste certain amino acids, this causes an ingesting reaction," Thill explains, "making them hold on longer. When they encounter other amino acids or the foreign feel and taste of purely artificial baits, this normally causes them to quickly spit out the bait. That's why, even when I'm fishing artificials—say a jig with a plastic tail—I usually put at least a small piece of natural bait on the tip of the hook."

About Leeches

Many anglers are still afraid of leeches, after all these years. They've seen too many movies where leeches take Manhattan, or eat four small boys for supper. Leeches, or more specifically *ribbon leeches*, the ones you fish with, are not bloodsuckers. Yes, leeches have suckers on each end, and they can attach to your skin. But they don't suck blood, and they fall off in a few seconds in most cases. A lot of anglers, in fact, let leeches grab on so it's easier to hook them.

For anyone who still refuses to handle them, Rick James (another well-known member of the Lindy-Little Joe Fishing Team) offers a simple tip that really works:

Before launching, put a small pile of sand somewhere in the boat. Let it heat up in the sun. Use a minnow net if you have to, to take a leech out of the bucket. Drop it on the sand, and it will stiffen up long enough to let you easily hook it on. Drop it in the water, the sand washes off, the leech goes crazy, and you're fishing!

Leeches are choice baits for a number of reasons. Most importantly, walleyes love to eat them. But anglers also like them be-

Tiny Eurolarvae, colored maggots from England, may have a place in jigging for walleyes. They cover the hook and lend a natural release of amino acids when a fish strikes, perhaps making the fish hold onto the jig longer.

cause they are tough. They do not come off when cast on a jig like minnows do, and they stay alive longer when hooked. They also tolerate warm water, remaining lively, enticing morsels at 50 degrees Fahrenheit and higher.

A few knowledgeable anglers trap their own leeches in the spring, often acquiring a season's supply in a week or two. They sink traps into small ponds, using butcher shop trimmings or fish parts for bait.

Most of us, however, rely on the local bait dealer, which is an especially good idea if you don't know the difference between a leech and a bloodsucker.

It is not difficult to distinguish between the two. Here are some tips that will help:

• Ribbon leeches are firm; bloodsuckers are soft, mushy and often grow to enormous sizes.

• Leeches have visible serrations, or edges, when they roll into a ball. Bloodsuckers look perfectly smooth.

• Medicine leeches, one type of bloodsucker, have a black back and orangey belly, with straight rows of red or orange dots on their back.

Ribbon leeches are clean, easy to handle and deadly on walleyes! Their firm body and visible serrations make them easy to tell from bloodsuckers, which are lousy walleye baits and "yucky" besides!

About Nightcrawlers

Nightcrawlers are a versatile bait. Fish them under a slip-bobber, tipped on a jig or on a spinner rig. One successful old-time technique was to impale a half a nightcrawler on the trailing hook of a Lazy Ike.

The point is to be creative. If you think a bit of meat will improve your chances, try it. Just make sure the bait is fresh and lively. Take the first step when making your purchase.

Be sure to open nightcrawler containers at the bait shop before deciding to buy. They should be big, plump and lively. Skinny, lethargic, mushy crawlers are about to die and should be left for the bait shop owner to bury.

You can do a lot with nightcrawlers if you buy them ahead of time. Get some good ones, and put them in commercial bedding, like Worm Paradise (HT Enterprises, Dept. NAF, 139 E. Sheboygan St., Campbellsport, WI 53010), which has worm food built in. Coffee grounds should not be used for bedding.

Make sure the bedding is moist, not wet. Add ground, moistened newspaper or organic material for bulk if necessary. Put it in an insulated container (Styrofoam coolers are the old standby), keep the lid on, and leave it in a dark, cool place. As time goes by, the critters just get bigger and healthier, waiting patiently for you to go fishing.

But before you hit the water, put the finishing touches on. This is known as "conditioning" your nightcrawlers.

The day before you're going fishing, dump some crawlers on a bed of crushed ice and cover them with newspapers. The ice will melt, the crawlers will soak up the water, and next morning you have bait that looks like it's been pumping iron. Try grabbing one now! It'll take you five minutes to hook it up.

"A good nightcrawler," says Tom Neustrom, "should scare everything smaller than 6 pounds. It should scare your dog."

If ice is not readily available, you can put crawlers in a bath of ice water (they can live a short time in water but will eventually drown). The effect, short-term, is nearly the same.

Lure Color

Several years ago, a device claiming to "take all the guesswork" out of lure color selection hit the market with a bravado befitting

A good nightcrawler should be large enough to "scare the fish," say expert anglers. Prepare for your next trip by purchasing good quality crawlers beforehand, storing them properly and "conditioning" them before you head to the lake.

the exciting nature of new fishing products. Talk resounded that first winter at sports shows as anglers prepared for their first season with the instrument. Finally! A way to know for sure the color lure to use.

When all the claims settled and the devices hit the water, they turned out to measure what wavelength of light most visible at the depth a probe was lowered to, in the prevailing water clarity. An underwater light meter, you might say, and not a very good one, according to impromptu tests done with identical units side by side.

Suffice it to say that lure color selection is still more art than science.

Some top anglers swear that it's a make-or-break deal, that even shades of a certain color will outproduce everything else. Others either seem to use a few colors exclusively or dismiss color's importance altogether.

Let's listen to both sides.

It Doesn't Matter—
Mike McClelland: "Let me put it this way...color consumes

way, way too much thought time for the fisherman. For as important as it really is, it's ridiculous. I mean, color is a two percent deal, and it consumes 70 percent of most people's thinking and time on the water. The key to your baits is what you do with them, not what color they are.

"I won't say it doesn't make any difference," McClelland continues. "What I'm saying is that I don't have time to mess with it. If I was running a big launch and had 35 rods out over the boat every day, I would have time to see which color seemed to be producing best. But the average guys should worry more about the spots they're fishing and the action they're putting on the bait, that's all I'm saying."

Jim Randash agrees: "Let's take crankbaits as an example. Open up my tackle box and I've got about 200 lures in there. They're all the same color, a natural paint that looks like a minnow; you know, silvery sides. I buy 'em by the dozen, and I buy one color. I don't always do that well with them, but I don't spend time screwing around trying to figure out if I have the right color. I spend my time worrying about more important things.

"Let's say you and I are fishing in a tournament," Randash continues. "We're trying to find the right color, so we're running through all these colors, spending all kinds of time changing lures. During that time, the lure is out of the water. You find a good color, but that color might change in a matter of hours or minutes. Believe me, I've thought this through. I know that consistently overall, a minnow-imitating color is my best producer, and I'm going to be a heckuva lot better off not screwing around with anything else. That's why I buy just one color. Then I don't have to worry about it."

It Matters—
Gary Roach: "Color is real important. One color is typically going to outproduce the others. I know it changes, but while it's working it's worth trying to figure out. It's not that much trouble to keep checking it, and it really comes into play when you're catching fish one minute and then they quit. Many times, by switching to another color, you can pick up a few more fish before they quit again. A lot of guys do that."

Gary Parsons/Keith Kavajecz: "Absolutely, color is important. We fish crankbaits for walleyes a lot, and we use a lot of chrome colors, like blue-chrome and silver-chrome, because they match shad and other baitfish populations we run into in various places. You see the studies that say walleyes can see chartreuse and orange best, and those two colors catch a lot of walleyes. We prefer broken patterns, though, rather than, say, a solid chartreuse. Not only that, but a white body, a white belly, seems to make a big difference in the number of fish we catch.

"The reason we feel lure color makes such a difference," continues Parsons, "is that we do so much crankbait trolling at specific depth contours. We're running four identical lures, with the only differences being the colors. We'll have, on any given day, certain colors that completely outproduce the others. As soon as we realize one of those patterns is developing, all four lures are that color. When things slow down, we start experimenting again. Color's effectiveness tends to change as light conditions change, or as water turbidity changes.

"Maybe the wind comes up, or some sections of the lake are clearer than others. Sometimes it seems like the fish just get tired of seeing a certain color, or it quits fooling them. Depth definitely changes things, too.

"It may change three times during the course of a day, it may change from day to day, or it may not change for a week," says Parsons.

When you add it up, you might conclude that lure color indeed does make a difference in some situations. McClelland's and Randash's point is well taken, however; until you get a handle on all the other important factors, like mastering sonar use, finding fish, controlling your boat, and building various actions into your presentations, don't let color rule your time on the water.

Remember Dr. Dwight Burkhardt's research, indicating that the walleye's eye is most sensitive to orange and green light (see chapter 5). They are, history says, good walleye colors, especially in jigs, spinner blades and slip-sinkers.

If you had to pick a few major walleye colors, they would probably be chartreuse (which has no doubt accounted for more walleyes than any other single color), fluorescent orange, silver (especially in crankbaits), and "no" color (such as unpainted jigs, or a plain hook with live bait on it).

Lately, phosphorescent, or "glow-in-the-dark" lures have been catching impressive numbers of walleyes, especially in low-light

One way of checking for color preference in walleyes is to troll different-colored lures on each rod, noting which baits the most fish come on. Here, Keith Kavajecz shows how he and partner Gary Parsons spread out four rods with the use of Wille planer boards.

conditions. (Low light can include water in late evening or early morning, water under overcast skies or heavy winds, or dirty water.) One handy way to keep phosphorescence on hand is to pick up a package of Firefly luminescent tape (Blue Fox Tackle Co. Dept. NAF, 645 N. Emerson, Cambridge, MN 55008), which can be applied to any crankbait, jig, sinker, etc.

Dick Sternberg, the inventor of the tape, says that the secret to its effectiveness is that its glow is not as strong as other similar products. "Walleyes' senses are pretty sharp," he says. "You don't have to hit them over the head to get them to notice something. I've seen a lot of instances with other luminescent tapes and things where they glowed like a tracer bullet, and they don't catch fish until they dim. It seems like if you use something too bright, it actually spooks the fish."

Put a short stripe down each side of a crankbait, Sternberg suggests, or small eyes on each side of a jig, just enough to help a walleye detect your lure's presence when its eyesight might be hampered.

A few last thoughts on lure color and performance of colors underwater:

• Fluorescent colors hold their true color much deeper than non-fluorescent colors. They are visible at greater distances than non-fluorescent colors of identical shades, regardless of water clarity. As long as any light at all is present under the water, it can "excite" the ions of the fluorescent paint, bringing out not only color, but the actual color of the lure!

In other words, say you are using a fluorescent orange jig at a depth that no orange light could penetrate. As long as there is some light—any light—the fluorescent paint on the jig will pick it up and glow orange. Talk about a lure that stands out against the background!

• In murkier water, longer wavelengths (green, yellow or all the way to oranges and reds in very dirty water) penetrate deepest. In extremely dirty water, though, all colors disappear quickly.

• In clearer water (oceans being the extreme example), blues penetrate deepest.

Boat Control

Every good walleye fisherman in North America has developed a versatility that extends beyond presenting different baits. You'll find that versatility helpful when it comes to controlling your boat.

In many walleye-fishing situations, you actually present the bait with the boat; that is, by moving the boat around, you move the bait—following contours, controlling speed and steering clear of spooky fish.

You need to become good at a variety of maneuvers. Foremost is either backtrolling or front-trolling with an electric motor (or in some cases, a gas-powered kicker). You'll see the pros doing both.

Consciously practice staying on depth contours, or following weedlines and other cover edges, by using the motor and sonar together.

(In the following, simply substitute "gas kicker" for "electric" if that's what you fish with.)

Boat control, when you break it down, is no more than common sense. Look the situation over, and do what you have to in order to control your boat. If your rear electric motor can't fight the wind by itself, either start the big outboard or run both electrics in unison! One—usually the bow-mount—provides the

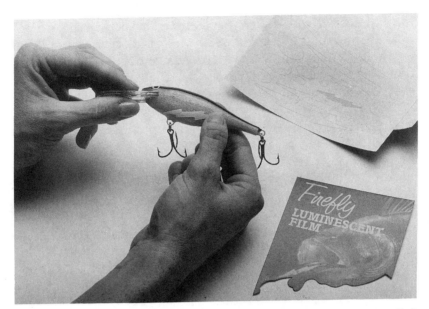

Firefly luminescent film, developed by fisheries researcher-turned outdoor writer Dick Sternberg, is an effective way of putting phosphorescence to work on practically any lure. He cautions NAFC members to avoid using lures or tapes that are too bright, as they will spook fish.

oomph to hold your position or gain ground against the wind or river current, and the other—usually the rear-mount—is used to control direction.

With the advent of extra-long power cords, such as the ones MinnKota puts on its remote-control motors, you can run both electrics yourself. One foot runs the bow-mount, one hand runs the rear- mount, one eye watches the sonar and one hand holds the rod, which is watched by the other eye. No sweat!

In a lot of cases, river fish want baits moving at exactly the speed of the current. By slowing boat drift to match the current, you can fish lighter baits than river fishing lore says are needed to get to the fish zone. And on lakes and reservoirs, you often want to backtroll against the wind along a certain course, then perform a slow "controlled drift" along the same course or area, going with the wind.

By taking control of your boat, you can not only slow down, but stay on precise courses as well. It's not necessarily easy, but it's a learned skill you can become good at with practice. When vertical jigging becomes difficult because of wind, or the combination of wind and current, Mike McClelland does what he calls "chasing his line" with his electric, or electrics. He keeps his jig in a vertical alignment at all times. When the wind or current pulls his bait to the left, he follows it with his boat and rodtip. Ditto for any other direction. Believe it or not, McClelland can fish $1/4$- and even $1/8$-ounce jigs in heavy current with this method.

Another way to control your drift in heavy waves is with a sea anchor like the Drift Sock (Skogstad Enterprises, Dept. NAF, 7145 Stevens Ave. S., Minneapolis, MN 55423). "It's a very good product," says Jerry Anderson, who guides on windswept Mille Lacs Lake. "I've used about all of them, and they all help to some degree, although the Drift Sock is better designed and just works better than any other one I've used."

The Sock will allow you to troll slowly, either forward or backward, even with a large outboard that doesn't troll down well. It won't take the place of an electric motor in shallow water, but it helps make a rough day fishable.

A sea anchor could also become a safety valve should your motor fail to start on high seas. This is no sweeping statement that it will save your life someday, but it would keep your bow pointed into heavy waves while you worked on the engine, keeping water

Strict boat control is essential to proper bait presentation. The advent of powerful electric trolling motors has turned boat control into a fine art that can be developed with on-the-water practice.

Sea anchors, such as the Drift Sock, help slow your drift (improving your boat control) in heavy waves. They can also be used to modify trolling speeds and can be a safety item if your engine breaks down in heavy waves.

from coming overboard by the gallon and swamping the boat.

Anchoring

A lost art, anchoring is perhaps the ultimate form of boat control. Tom Neustrom is widely known as a master of the anchor. He offers these tips:

• Don't anchor unless you know or strongly suspect fish are there and catchable. On known spots, especially those that require pinpoint casts, or even a slip-bobber presentation, anchoring can allow you to repeatedly put a bait in the exact locations you think are holding fish. Many times, Neustrom says, he catches big walleyes after casting a dozen or more times to the same little spot.

• "You anchor when you have to," he says, and that often means in heavy winds. Remember, wind activates shallow fish, and anchoring can let you forget about controlling the boat and concentrate on fishing.

• In heavy wind, always anchor off the bow. It's much safer!

• Most of the time, approach shallow fish from deep water. Anchor and play out rope until you are in fishing position.

• You can cover a wider area by sliding to either or both sides using the rear electric motor. This cuts down on the number of times you have to lift and reposition the anchor.

• Set, don't drop, an anchor into the water. You're fishing, not practicing for the world belly-flop championships. Be quiet!

• Get an anchor that can hold your boat. Neustrom recommends at least a 25-pound Navy-style anchor for a boat weighing 800 pounds or more, including passengers and all gear. He favors a 30-pound vinyl-coated Navy anchor. Don't skimp on anchor rope; get at least 100 feet and make sure it's silky-smooth—the person letting the anchor down and bringing it up will be forever grateful.

That wraps up our look at the "little things" that mean a lot to your walleye fishing success. Now, let's take an in-depth look at the major presentation methods and how to develop your skills so that you can become a versatile, walleye-catching machine.

24

Jigging And Rigging

J igs are the staple of the walleye angler's weaponry. You could forget the crankbaits, the slip-sinker rigs, the jigging spoons, the bottom bouncers or the slip-bobbers and still be okay on most waters. But don't forget the jigs, no matter where you're headed. What a simple thing, but give one to Daryl Christensen, Tom Neustrom or Mike McClelland, and it undulates, slides, dances, drags, hops and draws strikes from walleyes. It imitates and it aggravates. It can mimic a minnow or a mayfly. "Na, na, na, na,na," taunts an advertisement for Blue Fox's Foxee Jigs, "Bet you can't find me." Walleyes can, and do, find them.

The word jig used to mean a heavy, deep-water walleye bait reserved for bouncing on the bottom of "holes." A jig wasn't a jig unless it weighed at least $1/4$ ounce, and many favorites could bend your rod like you had a fish on. Almost as if to honor the jig's potential, creative-minded pros have taken them everywhere walleyes are found. After all, what could be simpler or more efficient than a hook and sinker in one?

Lightweight jigs have been around for hundreds, if not thousands, of years. Once the personal property of panfish seekers, they, too, have found their way into walleye anglers' tackle boxes. It might surprise you to know that a lot of today's top walleye fishermen use primarily $1/8$- and $1/16$-ounce jigs.

If you don't fish jigs yet, don't wait any longer to learn. Even if you do, there are countless variations to practice. A lifetime is too short to master jig fishing, but you can be catching fish the first day. They can be cast, trolled or drifted. There are many dressings (plastic tails, bodies, live bait) to choose from, and many types of jig heads as well. The standard, of course, has been the round-ball jig head, but many others have been developed to fulfill specific needs. The swimming head, for instance, does exactly what its name implies. It is designed to be presented horizontally, as if it were swimming through the water. Wedge-shaped jig heads catch the current in a river and are forced to the bottom more quickly than round-head jigs. The hook shank also emerges from the head at an upward angle to minimize snagging problems. There are banana-shaped heads and ones that look like bullets. Some even have a spinner or propeller for added flash and vibration.

There are so many options, an angler could get carried away just trying to decide which to use. But the experts tell us not to fret too much. Presentation is more important than the type of head or dressing used.

"I'm a little biased," says Daryl Christensen, considered one of the finest jig anglers on the MWC circuit, "but I think people should fish with jigs most of the time. If they learn to use them, they'll catch more walleyes with them than with anything else. Jigs do everything you need them to do, and the most important thing is they keep you in the fish zone at all times. You never pull a jig away from a fish, because if you do, it stops and comes right back to them when you make the next jigging motion. So you've got the ultimate presentation."

So many fish. So little time.

Jigs, Walleyes, Action!

Virtually any jigging action you can dream up will catch walleyes. Most, but by no means all, are *horizontal*. That means the jigging motion is done sideways rather than up-and-down. If you watch jigs worked both horizontally and vertically in clear water, you'll notice how much more "natural" the horizontal movements appear.

Most of the time, horizontal presentations will catch more walleyes. But that, like everything else in fishing, is not a hard-and-fast rule. Sometimes, "hippety-hopping," hard snapping and other vertical approaches trigger more fish.

The variables in jigging presentation are speed, length and height of the motion. You can control jigs directly by how fast you

Complete Angler's Library

The jig is one of the most effective walleye lures available. Many pros, if forced to fish with only one type of lure or presentation, would select the jig without hesitation.

Jigging And Rigging

reel and move the rod and how high you lift the rod. You can also control them indirectly by using lighter or heavier jigs, bodies or no bodies, and different live baits.

This may seem obvious, but lighter jigs sink more slowly. A jig with a body on it sinks slower than one without. Heavy live baits might make a jig sink faster, but if the bait is lively and strong enough to control the jig head, you can get an erratic, extremely slow drop. What do the walleyes want? That varies from lake to lake, day to day, and even hour to hour. Aggressive fish might want to chase a lively bait, while inactive ones shy away from the same thing.

One of the best ways to learn to catch walleyes on a jig is to watch and imitate a good jig fisherman. An afternoon sharing the boat with one can save you years of trial and error. Study their hand positions, and try to mimic their actions. The best ones change retrieve and jigging actions at regular intervals until they get a bite. They are looking for the key that unlocks the walleye's mouth and trying all the combinations until they find it.

"Watch someone else who is catching fish with a jig," says Mike McClelland. "Is he dragging the jig? Maybe he is holding the jig up off the bottom just a little bit, just letting it sit there and drift along. It isn't the jig, after all, that's attracting the fish; it's what the jig is representing to the fish. That's why, when you're jigging, you want to do different things. Too many jig fishermen just get into a rhythm of how they like to work the jig.

"When I'm jig fishing—say I'm casting—I may hold the rodtip high and take long strokes, hold it up real high and let the line glide through the water a long way. Or I may never take it off the bottom. Or I may pump it," McClelland adds. "In a matter of 10 casts I'll cover 10 different ways to present that jig, looking for the one the fish want."

Jigs are normally thought of as slow-poke baits, something to crawl along, trying to tempt reluctant walleyes. Daryl Christensen challenges that notion every time out and usually scores big with a style that some might consider frantic.

"A jig is a tool for putting the bait in front of the fish," he says. "It's nothing any more magical than that. I try to keep the jig off the bottom all the time. If you're fishing a jig and getting snagged a lot, you're not fishing right. I've had guys in the boat with me who lose 30 jigs to my one because they're fishing on the bottom. The

Carefully watch a good jig fisherman's hands. Study how he is working the jig: little hops, dragging along the bottom, swimming it. Little things make a difference when walleye fishing. The key to success is finding what those things are.

active fish aren't on the bottom, and they're not in the rocks or under the rocks. You want to keep that jig above the bottom, a foot to two feet, as much as possible.

"Gary Parsons, when he fished with me for the first time," continues Christensen, "said the one thing he was amazed at was how fast I work a jig and how many fish I catch doing it. Sure, I work it faster than most guys do, but still, compare my jigging speed with most guys' crankbait speeds. They can cast out three times to my one with the jig.

"Even if you're working it fast, you're obviously not working it too fast. With most fish, especially in shallow water (which typically holds more active fish), you couldn't take that thing away from them if you wanted to.

"I change up my movements a lot unless I'm having good success with one," says Christensen. "I usually start with a standard lift-and-crank retrieve if I'm casting and work from there."

Detecting Bites And Setting The Hook

Your jig fishing destiny is in your own hands. The ability to know when you have one will determine how many fish you

Here's an array of the best in walleye jigs. Clockwise from lower left corner: Northland's Fireball, Northland's two-tone jig head, Jack's Jigs, Lindy's Fuzz-E-Grub, Lindy's Flat Foot Fuzz-E-Grub, Blue Fox's Foxee Jig, Greg Bohn's Stinger jig, Blue Fox's Chewee Juice Jig Tipper (a new all-natural, biodegradable add-on body that gets slimy in water) on a Gopher Tackle Mushroom jig head, and finally, Blue Fox's Vibrotail.

catch. It's entirely possible to put the right thing down there, work it perfectly and catch nothing.

In less than an instant, a walleye can grab a jig and blow it back out. That's why live bait can be so important, even on aggressive biters. The natural reaction of a fish that bites into the real thing is to hang on, often long enough for even a beginner to react and set the hook.

Still, there are two distinct schools of thought when it comes to setting the hook. One says that there are times when you have to delay the hookset, often playing with the fish to get it to clamp down on the bait. The other says when you feel anything, set the hook and ask questions later.

Give 'em Time Sometimes

There is a group of anglers—and they catch a lot of walleyes—who say that it's necessary sometimes to wait before setting the hook with a jig. One classic piece of advice that has put tons of walleyes in the boat is to drop your rodtip and reel up the slack at the sign of a bite, then snap your wrist upward to set the hook.

Complete Angler's Library

"Walleyes don't suck on their prey like a banana," says Tom Neustrom. "They don't have teeth for nothing. They are biters, chewers, who grasp their prey and tear, rip and kill it. Walleyes don't hit a jig the same way every time, so there can't be any rule for when to set the hook. I've probably heard 50 different opinions on this, and they can't all be either right or wrong.

"Some guys will tell you to set the hook when you feel anything 'different,' " Neustrom continues. "But I say, many times when you feel that something different, wait for a split second, and feel for that sign of life. Raise your rodtip and feel for that fish to commit itself."

Neustrom is quick to explain that his "wait 'em out" theory applies mainly to bigger live baits, especially minnows (but also nightcrawlers). Most experts agree that walleyes normally take a leech in right away, and ditto for smaller minnows. And if you don't have live bait on, such as when you're fishing a plastic Twister or Swirl tail, the fish won't hold onto it, so you're forced to set right away.

"But I've seen times," Neustrom says, "especially when I'm using bigger minnows, where you even had to open the bail and let the fish run with it or you didn't get them. Believe me, I've tried everything, including setting right away, and it doesn't work all the time.

"What you do depends on how the fish hits it," continues Neustrom. "If it grabs the jig and runs sideways or away from you, go ahead and set right away. But if you just feel a little more weight, like the fish has mouthed the bait and is swimming toward you or with you, just hanging on, wait until the fish commits himself. Kind of pull up on him with a little pressure. Sometimes he'll drop it, but many times he'll grab it tighter if it seems like it's trying to escape."

Hit 'em Right Away

In this corner, wearing the red trunks, are the guys who say no matter which way the walleye grabs your jig, or how it feels, you "cross their eyes" right now. You feel something, you set the hook. Period.

"In jig fishing, the rule is, if you want to be successful you set the hook anytime you feel anything," says Mike McClelland. "Whenever my jig stops, I set the hook. One out of three times I still set the hook on a rock or weed or something, but I don't miss many fish, either. I never wait to see if it's a fish. If it's a rock or a snag, get it over with—break it off if you have to—and get back to fishing. Don't lift up to see if it's going to swim away. That technique worked on suicidal fish 20 years ago, but it doesn't work anymore.

"The first little tick you feel, that's as good as it's going to get. The fish is going to have it all the way in," McClelland says. "He isn't going to swim off and swallow a quarter ounce of lead. I can take someone who's never fished jigs, and with the proper attitude I can have them 95 percent as good as they'll ever be in their life in half an hour. I did it all the time when I was guiding.

"The key to jig fishing," continues McClelland, "is light line presented in a manner so that when the fish hits the jig it can go with the flow of the water being sucked through its mouth. That's why, when you feel something—additional weight, a tick or anything at all different—you know the fish has the thing all the way in, and you should set the hook right away."

What's Best For You

We've said it before, but fishing pros go by their own experiences. They are all good anglers. If some say they've encountered situations where a delayed hookset meant more fish, there's no reason to doubt them. Others are best served by always ramming the hook home at the first hint of a bite. Try it both ways and see which works best for you.

One thing everyone agrees on: Successful jig fishing demands that you pay attention. "You have to be very intense," says Daryl Christensen. "If you spend eight hours in a boat intensely jig fishing, it wears on you. You're worn out, but the more intense you are, the more fish you catch.

"Most people lose their concentration in about 15 minutes," asserts Christensen. "So they jig fish all day and miss a lot of fish. They don't detect many of the bites they had and come in saying, 'I jigged all day and didn't get anything.' Well, they were fishing all day, and there was a jig tied onto their line, but they weren't jig fishing all day.

"The touch for detecting bites comes from intense concentration, a good rod and experience. It doesn't come overnight. Some guys are mainly line watchers, and others do it by feel. Me, I'm kind of a combination. No matter how you do it, realize it's going to take time to catch on. Practice at it, and don't let your mind wander if you want to get good."

Final Thoughts On Jigging
• The trend, as we said, is definitely toward lighter jigs. Stock up on $^1/_8$- and $^1/_{16}$-ounce heads, and have a few $^1/_{32}$-ouncers for clear, shallow water and extremely finicky fish. The slow drop can be the answer. Top anglers can vertically fish a $^1/_{16}$-ounce jig in water down to 20 feet by keeping the line going straight down, moving slow and being patient.
• The size of the hook varies a lot from brand to brand. Most anglers agree that a bigger hook helps catch more fish. You can find $^1/_8$- and $^1/_{16}$-ounce jigs with fairly large hooks, or with tiny hooks, more suitable for sunfish.
• Line weight is an often-discussed factor. Six-pound-test is the unanimous overall choice of the pros, and many use 8-pound a lot of the time. A few believe strongly that 4-pound line can make a difference on negative walleyes, but others say it doesn't matter, as long as you can put the bait in front of the fish. Drop rates and

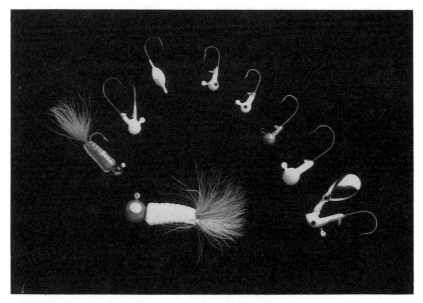

The trend is toward lighter jigs for many walleye-fishing situations. The jig at bottom is a standard $^1/_2$-ounce Fuzz-E-Grub. Notice how small the $^1/_8$- and $^1/_{16}$-ounce jigs look in comparison. Sometimes, their slower drop rate and tantalizing action can help you trigger reluctant fish.

the way you work the jig are probably the most important factors. The thought that walleyes can be line-shy hasn't been proven, but a lighter jig just plain works better and looks more natural on lighter line.

• The way you hook live baits on makes a difference. Stick leeches once in the fat end, right by or in the sucker. That way they won't ball up on the hook.

• Either thread nightcrawlers onto the hook, leaving the end trailing behind, or hook them in the middle, leaving two ends flapping through the water. Some anglers believe that makes the crawler look bigger and more appealing. Experiment each day on each lake to see which the walleyes prefer.

• Minnows can be hooked through the lips, through the top of the head, through the bottom of the head, or along the body and out the mouth. On a bodyless jig, try running the hook into the mouth, out the gill and along the body (from belly to back), just under the skin and as far back as possible. This keeps the minnow snug against the lead head and puts the hook in a position to catch short-biting fish. Hooking them through the lips, or upside down through the lips, tends to make the minnow struggle more, if that's what you want. Hooking them through the head or body kills them, and you have to put the action into the bait yourself.

• Punching the paint out of new jig hook eyes can be a pain. You can use another jig, but that tends to dull the hook point. The Eye-Buster (Mertens Tackle, Dept. NAF, P.O. Box 1753, Fond du Lac, WI 54935) is an inexpensive answer that really works. You'll see them on the floor of most pros' boats. They're available through many mail-order houses and sporting goods stores. Put one in your jig box.

Live-Bait Rigging

If the Fresh Water Fishing Hall of Fame ever decides to accept lures, the Lindy Rig would have to be one of the first inductees. Lindy Rigs have been around such a long time and caught so many fish that they've become the generic designation for live-bait rigs, literally the Kleenex of walleye fishing.

Since they were introduced in the 1960s, more than 30 million have been sold, and the number of walleyes they've caught is incalculable.

It's believed that the basic concept of live-bait rigging was in-

An Eye-Buster is a valuable addition to your jig box. With it, you can quickly clear paint from the jig eye without having to use another jig or lure to complete the task. It's safer and keeps all your hooks sharp.

vented decades earlier by carp fishermen who free-lined stink bait through an egg sinker. The late Bill Binkelman, along with Al and Ron Lindner, took that concept the next step, developing a system for presenting bait to finicky Midwestern walleyes.

The Lindners teamed with a fellow named Nick Adams, formed Lindy Tackle, and began packaging the original Lindy Rig, complete with instructions.

There was fear that the item was too easily made at home to sell well; who would pay hard-earned money for a hook, line and sinker? Their fears were unfounded.

They packaged the rig complete with inside tips on fishing with it. Enlisting the help of professional guides like Gary Roach and Rod Romine, they took their dog-and-pony show on the road, catching limits of walleyes from lakes thought to be fished out. They called it their "magic act."

The rest is fishing history.

The concept has been further developed, in fact, by companies like Northland Tackle, who with Gary Roach developed the Roach Rig, a live-bait rig that employs colored sinkers that easily slip on and off the line without retying.

Rigs are the essence of simplicity in a sport fraught with bells and whistles. They are nothing more than a monofilament snell with a hook and a shoe-shaped weight called a walking slip-sinker. The bait—usually a nightcrawler, leech or minnow—is impaled on the hook and dragged slowly along the bottom. All the fish sees is a slithering leech, squirming crawler or struggling minnow.

Originally, we believed that walleyes would mouth a bait, slowly rolling it up on their tongue. Lindy Riggers would feed line through the slip-sinker until just the right moment, then set the hook. Recognizing when that moment had arrived was the trick. Set the hook too soon and the fish got half your bait. Wait too long and the fish lost interest and spit out the bait, or had it half-way down its stomach.

One way of judging when to set the hook was the "count" method. Anglers would count to 10 before setting the hook. If they missed, next time they'd count to 20. Other anglers used the "feel" method. They'd pick up their rod until the pull from the other end felt solid before setting the hook. Unfortunately, these systems were far from foolproof.

Skilled riggers learned that by fishing the smallest possible sinker on light line, they enjoyed a higher degree of success. Heavy line and big sinkers were thought to spook fish. Anglers also discovered that by constantly working their rodtip, giving the bait a stop-and-go action, they caught more fish. It seemed as if the additional action attracted fish by making the bait look more lifelike.

In recent years our understanding of walleyes has increased, and today we recognize that—at least in many cases—our inability to consistently hook walleyes on rigs had to do with how a walleye feeds.

Mike McClelland was perhaps the first to identify how a walleye feeds. According to Mike, a walleye most often takes a bait much like a bass does, opening its mouth, flaring its gills and inhaling the water around the bait. If your fishing line is tight, the bait can stop before it flows all the way into the walleye's mouth. That bump we often feel, Mike maintains, is not the fish picking up the bait, but the sinker being lifted off bottom.

Walleyes don't always feed in this manner; they sometimes get in aggressive feeding moods, hitting and slashing at their prey like

Complete Angler's Library

The Lindy Rig, granddaddy of live-bait rigs, was developed for walleye fishermen in the 1960s. Its huge success spawned a new generation with new twists, like the Roach Rig, which features adjustable leader length and a splash of color.

a pike, salmon or muskie does, biting and tearing.

Nonetheless, a stop-and-go action creates slack line, allowing a walleye to more easily get the bait all the way into its mouth. Light line and small sinkers have less resistance in the water, enabling a fish to take a bait with one gulp, if it's so inclined.

But what about the thought that heavier line spooks walleyes? "If fish are spooked by line," McClelland asks, "why do so many walleyes get caught in gill nets?"

Mike reasoned that if he could figure a way to keep slack in the line at all times, he could at least reduce the short hits. He and tournament partner Bob Propst experimented with coiled "memory" leaders. They'd wrap six-foot Lindy snells around a snell-holder and leave them in the hot sun. Monofilament line develops *memory* over time, meaning it retains its configuration, explaining why old line comes off your reel spool looking like a Slinky.

It worked. McClelland proved that during the 1985 Mercury National on Lake Winnebago near Oshkosh, Wisconsin. It was the second day of the tournament and a big wind came up. After searching most of the day for fish, he found a school off a tiny underwater point. Trouble was, they were very lethargic and often hit short. Mike missed the first three, so he went to lighter line—2-pound test.

His experiment worked. Well, almost. He hooked the next few fish, but they all broke his line. Mike went back to the drawing board. He knew he had to give the fish more opportunity to take the bait, but the wind made it almost impossible. He finally decided to try a coiled leader.

The result: seven hits and seven fish and another tournament championship.

Coiled leaders allowed the bait to move into the fish's mouth with no resistance. Mike found he could set the hook the instant he felt something suspicious. Trouble was, once the line soaked up some water or was stretched by a fish, the coil disappeared.

Working with McClelland, Lindy Tackle developed a process that created a permanent coil in the snell, and the Coiled Lindy Rig was born. A tight, pigtail coil just above the hook provides the necessary forgiveness that turns even novice riggers into fish-catchers.

The fish's activity level will dictate which rig is preferable. With fairly active walleyes, a standard live-bait rig is plenty effective. If they're on the finicky side, a coiled snell will put fish in the boat that would otherwise be missed. With some baits, like large suckers or chubs, it may be necessary to feed line while the fish turns the bait to swallow it head first.

Numerous other variations on the original Lindy Rig have evolved over the years. Floating rigs have an adjustable float on the snell that holds the bait off bottom, unless you are moving the bait fairly fast. Floating rigs have the advantage of color as an attractant, and also help create slack in the line. Floating jig heads on a snell accomplish the same thing.

Under the right conditions, old-timers prefer to use just a tiny split-shot for weight. A split-shot has far less resistance in the water, again allowing fish to get the bait in one gulp.

The equipment necessary for rigging hasn't changed much. A 6-foot rod with a fast tip, a spinning reel and light line (there's no reason to use line heavier than 8-pound test, and 6-pound is preferable) still get the nod from most rig fishermen.

The idea is still to keep the bait in the fish zone on or near bottom, moving it slowly and keeping a slight amount of slack in the

The Coiled Lindy Rig is designed to give finicky walleyes slack line, allowing your bait to flow into their mouths with very little resistance.

Jigging And Rigging

line. Most experienced riggers instinctively hold their rod fairly high off the water, with the bail open and the line notched in their index finger. At the first sign of a hit they'll drop the rod and release the line, allowing the fish to move off with the bait.

When using coiled snells, anglers have learned to take up the slack and set the hook the instant they feel anything that could be a fish.

Live-bait rigs have likely produced more walleyes than any presentation, except perhaps leadhead jigs. And if recent developments are any indication, the original Lindy Rig—and the variations it has spawned—are going to be around for a long, long time.

25

Hot Presentations

While jigs and rigs have been and probably will continue to produce more than all other presentations combined, there are other techniques that will outproduce them in certain situations. Mastering these techniques will give you the versatility to catch walleyes wherever you are and wherever you're going.

Spinners

Lindy Rigs effectively rendered spinners obsolete, at least in the minds of many. Prior to the movement toward a more natural presentation, spinner rigs were the most popular summertime walleye weapon. The Prescott, Weller Strip-On and June Bug spinners ruled the roost until the Little Joe, the first monofilament-snelled spinner, came along.

Once rigs hit the marketplace, however, spinner sales declined. The rationale of the day was that walleyes had so much to eat they could only be tempted to take a tiny morsel presented in the most natural way possible. In their seminars, theoreticians developed a popular analogy about people who, after a large meal, still can't resist an after-dinner mint. Walleyes with a full stomach, they said, didn't want another meal, but they'd surely take a tidbit like a juicy crawler or lively leech.

When the Missouri River impoundments came of age, anglers quickly discovered that a spinner/crawler combination would produce fish that snubbed their noses at a Lindy Rig. The purists

Spinner rigs were considered too crude by many anglers for today's "sophisticated" walleyes. But the spinner/crawler combination continues to take fish and, in many situations, is the best way to go.

winced. Some reasoned that all the stupid fish had been harvested from Minnesota and Wisconsin waters, leaving a wary strain of walleyes too clever to be fooled by a spinner. Dakota walleyes, some boldly proclaimed, were stupid.

Missouri River angler Dan Nelson, a long-time devotee of Lindy Rigging, wrestled with this question for several years. At first reluctant to even tie up a spinner, Nelson had to admit they were far more effective than rigs during most of the warm-water period.

Forage certainly didn't have anything to do with it; walleyes in the smelt-based Missouri had more food at their disposal than they could possibly consume. So much, in fact, that it was not uncommon to catch walleyes with the tails of a dozen undigested smelt sticking out of their throats.

Eventually Nelson came up with a theory of his own, one that explained activity levels on the basis of populations.

"A big muskie feeds whenever it chooses," Nelson says."You can make a thousand casts to a muskie and it might not move. But toss a piece of worm into a school of bluegills and watch them rip it to shreds. It's not that muskies are any smarter than bluegills, it's just that they're not as competitive. They don't have to be. The bluegill has to grab what it can get.

"It's the same with walleyes," Nelson says. "When a population is fished down, walleyes become less aggressive. But with a huge school of walleyes, like many of those on the Missouri, fish are more apt to be triggered by a flashy, fast-moving bait. They're as competitive as a school of bluegills."

If there were any doubts about Nelson's ideas, they vanished in the mid-1980s when high water levels coupled with reduced populations resulted in smaller schools of fish on the Missouri. For several years, a Lindy Rig was the most productive presentation where spinners had once ruled. When water levels dropped dramatically and the fish were concentrated, you guessed it, spinners made a comeback.

Water clarity is another part of the answer. In stained water, the vibrations given off by spinner blades help fish locate the bait. The darker the water, the bigger the edge for spinners over rigs.

Spinners are best fished behind a bottom bouncer, a type of weight developed specifically for Missouri River fishing. Rods and reels are a matter of personal preference, with spinning and bait-casting outfits working about equally well. Heavier line is acceptable because these more aggressive fish will actually overtake a bait rather than inhaling it.

Blade size and color can be important factors. Missouri River anglers found that bigger blades tend to take bigger fish. Color preferences can change from day to day, but various shades of chartreuse and green are consistent producers. In badly stained water, reds and oranges have historically produced best.

Speed is another important variable. Spinners can be fished so slowly that the blade barely turns or as fast as two or three miles per hour.

Spinners are particularly effective in reservoirs, but also work well in shallow, dishpan lakes trolled along the outside weed edge.

Weight-Forward Spinners

About the same time Missouri River anglers were deploying spinners, Lake Erie's Western basin was making its legendary comeback as a walleye fishery. Erie anglers insisted that weight-forward spinners were the only thing that produced walleyes for them.

Purists scoffed. Their attitude was "give me a rig or a jig and I'll show those lead-slingers a thing or two about catching walleyes." Once again, gamefish population densities and forage dictated the most effective presentations. Erie walleyes were suspended, feeding on smelt and alewives just under the surface. Lindy Rigs were designed to be fished on the bottom. What's more, those shallow fish flared from passing boats, making it necessary to cast to the schools, not troll over them.

Weight-forward spinners were pitched off to the sides of the boat, counted down to the appropriate depth and retrieved with an up-and-down action. Because the weight was up front, the lure snapped through the water with an enticing action, its blades getting the attention of those active, competitive fish.

Baits like Tom's Walleye Lure and the Erie Dearie catch bottom-feeding fish as well. Trolled along the bottom with the same herky-jerky action, they take walleyes as well as a regular spinner, at times even better.

Walleye fishing, you might say, had yet another wrinkle.

Bottom Bouncers

At first glance, the "Missouri River bottom bouncer" doesn't look like much. It doesn't get any prettier after you study it, either.

Bottom bouncers are an L-shaped piece of wire with a hunk of lead molded into the knee. As far as anyone knows, the first bottom bouncer was made back in the mid-1970s by a fellow named Bob Meter out of Bismarck, North Dakota, for use on Lake Sakakawea. Meter would attach a spinner to his odd-looking conglomeration of wire and lead, fishing the whole package at speeds that made old-time walleye specialists snicker.

The general reaction to bottom bouncers was that Dakota walleyes had to be intellectually inferior if they'd give a second look to anything so ludicrous. The MWC tournament trail changed all that in a hurry.

When Propst and McClelland showed up at a Minnesota MWC event with their bottom bouncers riding front and center, they were nearly laughed off the water. "Our walleyes are too sophisticated to hit anything like that," the Dakota fishermen were told.

The laughs subsided, however, when Propst and McClelland stepped to the victory stand to accept their first-place check.

NAFC member Eric Kraemer of Pittsburg, Pennsylvania, caught this 8-pound-plus walleye on a weight-forward Parrish lure while fishing Lake Erie out of Port Clinton, Ohio.

The job of a sinker is to keep the bait on the bottom, period. And bottom bouncers perform that task exceedingly well. The wire leg below the lead makes bottom bouncers more snag-proof than other sinkers. Because of their design and sheer weight, they stay on the bottom regardless of speed or depth. As McClelland puts it, "They have no conscience...they're always on the bottom."

There are lots of ways to fish bottom bouncers. Rigged with a spinner, they're deadly for aggressive walleyes in off-colored water. Propst and McClelland also like to attach a six-foot Lindy snell tipped with a leech and use it as their second rod or prover-bial "silent partner." These "dead lines" have probably put more tournament-winning fish in their boats than the rod they hold in their hands and work. Floating rigs are another great partner for the bottom bouncer.

Still another tactic that has its roots with the Missouri River anglers is to use a shallow-running crankbait on a five-foot leader behind a bottom bouncer. It's an ideal way to work a bait up and down a sharp vertical drop. The same setup is deadly for drifting fast current in the tailwaters below dams.

Bottom bouncers are extremely popular on Kansas' reservoirs

and have been gaining acceptance on other Southern waters as well. No matter where you fish walleyes, if you haven't at least tried them, you may be missing out on a great tool.

Slip-Bobbers

In walleye fishing, necessity is truly the mother of innovation. Many of the presentations we've examined were developed to meet a specific need, and the slip-bobber is no exception.

They came into their own on Minnesota's Mille Lacs Lake, a legendary walleye factory. When the wind blows, Mille Lacs walleyes move shallow on many of the rock reefs that dot the lake. Fishing here is almost impossible; not only is it easy to spook the fish, but the fishing is downright dangerous as well.

Enterprising anglers solved the problem with slip-bobbers. They'd anchor a safe distance from the reefs and cast these crazy setups, which kept the bait suspended just above the rocks and in the fish zone.

Slip-bobbers, in most cases, have the line threaded through the center. An adjustable "bobber stop," a tiny knot tied to the monofilament line, holds the bobber at the desired depth. Under the bobber, split shot or lead jig heads are used to weight the whole package. The bobber stop reels onto the spool with the line while fighting a fish or making another cast, allowing the angler to fish deep water without complications.

Usually tipped with a leech, the rig is cast to the spot and allowed to sit as the shot pulls the bait down until it's halted by the bobber stop. After that, it's just like fishing a regular bobber. When the thing goes under, you have a fish on.

Slip-bobbers are not only great for fishing shallow. They work well in weeds, too. It's possible to cast a slip-bobber rig into dense vegetation and not get hung up.

Most veteran slip-bobber fishermen like Jerry Anderson believe it's best not to get overanxious about setting the hook. In a wind, there will be slack line between your rodtip and the bobber. It's impossible to get a good hookset until the slack is taken in. Good bobber anglers hold their rodtip high, taking up the slack without exerting any pressure that might alert the fish. Only after the slack has been removed should the hook be set.

Lindy's new Coiled Rig has definite applications for bobber fishing. The coil allows a fish to inhale the whole bait before feel-

Slip-bobbers make it possible to suspend baits in front of inactive walleyes, often tempting them when nothing else works. They work equally well in deep or shallow water.

Hot Presentations

ing any resistance from the bobber, reducing the chances it will spit the offering before the hooks can be set.

European Float Systems For Our Walleyes

Slip-bobbers certainly have their place among North American walleye tactics. Tournaments and money have been won with them. For plunking a live bait in front of concentrated or negative fish, the precision and patience of this method are unquestioned.

Wait a minute. There's another guy over here with his hand up, who wants to say something about bobber fishing—or as he calls it, *float* fishing—for walleyes.

We've already met Mick Thill, who gave us those live bait tips earlier in this section. He hails from Chicago, but lived most of his life in England, where he became a genuine match-fishing superstar. He is the only American ever to win a gold medal in the World Fresh Water Fishing Championships, a feat he accomplished in 1982 on the River Arno in Florence, Italy.

Thill has mastered the sophisticated light-line shorefishing techniques that have been honed to a science and an art across Europe. In 1986, he returned to the United States, bringing all the knowledge he had gathered. He has spent the recent past adapting European float technology to our fish, which he considers typically more aggressive and less pressured than those in Europe.

Not surprisingly, Thill finds our floats and techniques a bit behind the times.

"There's absolutely no sophistication in any float-fishing styles in America," he says. He doesn't mean it sarcastically; he is out to show us a better way. "I know the classic walleye bobber in North America, the sort of plastic tube, foam body, with the bead at the top. I've been astounded since I first saw them."

Astounded, in this context, should not be confused with "impressed."

It's going to be a gradual education process, Thill stresses. He doesn't expect us to embrace everything he says or soak up his lifetime of experiences in one sitting. Still, here are the basics for putting European float technology to work in your fishing.

Our floats are too buoyant:

Thill, who designs floats exclusively for Thill Fishing Tackle (Dept. NAF, 706 W. Bradley, Urbana, IL 61801, (217) 384-5240), has not been able to make floats as subtle as he'd

Press clippings continue to pile up for Mick Thill, a Chicago native who spent most of his life in England, where he became a genuine match-fishing superstar. What he has learned (and developed) about float fishing can be adapted to our walleye fishing.

like, because in testing, American fishermen have been breaking them right and left. European floats are hydrodynamic and aerodynamic marvels, polished and painted wisps of balsa wood, an instrument of subtle presentation and bite detection in educated hands. It's going to take us time, he says, for us to learn what it takes to fish this delicate system.

To be functional in the European sense, a float has to be barely floating. Intricate patterns have been developed for putting lead shot on the line, so just the tip (a pimple, it's often called) is visible above—or even slightly below—the water's surface. Then, when a fish takes, even if it makes only a halfhearted sucking motion through its gills, the bait goes in without resistance. Should the fish move off with the bait, it still feels little or nothing.

Now, take a good look at the slip-bobbers in your tackle box. Even if they're weighted properly, their sheer bulk causes enough water displacement for the fish to feel something, and that resistance, Thill maintains, often prevents a walleye from getting the bait fully inside its mouth. European floats, in contrast, are streamlined to pull down and through the water at the slightest tug.

Hot Presentations

You have to get used to fishing a float that's almost under:

"The average American," Thill says, "expects to see a lot of the float sticking out of the water. Ninety percent of the time, that's bad, for all the reasons we've already discussed. Unless the fish are really aggressive, which they usually aren't, they just won't pull a buoyant float all the way under."

Choose the type and size of float according to the conditions and how you're fishing:

Look the conditions over carefully. How deep are you going to fish? How much wind or current is there? How heavy is your bait?

• As you go deeper and use heavier baits, the float has to be thicker-bodied and more buoyant.

• In rougher water you need a longer-stemmed float, which can fight the tendency to drift and wash out of control.

• If you are fishing vertically (straight down from the boat), a "center slider" float becomes functional. This is a float with a tube running the length of the body, which the line passes through, such as most of our traditional slip-bobbers. This is effective because you're setting the hook straight up, through the float.

• If you have to cast or let the float drift away from the boat, you get a severe angle in the line with a center slider, making hooksetting difficult, unless you strike straight up.

"What happens," Thill says, "is what I call 'bumping the fish off.' When you strike, the float folds over, and you literally bump the fish off the hook, especially with a short rod. Not only do you lose that fish, but it can create a lot of noise, which can put a whole school of fish in a negative mood."

The solution to fishing away from the boat, or casting from shore, Thill says, is usually a "waggler" or "bottom-only" float, such as the TG Waggler and TG Bodied Waggler. These are long, streamlined floats that have only one attachment point for the line, a small hole at the very bottom, hence the name. They are used as slip-floats, but because the line only passes through the bottom, the severity of the angle in the line is reduced, giving you more control in setting the hook and fighting fish.

Floats such as the River Master, with more bulk and buoyancy at the top, are good in heavy current or wind.

Use the smallest float possible for the water conditions and bait, and work hard to balance the entire rig.

"Select the smallest one that allows you to fish at the depth

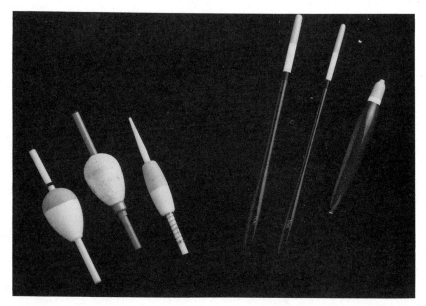

A quick glance says a lot about the differences between standard American slip-bobbers (left) and Mick Thill's floats, being made and marketed by Thill Tackle. It's easy to see that American floats displace more water and therefore are more difficult to pull under.

and wind conditions you're facing," Thill advises. "Shot the float down so a minimum amount sticks above the surface. The fish feels less, but it forces you to pay more attention.

"Many times," Thill continues, "the float will disappear for a second because the bait pulls it under. But you get used to this, and it's the ultimate in sensitivity. You learn to read the rhythm of the bait popping down, coming back up, popping down and so forth. When the float doesn't return, it often means a fish has taken the bait.

"You carefully check, feeling for the presence of the fish, and set the hook and you've got him," says Thill. "And the fish didn't feel a thing. It was just like gobbling up any other minnow or worm or whatever it's used to eating.

"Really, you should think about balancing the hook, line weight, float and bait, not to mention the rod and reel, into a workable unit. That's just common sense in Europe: balancing everything together into a simple, basic, effective system."

Weighting, or "shotting" the setup, is the critical step, Thill says, to beating the conditions—water depth, surface drift and weight of bait and hook.

Hot Presentations

Shotting: A Primer

Where you place shot on the line is as important as having enough to almost sink the float. Some basic principles:

• Normally, you don't want to bunch all the needed shot into one group. The Europeans call this "bulking." Even if the float is well balanced, a fish is more likely to feel resistance with bulked shot, especially if it's close to the hook. You can get away with bulking only when fish are aggressive.

• Shot placed closest to the hook are called "drop shot." The amount of weight close to the hook determines how fast the bait drops. If you want a slow, tantalizing drop, use less drop shot. As a rule of thumb, drop shot are put about 12 to 24 inches up from the hook.

• The rest of the shot, also known as the "bulk" shot, are placed farther up the line. The basic rule here is to have the bulk shot twice as far from the drop shot as the drop shot is from the hook. This is normally about 24 to 48 inches from the droppers. Space them somewhat evenly for a simple setup.

These are just the basics, Shotting 101. From here, a huge can of worms awaits and a science of shotting patterns evolved through the demands of European match fishing.

A Few Words On Tactics

First things first. You have to find the right depth. Europeans use a lead "plummet," a heavy weight that attaches on your line, essentially the same thing North American ice anglers use to find the bottom. You cast it out, adjusting the depth of the float on successive casts to determine bottom contours when fishing from shore without sonar or when you don't want to go on top of a spot with the boat.

With a plummet, it's easy to find the exact bottom setting, difficult even with sonar. Then, it's just as easy to set a float an inch off the bottom, six inches, a foot, two feet, anywhere you suspect walleyes might be holding.

If you have heavy shot placed near the bottom, and the float is set too deep for the water, it will lie flat across the surface. When you shorten the line sufficiently, bringing it taut, the float will "cock," or snap upright.

Less shot near the bait, and smaller hooks, allow the bait more freedom, giving your presentation more action. Some days that's good; sometimes, with negative fish, it's too much. Experiment!

Most days, keeping your bait from washing with the wind or current can mean more fish. You can accomplish this by lengthening the line a bit from the position that just balances the float and putting enough shot close to the hook to anchor it to the bottom. Again, experiment with the length of line between the "anchor" and the bait, similar to experimenting with snell lengths on traditional slip-sinker live-bait rigs.

Moving the bait slowly along, especially in calm or still waters, will sometimes trigger more strikes. Try slowly reeling along, noticing how the float is moving with you. When it stops at all, it will begin to dig deeper. Gently feel for the presence of life, and set the hook if you detect a fish. That's what you're there for!

Experiment each day to read the aggressiveness of the fish. If you set the hook immediately on your first three bites and come up empty, try giving them more time. Mick Thill says it only takes him a bite or two to have the pattern wired.

For the rest of us it may take longer, but after all, he's been at this business longer than we have. He's come home to teach us, though, not to laugh at our primitive bobbers.

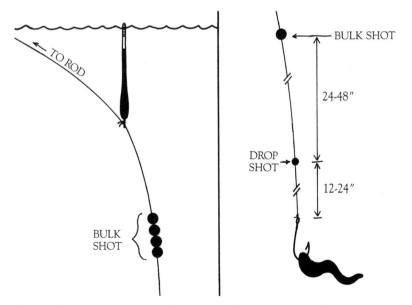

When the line is properly shotted, only the tip of the European float is visible. The advantage of this system is twofold. Its reduced resistance makes it easier for the fish to take the bait and lessens the chance the fish will drop it.

Crankbaits

Crankbaits run hot and cold with walleye fishermen. Just ask any fishing tackle retailer or distributor; fluctuating crankbait sales have produced more ulcers and gray hairs than the stock market. One year cranks are the rage and the retailer can't stock enough of them. The next, he buys a truckload and gives them to his dog to chew on. If trying to anticipate the demand isn't perplexing enough, the tackle shop owner is expected to stock the right model and guess which colors will be the best sellers.

Considering the mind-boggling array of baits and color combinations available, buying crankbaits is for the seller like drawing to an inside straight.

But if hard bait sales are fickle, the walleye's affinity for them is not. Crankbaits catch walleyes and, most experts believe, bigger walleyes than other presentations, over the course of time. So why the fluctuations of popularity and success, given the proven track record? No doubt it's because most fishermen still don't understand how to consistently catch walleyes with them.

Crankbait fishing is actually quite simple. It requires selecting a bait that runs to the required depth, and making sure the bait is properly tuned. It sounds easy enough, until you inject human nature into the equation.

Let's follow the adventures of the average angler. Acting on a rumor that Shad Raps are tearing up the walleyes on Muddy Lake, Joe buys a dozen assorted Shad Raps and hits the water. As it turns out, the reports are accurate and Joe catches a dandy limit of walleyes trolling No. 5 perch-pattern baits in seven feet of water off a weedline.

For the rest of his life, Joe wants to fish nothing but No. 5 perch-colored Shad Raps, which have become his "confidence lure." On his next outing, the fish are in 28 feet, but Joe can't bring himself to tie on a different bait. Guides call it the "one-lure syndrome." When they ask a customer to change baits, the response is typically: "I caught fish on this lure up in Canada back in '69 and..."

The No. 5 Shad Rap is a great little lure, but the walleye wasn't born that would swim 20 feet vertically to hit one. Rule number one in walleye fishing is to pick a bait that runs to the depth that's holding fish.

Knowing how deep a crankbait dives requires a bit of elbow

Crankbaits catch a lot of walleyes, and impressive numbers of larger-than-average fish. Here, a nice fish falls prey to a black-and-silver Shad Rap fished over a shallow rock bar. A deadly method to try day or night.

grease. Not only are different baits designed to reach different depths, but there are also the variables of line diameter and speed of retrieve. Because of this, many manufacturers are reluctant to label the depth ranges of their baits. The smaller the line, the deeper a bait will dive, generally speaking. And the faster you move, the more it will dig. The more line you let out—to a point—the deeper the bait will go.

The best way to determine a bait's depth range is trial and error. Find a long stretch of hard-bottomed shore with a constant depth and drag different lures, noting how deep each runs.

It's possible to stretch a bait's potential by adding weight. You want to get the weight at least 24 inches above the lure. Bead-chain sinkers twist in the water less than other types, but you have to cut the line and tie them in. Rubber-core sinkers are easy to twist on the line, but they tend to spin around in the water even at normal trolling speeds, often affecting the action of the lure. A three-way dropper rig can also be used with a crankbait, and the amount of weight tied to the dropper adjusted to how deep you need to go. Split-shot are a convenient way to add a foot or two without affecting lure performance much.

Rule number two is: Most crankbaits need some tuning. An untuned bait won't dive to its intended depth or throw those fish-attracting vibrations. The angler must inspect each bait, hand-tuning those that don't track.

Tuning is best accomplished in a swimming pool or off a dock. Cast a bait and retrieve it as fast as the handle will turn. The speed is important, because every bait appears to be running straight when fished slowly. If the bait broaches, or turns to one side while being retrieved fast, it needs to be tuned. (Catching fish can knock a previously tuned bait out of tune.)

If the bait runs to the right, bend the eyelet (the part you tie the line to) slightly in the opposite direction, in this case back to the left. A slight adjustment is usually all that's needed. A properly tuned lure will swim on a perfectly straight line back to the rod tip.

Once a bait is running true, it's helpful to brand it for future reference. Scratching a little paint off the back is a good way to remember which baits run true.

Not all crankbaits are created equal. Out of 10 seemingly identical baits, only one will be a fish-killer. The other nine will catch fish, but only one will drive fish crazy. You can almost feel the difference when you drag it through the water. It pulls a little harder and makes your rodtip twitch faster. Every serious crankbait fisherman has a few such baits, the ones with so many tooth marks the original finish is all but obliterated.

Crankbaits are best fished on 6- or 8-pound monofilament line and there's rarely a reason to go heavier than 10-pound. The line should be tied directly to lures with split-rings in the eyelet. On cranks without split-rings, use a loop knot like the Rapala knot, or a crankbait snap like the solid black versions sold by Lindy and Berkley. Never use a snap-swivel with a crankbait unless you want to go fishless.

Color can make a difference, although it seems that many anglers get excessively hung up on color patterns. It's best to experiment with colors from day to day, letting the fish tell you what works best.

For years we believed that crankbaits produced only active walleyes. Recently, however, we've found that cranks sometimes turn walleyes that refuse every other presentation, and a lot of skilled walleye chasers are using crankbaits as fish finders. Because they can be trolled at such fast speeds, crankbaits allow the angler to eliminate unproductive water quickly.

The next questions are where and when to fish crankbaits, and those can only be answered by the fish. There are, however, some situations more likely to produce crankbait walleyes than others. Stained water is always a good candidate. When the fish move shallow to feed in muddy water, crankbaits are an excellent choice because the vibrations help the fish zero in on the bait.

Cranks are deadly on dishpan lakes with heavy weed growth and a shallow mud basin. They can be cast to pockets in the weeds, trolled at high speeds on the outside edges of the weeds and dragged over the lake basin. In the basin some walleyes will be suspending and others relating to the soft bottom.

Because these lakes don't contain the structural elements or forage that typically attract walleyes—remember, walleyes don't know they are living in an atypical environment—the fish are forced to relate to the lake any way they can. They go where their food is.

In fact, crankbaiting for walleyes likely got its start with bass

Adding weight can put crankbaits to just about any depth walleyes are found. The better options include, from the top: bottom bouncer, split shot, rubber-core sinker, and bead-chain sinker. Rubber-cores can twist your line and affect a bait's action more than bead-chains, which are probably the best choice for getting to intermediate depths.

fishermen pitching plugs to the weeds and catching walleyes by "mistake."

If these same types of lakes contain shallow rock piles, cranks can be deadly during the post-spawn period. The rocks soak up sun and radiate warmth, attracting baitfish. By midday a few big walleyes will move up to investigate, and casting crankbaits is one of the best ways to catch them.

Crankbaits are an excellent choice on reservoirs from the post-spawn period right through the early fall. When the wind blows over these sprawling impoundments, walleyes head for the shallows and are easy pickings on crankbaits.

Cranks work well on large, shallow lakes like Mille Lacs, Wisconsin's Winnebago and Lake of the Woods, to name a few. They can be cast to structure-relating fish and trolled for suspended walleyes.

Crankbaits also work well in rivers. Experts used to insist that any effective river presentation required moving with the current flow, thereby "washing" the offering into the mouths of waiting fish in the manner they were used to. Back in the early '80s, Gary Roach shot holes in that line of thinking when he pulled limits of trophy walleyes from the Columbia River trolling Shadlings upstream. The tactic quickly spread to the Missouri River, where North Dakota anglers broke two of walleye fishing's hallowed rules by catching crankbait walleyes trolling against the current, and doing it during the pre-spawn period to boot.

Finding areas of reduced current, Bill Mitzel of Bismarck would troll Shad Raps or Shadlings over sandbars or through backwater pockets for pre-spawn fish. Not only did he catch walleyes, but in some instances crankbaits produced larger fish than those coming on jigs.

While crankbaits are still a touchy subject with retailers who can never seem to guess what to stock, they've been accepted by the walleyes as a substitute for their regular food. For those walleye anglers who have taken the trouble to figure out how deep their lures run and put them in front of fish, a deadly tool has come of age.

Super-Deep Crankbaits

Super-deep crankbaits are one of the most exciting developments in walleye fishing since the Lindy Rig. These big, spoon-

Super-deep crankbaits like Lindy's No. 9 Deep Shadling and Bomber's 25A are taking deep, summer walleyes that some thought were uncatchable. Lake Erie fishermen, take note!

Hot Presentations

billed baits could prove to be a missing link during a few of those times of year when fishing is tough.

How deep is super deep? These baits will dive from 20 to as much as 35 feet without any added weight. Most are $4^1/_2$ to 6 inches long and look more like muskie or pike baits, but walleyes, especially big ones, love 'em.

The conventional thinking on walleyes was that when they went deep, they were inactive and could only be coaxed with a slow-moving rig or jig. That's what Don Palmer thought, too.

An upper Lake Oahe guide out of Mobridge, South Dakota, Don was one of the first anglers to experiment with super-deep cranks in the early 1980s. Frustrated by his inability to consistently catch walleyes in July, August and September, he began playing with off-the-wall tactics. Using his electronics, he'd locate a school of fish on the deep edge of a mud flat. He rigged them and jigged them, worked them with spinners and spoons and was on the verge of trying dynamite when he noticed Bomber's 25 Long A in a distributor catalog. Figuring "why not?" he ordered a dozen and gave them a try. Sure enough, he boated two hefty walleyes on his initial pass down a flat.

It wasn't until a couple years later that Don gave the system a real workout. Needing fish for a large party he had booked, he got desperate and dug out the Bombers. At that time, Mobridge was considered a "cigar factory," an area that kicked out lots of small walleyes but few big ones. That September, though, Don and his clients did a number on big fish.

Several years later Palmer introduced the tactic to Dave "Hot Tip" Jenson, an old friend from Fargo, North Dakota. That same summer Jenson went West for a trophy walleye trip on the Columbia River.

When his favorite Columbia tactics failed to produce, Jenson resorted to dragging Bombers and No. 9 deep Lindy Shadlings off the edge of lava rock reefs. It worked. Jenson pulled more 10- to 14-pound walleyes in two weeks than many lakes yield in a decade. Subsequent trips provided a similar story.

A new walleye pattern was emerging. Anglers on the lower end of Lake Oahe share Palmer's success, as did anglers in other parts of the walleye range. Charter captains in the Central and Eastern basins of Lake Erie were learning to use the same baits under planer boards. Before long, super-deep crankbaits were turn-

One of the pioneers of deep-cranking for walleyes, Don Palmer, nets a nice fish for Kim Nelson on South Dakota's Lake Oahe.

ing fish when nothing else worked, and another walleye rule was scratched off the books.

Freelining a crankbait to 25 feet is no easy task. Over the years Don has developed a system for bottom bouncing a lure to unheard-of depths. First he makes certain that all baits he intends to fish are perfectly tuned. Each outing begins with a ritual, a bait-tuning session on the docks overlooked by Jed's Landing.

On the water, he searches for deep fish with his sonar. Once he locates them, Don lowers the bait into the water slowly, letting out eight or 10 feet of line and drawing it tight before relinquishing any more. By keeping the straightest possible line between rodtip and bait, Don retains enough sensitivity to know when his lure is bumping bottom. Also, by keeping the line tight while paying it out, he avoids the inevitable bow in the line that would come if he just tossed out a cast and engaged the line, as many anglers do.

A hard bottom is easy to detect with a vibrating lure; mud is something else. Don watches his rodtip for clues. When his bait is plowing mud, the rod will get mushy as the tip-quivering vibrations disappear. Over mud, Don will take in a foot or so of line and start working the bait.

Don developed a drop-and-pump technique that's deadly. He'll pull the rodtip forward quickly, then drop it back, allowing the bait to flutter on slack line. That's when most of the strikes occur. This tactic not only encourages strikes, it also allows a waiting fish to inhale the bait with no resistance.

Don usually trolls fairly fast while working the bait to the bottom, but he's learned that once the bait is down, less speed is required to keep it there. When one of his party hooks a fish, Don will put the engine in neutral and retrieve his bait with a pump-and-reel motion. The big-billed lure will stay close to the bottom until it's almost directly under the boat, allowing him to pick up a lot of bonus fish.

The deepest of the super-deep cranks is Lindy's No. 9 Deep Baitfish, a lure that dives to 35 feet. Bomber's 25A is consistently good for 25 feet. Other super-deep crankbaits include Storm's Thunderstick, Lindy's No. 9 Deep Shadling, Rebel's Fastrac and Bagley's Bang-O-Lure.

Super-deep crankbaits are a relatively new innovation and much is still to be learned about using them. By the end of the '90s, however, they'll be one of walleye fishing's hottest baits.

Planer Boards

Walleyes are boat-shy. It's not that the fish are clever enough to recognize boats as a potential threat. But they instinctively understand the basic rules of survival, one of which says: "Never mess with a critter that's 18 feet long."

This is especially true of suspended, open-water walleyes because they can't bury their noses in the mud, tuck behind a rock, or vanish into the weeds. Their only option is to flare from the passing boat.

Great Lakes fishermen solved the problem by using planer boards, or skis, to carry a bait to close-to-the-surface brown trout. Boards also are effective on chinook salmon and even lake trout early in the year when they're close to the surface. Recognizing the application, a handful of walleye fishermen incorporated the same tactic into their repertoire.

One of the first to successfully use boards on walleyes was Wisconsin dentist Gary Parsons, who later teamed with Keith Kavajecz to capture MWC Team-of-the-Year and National Championship titles. Dr. Parsons lives in Chilton, a small town on the eastern edge of Lake Winnebago. Parsons' dad, Don, became bored with the smallish fish regularly caught from Winnebago's shoreline shallows and one day decided to troll crankbaits across the lake's shallow basin. He enjoyed just enough success to get his son's attention.

After much trial and error, Gary borrowed an open-water technique from trout fishermen who worked nearby Lake Michigan. Using planer boards, he started catching bigger fish than the shore-bound anglers ever dreamed existed in the lake.

At the same time, Ed and Sam Concilla, the charter captains who discovered Lake Erie's Eastern Basin walleyes, fell back on their salmon fishing expertise to discover a consistent approach on their waters. Boards did the trick there, too.

Walleyes suspend a lot more than we once suspected. And boards are one of the most effective tools ever devised for finding and catching those suspended, open-water fish.

Boards can also be used to run a bait through water too shallow to be trolled. Walleyes lying in three or four feet of water on a calm day are unapproachable with a boat. Casting is one alternative,

Planer boards can take your lures away from the spooking influence of the boat. Daryl Christensen lands a dandy sauger that hit a planer board-trolled Lindy Shadling.

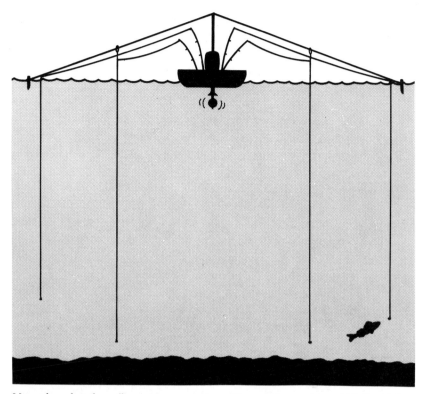

Using planer boards, walleye anglers can cover a wide swath by running multiple lines (where legal) at various distances from the boat with baits that reach different depths.

but that doesn't allow the angler to cover as much water as trolling does. With boards, an entire stretch of shoreline can be checked quickly. Once a pocket of fish has been located, casting becomes an effective alternative.

Whether walleyes are near the surface, in the shallows or down deep, innovative anglers have come up with methods to catch them. Some of these new presentations, like planer boards, are unfamiliar to many fishermen, and some may even seem out-landish. But they do work in a wide variety of conditions. Walleye fishermen who learn these techniques and adapt them to their own angling situations will see more action when traditional methods fail to produce.

Downriggers

Who would have thought that downriggers would ever be incorporated for walleyes? Here's a fish we all credited with almost human intelligence levels—so finicky it could tell 4-pound line from 6-pound. And now we're catching them on lures trolled behind a 10-pound cannonball.

Yes, we may have overrated the walleye's IQ just a bit. It's really no smarter than other fish. It seems that the most important thing is to put a bait in front of the fish's mouth. Of course, in 80 feet of water with scattered schools of suspended fish, that's no easy task.

But downriggers make it possible, and a lot of walleyes have been caught with them in recent years. Before BC plankton came into the system, pulling walleyes closer to the surface, Lake Erie's Eastern Basin anglers routinely caught their walleyes on downriggers from 70 and 80 feet. Even today, Eastern Basin walleyes will go deep, requiring the use of downriggers.

But Lake Erie is not the only home for downrigger walleye fishermen. Lake of the Woods and Devil's Lake, North Dakota, are two more of many, many bodies of water with documented success stories.

The development and popularization of super-deep crankbaits will likely eliminate the need for downriggers in some cases, where most of the fish are coming from 25 to 35 feet of water. But when they drop beyond that, downriggers will continue to be the ticket.

Now that you have armed yourself with the latest and greatest walleye presentations, don't wait to try them out. Next time your favorite methods don't work, dig into your bag of tricks and see what develops. Better yet, try these tactics when your methods are hot and see if it is still the best way to fish. You may be surprised.

26

Pressured Walleyes

The presence of humans, with their boats and attachments (like waterskiers), can affect walleyes. We've already considered the possibility that night fishing might be your best option on waters with heavy traffic. But it's not the only one.

You have a number of options when boating and/or fishing pressure have slowed the walleye action. Generally, the experts say "try every trick in the book." Try fishing among the crowds. If that doesn't work, go off by yourself. Look for fish both in deeper and shallower water. Scale down your tackle, fishing slowly with smaller rigs and baits, but also try ripping fast-moving lures. If possible, fish when the pressure is lightest.

Specifically, here are some tactics you should try:

• First, with your sense of humor turned up high, head right into the circus. Join the parade of boats, and study what's going on. Normally, advises Mike McClelland, one or two boats are catching most or all of the fish. Watch what they're doing down to the finest detail. "See how deep they're fishing, which part of the structure they're on, what they're using for bait, how they're working it and anything else you can see."

• Now, with a good idea of what type of spot the party is on and what the successful anglers are doing, head off on your own. Look up similar spots and try similar tactics. "Doing that," says McClelland, "has salvaged guide days for me and even won me money in tournaments."

• Sometimes, you can catch fish from right among the crowds of boats by trying a slightly different presentation than everyone else. After a few dozen walleyes are fooled by a certain bait, they tend to get smart. Often, using something lighter in weight (which gives a more tantalizing, subtle action) or a different color can trigger a few walleyes for your boat.

Jerry Anderson, an MWC tournament veteran, calls it finesse fishing. He parlayed it, in fact, into a Team-of-the-Year title during the inaugural MWC season. "When the fish are spooked," he says, "you have to go with light tackle and really slow down. If I'm fishing jigs, I might step down to a $1/8$- or $1/16$-ounce jig on 4-pound line. If I'm Lindy Rigging, I'll go with a lighter slip sinker. It's important to slow down as much as you can, especially if you know you're over fish. By using lighter tackle, it forces you to slow down. You don't have any choice."

• Somewhat surprisingly, an even wider change of tactics can sometimes do the trick. Dan Nelson says, "If live bait isn't producing, try a fast-moving crankbait. It sounds crazy, but it has worked for me."

• Don't add to the spooking influence of a group of boats. Researcher John Pitlo observed in a study done on Iowa's Lake Okoboji that walleyes would move aside for a boat but didn't seem spooked by it if the water was at least 12 feet deep and the motor ran at a constant speed. The critical depth varies, depending on water clarity, wind and other factors. But the thing to avoid is throttling up and down, starting and stopping.

• If the walleyes seem to have vanished, look both deeper and shallower. Normally, they'll be forced deeper by pressure, say the experts. But you never know.

• Gary Roach says that fishing pressure often bunches walleyes together, even if they were scattered and feeding to begin with. "If a bunch of boats are all hammering fish and they suddenly quit," he says, "start searching long stretches of the structure. Sometimes, you'll find a group of fish all huddled together, and you can pluck a few out if you fish slow and quiet. That's why they invented electric motors!"

• Walleyes are usually on a spot for a reason, and it's usually the presence of food. If most of the fishing traffic comes on the weekends, see what you can do about getting out on the weekdays. Those same crowded spots are often wide open, and the fish will

Most eager walleye anglers camp on the first good school of fish they find. The result can be a "party" of boats, all catching fish, but precious few lunkers. If you really want a trophy, you may need to leave the party early and go searching.

be less pressured and more likely to take your bait.

• If the wind comes up, a lot of casual anglers will get off the water. If you have a boat that can take the rolling, stay out. Even on pressured waters the fish can go on a rampage, often in shallow, wind-affected water.

• Adopt a strategy similar to that of a basketball team trying to cut a big deficit: run-and-gun.

"We call it the milk route approach," says Jerry Anderson. "You might try this 'move, move, move' all day long. Chances are you won't take more than one fish off any one spot.

What you're looking for is that one active fish out of a pounded or lethargic school. Work an area for five minutes and run to the next. You might hit 50 or more spots in the course of a day that way, and you can put a lot of fish in the boat if you pick up one in every fifth spot. Think of it that way; you're just trying to improve the odds of putting your bait in front of a fish that's willing to bite."

North American Fishing Club members have to face the reality that virgin walleye fisheries are mainly a thing of the past. Save your money and fly in to a remote Canadian lake once or twice in your lifetime, just to feel what it's like to have fish waiting in line to hammer anything you throw in the water.

The rest of your outings, however, will be closer to where your family and job have you anchored. That's life. You have to learn to cope with all types of situations—unstable weather, changing seasons and the fact that you're not the only one who owns a boat and a lake map. Keep a smile on your face and your thinking cap on, and walleye fishing can be rewarding, no matter what the situation.

27

Trophy Walleyes
On Purpose

The Columbia River of the Pacific Northwest is home to perhaps the greatest population of titan walleyes in North America. Most educated observers think the next world record, assuming anyone ever tops Mabry Harper's 25-pound fish from Old Hickory Lake in Tennessee back in 1960, will come from these waters.

Big walleye specialists travel here to try their hand. Gary Roach, Dan Nelson and other members of the fabled Lindy-Little Joe Fishing Team pioneered the way, closely followed by teammates like Dave "Hot Tip" Jenson.

Jenson, of Fargo, North Dakota, knows the Columbia well. During just one extended trip in 1988, he and his party caught 80 walleyes more than 8 eight pounds. Of those, seven topped 14 pounds; 11 weighed more than 13.

The point is, "Hot Tip" knows big walleyes. He thirsts after them. He is willing to rearrange everything in his life for a few days on the Columbia. During that same trip, he hooked a fish that some people say had a chance...you know, the same way baseball announcers watch long fly balls and say things like, 'It's deep, way back, this one has a chance'...to break the world record.

Here's what happened that September night:

"Most of our fish came on the outside rods," Jenson begins, "so I had two friends fishing the outside rods, and I was trolling with the line going straight off the back. It was pitch black, the middle of the night, and all of a sudden my rod bent like it was going right to the bottom of the river. I knew it was a big fish right away, so the other guys got their lines in and we got the motor up.

"Eventually I steered the fish around to where we could get a look at it, and we shined the spotlight on it," Jenson continues. "About 30 to 40 yards away, this fish comes to the top and I mean it was huge, the most ungodly big walleye I've ever seen. I'll guarantee you if it wasn't 20 pounds it wasn't an ounce. Anyway, as this thing comes up and we've got the light on it, we're not saying a thing.

"John Tobolt of Moorhead, Minnesota, is an experienced muskie fisherman," Jenson says, "and I've fished a lot of muskies, so both of us can pretty much estimate the length of a fish within an inch or two and about how much it weighs.

"So anyway," says Jenson, "this fish comes around for a good look and I can't believe it. It's too big to believe it's a walleye, but it's a walleye; we could see it perfectly. It was like a midnight dream, that fish. We were drifting down with the current, and I was fighting the fish and all of a sudden I felt my line go slack. It tightened right up again, but because the light was still on it, I could see that all that was hanging in the fish's mouth was the front treble, just barely nipping the meaty part of the flesh.

"I backed off the drag, because that's all I could do. The thing was finning only about five or six feet from the boat now," Jenson continues. "John was sitting there waiting to take a shot at it with the muskie net, but I kept telling him, 'John, it's too green yet; let it go.' I let the fish go, and she swam down about two or three feet and 'pop' the crankbait came out.

"I lay on the floor, stomped my feet, hit the floor and lay my head on the seat," Jenson admits. "Now, I might cry at a funeral or something, but right there, I was damn close, as close as I've ever come, to crying over a fish."

* * *

It's a safe bet that walleye anglers everywhere would die for a shot at the fish Jenson had on, and that he's not the only one who would cry if it got off. The pursuit of big fish is appealing to beginners, but it can begin to consume veterans like "Hot Tip." Setting the hook into something solid, something really solid, is heart-pounding time. It's too late at that point to check your knots or line, sharpen your hooks or get the landing net out where you can use it.

Trophy walleye hunter, Dan Nelson, knows his fish. He holds the IGFA 20-pound line class world record with a 15-pound, 3-ounce fish from the Columbia River in Oregon. This fish is more than 10 pounds.

Trophy Walleyes On Purpose   293

Big walleyes, like big fish of any kind, feel different, and a seasoned angler knows from the first head-shake what he's got.

"You can feel the distance that head moves back and forth, and that's one sign," says Mike McClelland. "Beyond that, you just know. Big fish don't fight with any panic, they just give you solid, heavy pressure. You know you're in for a battle."

Big walleyes are the dream, and for many, that's what they remain. The average size fish we all catch (unless we live on a secret lake), is almost embarrassingly small, a little more than 1 pound.

"Most walleye fishermen," believes McClelland, "are still looking for their first 5-pound fish."

Why is that? There's a variety of reasons. To catch big walleyes you have to spend time fishing for them, deliberately and consciously directing your efforts their way. Because, our experts say, they may not be in the same places or looking for the same meal as the smaller fish.

This may sound obvious, and you've probably heard it before, but the first rule of lunker hunting is to fish waters that have big walleyes in them. Says Hot Tip Jenson: "You have to go to a place that has big fish, like the Columbia River, the Missouri River system or Greer's Ferry, Lake Erie, Mille Lacs, places like that."

Most walleye anglers recognize all the places Jenson named as being "big water." That's no coincidence. As a rule, large bodies of water will hold more big walleyes than smaller ones. There is more total forage available, and small walleyes do not have to compete as intensively for food. Therefore they have a better opportunity to grow to a larger than average size.

But simply floating your boat over hog-infested waters won't put trophies on the wall. McClelland, who has caught more big walleyes than he can remember, has also caught his share of "cigars," a common term for smallish fish. Experience has taught him to keep looking when babies are biting.

"Big walleyes don't school," he says (although in rare cases, "pods" of big fish are found together). "People catch small fish because they tend to fish schooling fish. I've never found a school of 9-pound walleyes. They don't have to school; see, walleyes don't school for company. That's us again, relating our feelings and thought processes to fish, and that doesn't work. They'll all end up in an area if the right size food is there, but when the food supply is depleted, they scatter in every direction. We have learned that through telemetry studies. So what happens is that forage creates a school, a loose concentration of fish.

"Big fish are very independent," McClelland says. "They're loners, because of the size and variety of food available to them, because they're big. It all makes sense if you think about it. Small fish, on the other hand, are concentrated by a certain size of food.

"In most cases, there's no reason for big fish to be together and compete for food," continues McClelland. "Their food is everywhere. They may be suspended, they may be very shallow in a brush pile or other cover source, or in just about any key spot. They are individuals, and you have to learn that if you want to fish them. One thing is for sure: there won't be 1-pounders with them, because the big fish will eat them. Different size walleyes just don't hang around together in most cases."

Dan Nelson, another admitted trophy addict, agrees. "Small walleyes are a lot easier to catch," he says, "partly because there are more of them. But they're also much more competitive feeders. In a big school, you might say it's first come, first served. It's not that way at all with big fish."

The lure of quick action, and the hope that the next bite might be a big one, are what prevent most of us from catching more good fish, McClelland believes.

"Anglers' biggest mistake," he says, "is that they go find the first walleyes that will bite, and they never leave them. They think that sooner or later a bigger fish is going to come along, but it will probably never happen to them in their lifetime. They have to go fish big fish."

Now, again, even McClelland admits that this isn't always the case. In some systems, fish of different sizes will be found in the same general areas—with the biggest ones commanding the best feeding positions. But he maintains that more big walleyes are caught by accident than by design. Bass fishermen casting plastic worms into prime shallow cover, crappie anglers soaking minnows in the weeds, kids fishing off docks, muskie fishermen casting big baits, all "luck" into trophy walleyes over the course of every season.

"Ninety-nine percent of them are taken in shallow water, in locations you wouldn't consider walleye spots," McClelland says.

He's probably right.

So, to take fish, you have to leave the party early. Catch a few smaller fish to satisfy your need to set the hook, then look elsewhere. McClelland searches potential shallow-water feeding lies, as he details in the section on shallow walleyes (chapter 21). His tournament partner, Bob Propst, goes the other way, to nearby deep-water haunts.

Near boats that are "jerking lips" (another favorite term of anglers), you might expect to see Propst probing the deeper water, searching for individual "hooks" on his sonar unit, dragging Lindy Rigs with large live bait on them. It's a slow process, a search in every sense of the word, but if you really want a bigger fish, the reward is worth waiting—and working—for.

Another Dakota-type experience brought this to life for me a few years ago. Dan Nelson and I were taking a few days to fish the Mobridge area of Lake Oahe (Missouri River), another of those working weeks on the water in Nelson's "second office" (a 16-foot Yar-Craft).

Everybody was bringing in limits. Lines were forming at the public fish-cleaning tables. But the biggest fish in anybody's stash was about 3 pounds—except ours. By cleverly staying in the front seat of the boat, I followed Nelson to deep flooded railroad grades, shallow wind-affected flats and shorelines, and other isolated spots.

In three days, we rarely fished in the vicinity of other boats, though there were plenty out there. Smug smiles were replaced with looks of disbelief when we hoisted the only two fish we kept, an $8^1/_2$- and a 9-pounder, for photos.

We caught others, far from the crowds.

Tempting A Big Fish

One more piece of advice that resounds from every top trophy hunter: use bigger-than-normal baits.

"Whenever I go for big fish, I'm using big bait," says Jenson. "I'm talking about big crankbaits, huge jumbo leeches, minnows up to 8 or 10 inches long. Catching big fish is fairly simple, but it just takes a time commitment. Fish in the right locations and use big baits."

He mentioned crankbaits. That word—surprisingly to many walleye anglers—is magic to anglers in the know. "Crankbaits are big walleye baits," says Jenson. "We have proven this to ourselves many times, and other people will tell you the same thing."

Complete Angler's Library

It's been theorized that crankbaits, especially bigger ones, not only look right to big fish, but they feel right to their lateral lines. The exaggerated wobble registers "big, satisfying meal" to their predatory instincts. There is no unanimous rule of thumb for depth, retrieve speed, or action for triggering bigger fish, so experimentation is needed.

"In general, though," says Don Palmer, a highly respected guide and tournament angler from Mobridge, "you want to work in a stop-and-go action." Palmer is famous for his ability to troll up monsters when others are catching dinks, by using the "Palmer Drop," a series of movements where he pulls the bait forward, speeding it up, followed by a pause that lets the bait stall and flutter. Vicious strikes often come during the pause.

Many top walleye fishermen prefer the No. 9 Deep Lindy Baitfish, the No. 9 Lindy Shadling, the No. 18 Floating or Magnum Rapala or the larger Bombers, such as the 25A. To look these baits over, you might not consider them walleye ammo. A few big fish, though, will quickly change your mind.

One secretive southern Minnesota trophy walleye specialist who fishes at night on the huge lakes of the Canadian shield re-

Big walleyes key in on the "feel" (vibration) given off by big crankbaits. Lunker-slayers include (from left): Lindy's No. 9 Deep Baitfish, No. 9 Deep Shadling and Rapala's No. 18 floating minnow. A No. 7 Shad Rap is shown for size comparison.

veals that he has "a tackle box full of one thing." His secret? No. 18 silver-and-black Rapalas, which he retrieves slowly over shallow rocks, weed edges and incoming rivers.

"Big" can mean more than physical size, according to Dan Nelson. Years ago, he discovered that replacing the smaller willow-leaf blades on his spinner rigs with larger, No. 5 Colorado blades yielded bigger walleyes.

"The size of the bait is not as important as what the fish thinks the bait is," Nelson reasons. "The vibrations given off by a No. 5 Colorado blade are something the fish recognize as a meal of big proportions. Especially in dirtier water—although that isn't always the case, either, because they can work well in clear water— the bigger blades can make a big difference."

To "call" specifically to bigger fish, then, you need to make a big sound. Remember that, and arm yourself with the right stuff.

Chasing lunkers can get into your blood. It's another side of fishing that takes years to refine, and it's very difficult to cover thoroughly on paper. It demands an on-the-water commitment from you.

Here are a few final tips from our panel:

• Big walleyes are spooky. That's how they get to be that big. So the angler must also be cautious, moving slowly and quietly. When casting or trolling, fish from a distance. Make long casts. Troll with at least 100 to 150 feet of line behind the boat.

• Shut off your big motor long before you reach actual fishing territory. Drift in quietly, or sneak with an electric motor. Many top anglers believe it's worse to turn an electric on and off than to turn it on low and leave it running all the time.

• This doesn't always pay off, but consider fishing waters known to have walleyes, but not good numbers. These "sleepers" can have the fish of a lifetime. Don't make a career out of getting skunked, but give them a fair shot.

• Again, this is not a cure-all, but night fishing can yield a lot of big walleyes. Prime candidates: ultra-clear water, and lakes with heavy boating and/or fishing pressure.

• There are also seasonal variations in big-fish vulnerability. The "scarce forage" periods of spring and fall force all fish to search longer each day for food. Late fall is a famous time for eye-popping catches, mainly because female fish (which most trophies tend to be) feed heavily at that time of year. They require abun-

Late autumn is a good time to bust big walleyes. You may have to face cold, stiff winds, but dandies like these certainly reward the effort.

Trophy Walleyes On Purpose

dant nourishment to develop the eggs that will be deposited the next spring. Try steep-breaking structures that lead off shallow food shelves into deep water (down to 70 feet or more in many cases!). Work slowly with very big minnows on live-bait rigs or jigs, or slowly troll big deep-running crankbaits. Also work the shallow shelf areas.

It can mean putting up with some mean weather, but it can also be the end of your search for a 5-pounder. Or an 8-pounder. Or a 10-pounder.

28

Walleyes: What's In Store?

We've reached the final chapter, a time for pondering what happens to our characters after the book ends. The number of anglers is growing. Fishing may one day become the most popular participative sport in North America. The average fisherman is much more knowledgeable and proficient than just a few years ago.

For a long time we operated in naivete believing that sportfishermen could not have a significant impact on fish populations. We know better now; in less than a summer, a parade of high-tech boats with "good sticks" (slang for deadly anglers) can change the balance of a small- to medium-sized body of water by creaming off large numbers of adult walleyes.

Today's anglers are generally good, but they all seem to want to get better. How-to fishing education has become big business, with professionals waiting in line to fill seminar-goers, readers and television or video viewers with the latest hot methods.

To paraphrase a popular saying, "They ain't making any more walleye lakes." That's not entirely true, if you consider the possibility of future reservoir construction. But it's true in spirit. We are dealing with a finite amount of water, and an increasing number of walleye fishermen, who are better at catching fish. You don't have to be a genius, as they say, to realize something has to give somewhere.

Providing Walleyes For The Future

There is no magic cure, no instant puddin', for filling the water with big, hard-fighting walleyes waiting to bite our hooks. Entrusted with the management of fish stocks, and often embattled for their efforts, are state, provincial and federal fisheries biologists, researchers and managers. They're in a tough position, and they know it all too well.

"We're asked to balance the wishes of many groups," says Don Peirera, a former fisheries biologist who is working on a Ph.D. in applied statistical analysis, hoping someday to develop complex computer models for managing fisheries. "You take any lake anywhere in the United States or Canada, and you're going to have crappie fishermen who want more crappies, bass fishermen who want more bass, northern pike or muskie fishermen, walleye fishermen, catfish fishermen and on down the line. And they all want bigger fish, too."

Peirera points out that there's only room in any given system for so many pounds of fish per acre of water, a biological concept called carrying capacity, which is influenced by the fertility of the water and other factors. And, as he says, certain lakes are naturally meant for walleyes and others aren't.

So, you have this variety of systems throughout North America:

• Some with ecological "holes" for walleyes to fill;

• Some with good or formerly good walleye populations that can be maintained or bolstered through management efforts;

• Others where you can artificially build walleye populations with stocking, often at the expense of other species;

• And others that will never support good numbers of walleyes. Zealous anglers who live on or near this latter type of lake don't want to hear about such things if they like to fish walleyes. They just want natural resources people to come and dump trash cans full of walleyes into "their" water, which they support with tax dollars.

There will always be a place for stocking in walleye management. If we are going to continue expanding the fish's range, which is planned in certain cases, it's the only way to get started. And in waters that will sustain walleye life but lack good spawning habitat, a "put-and-take" fishery, as it's called, can be created and sustained with stocking.

Stocking will definitely put walleyes into a system, but the makeup of that system will help determine whether a quality fishery develops. And in some cases, walleyes might become part of the picture at the expense of other species.

Rehabilitating once-great walleye fisheries, even on huge, sprawling waters, can be accomplished by initial stockings that let the fish take a new hold. For instance, stocking helped revive the walleye fisheries in once-proud Great Lakes walleye waters at Saginaw Bay, Green Bay and Little and Big Bays de Noc—after water quality was restored. There are other examples.

But, fisheries professionals realize walleye numbers in those waters could never be maintained, much less built, through artificial means. The hope is, given an abundance of spawning habitat, the populations will multiply through natural reproduction.

The consensus among scientists seems to be that stocking should be reserved for situations with a high demand for walleyes, and chances that a fair percentage will be caught by anglers. Stocking has been successful in small lakes that "freeze out" occasionally in winter. "You can gamble with inexpensive fry in those situations," walleye researcher Dennis Schupp says, "and hope you get enough years between freeze-outs to provide some excellent short-term walleye fishing."

After all, fisheries management is run with budgetary constraints, just like any other business. And the cost of stocking

Walleyes: What's In Store?

walleyes is high; much, much higher than most anglers would imagine.

Even in places like walleye-rich Minnesota, which has an impressive hatchery network, less than 5 percent of all walleyes caught have been stocked. Estimates conclude that even if fishermen dedicated all license dollars to providing more walleyes, each angler would be entitled to take home three or four walleyes per year.

Sometimes local sportsman's groups will buy walleye fingerlings to stock in a pet lake. They usually pay about $1 apiece for them. Generously assuming that 5 or 10 percent survive until they reach about 1 pound in weight, and figuring about $3^1/_2$ percent of those will reach the angler's creel, based on several studies, those people just paid $25 to $30 to catch each of those 1-pound fish. The economics are not real bright.

Stocking, as you can see, is a management tool, not a cure-all. You have to ask tough questions, not the least of which is, "Does everyone want walleyes in Lake XYZ?" Research shows that introducing walleyes into some systems cuts into the number and size of other species like largemouth bass. Like so many things, stocking should be reserved for situations where it can make a bang for the buck, and fisheries professionals—armed with public opinion and scientific perspective, which average citizens too often lack—should decide when and where to apply its tonic.

It is rare for special regulations to be applied to stocked lakes; after all, the whole goal of stocking is to return as many walleyes as possible to the angler's creel. By letting us "at 'em" right away, stocking money is better spent. But, when special regulations are applied, several options are considered:

• *Minimum size limits*, where you make anglers throw back walleyes under a certain length, can help in systems with a high food supply but low walleye numbers. Giving each walleye a better chance to survive from year to year and feed on the abundant forage, can build a quality fishery in time.

• *Slot limits*, where anglers can keep smaller and very large fish but have to release those within a designated length range, can work where fishermen want to catch more big walleyes.

This management tool would not likely be applied unless the lake had strong natural reproduction. The whole purpose is to provide a fishery with a higher percentage of larger, adult fish by protecting the medium-sized fish, tomorrow's lunkers. "What you're trying to do," says Schupp, "is tie up more of your biomass in larger, adult walleyes."

But hey, hold the phone. What's all this about letting walleyes go? They're good to eat, right?

A Candidate For Catch-And-Release

Sportfishermen, people with one or two lines apiece, can catch enough walleyes to affect a population. We haven't always known that, believing as humans do that good things can last forever. During the 1970s, when the modern revolution in fishing tactics and equipment found its way to a good percentage of anglers, there was one main way to define success: a fanned-out stringer of dead fish you had to struggle to hold up for a picture.

The leaders of this thinking—and they can't be blamed because they probably didn't know what they were causing—were the emerging teaching pros, whose badge of office was an 8x10 glossy of impressive stiffs hanging from meat hooks. They signed them for adoring fans, who wished they could be like the pros.

"We really thought we could catch all those fish," remembers Dan Nelson, who heads up perhaps the most prestigious lineup of today's walleye pros, the Lindy-Little Joe Fishing Team, "and still leave plenty for everybody else."

Nelson and others like him have become the most ardent proponents of catch-and-release walleye fishing. They've all been walked through the same figures found in chapter 6 about how many walleyes live to be barely catchable size, and the scary few that beat the odds to become decent fish.

The facts stare back at us like the unblinking brilliance of a walleye eye hit with a spotlight. In recent years, anglers have seen the decline of many walleye fisheries. They still have an unquenchable thirst for solid bites, and they still want to produce a Polaroid of themselves beaming from behind a "whooee" stringer of adult walleyes. What's going to happen?

"The answer to that one is really quite simple," says Dennis Schupp. "We have to kill fewer walleyes."

Catch-and-release fishing involves personal restraint on the part of the angler, even in many instances where the law says it's OK to fill your livewell. In recent years, spot road checks by game wardens have turned up disappointing compliance with existing, fairly liberal, fish limits (violations have been uncovered in nearly half of all vehicles stopped in some cases). How can we expect voluntary help from these same anglers?

Even if we accept the idea of putting some of our catches back in the water, do released walleyes live? Scientific studies on the subject answer a resounding yes.

Three separate studies done in the 1980s involving catching, releasing and monitoring survival of released walleyes turned up a worst-case scenario of about 10 percent dying after being immediately returned to the water. Not surprisingly, mortality has been shown to be higher for walleyes caught on live bait—which tends to result in more fish being hooked deep in the throat—than those caught on artificial lures. In one study, virtually no deaths could be attributed to catching walleyes on artificial lures, then releasing them.

Keeping a walleye in a livewell before letting it go appears to cut into survival, but not much. At a recent walleye tournament on Mille Lacs Lake in central Minnesota, biologists monitored the weigh-in procedure, kept fish in holding pens in 12 feet of water for five days, then checked fish condition before releasing the survivors. The result? About 60 percent lived, despite being pounded across big waves to the weigh-in site and carried in plastic bags to a series of measurement and weight scales before being returned to the water in the holding pens.

These numbers indicate that walleyes are not as fragile as once thought, and that they are, indeed, good candidates for catch-and-release practices.

"A released fish is a stocked fish," the biologists like to say. A stocked fish that in most cases was reared in the wild, they might add.

Still, walleyes, like other fish, should be handled carefully before being released.

Evidence mounts from all sides, telling us that we are going to have to build new images of fishing success. The scars of human pollution are still growing, despite our best efforts to clean up our collective act. More, rather than fewer, health alerts advise us not to eat fish from contaminated waters. Some are exaggerated or without foundation, but many others are real and should be heeded for personal safety. In some regions, the future could dictate catch-and-release, even for reluctant participants.

Tournament studies show that walleyes kept in livewells before being released don't survive as well as those released immediately after being caught. Still, enough "livewelled" fish do survive that you can consider letting them go even after driving around with them.

The Role Of Tournaments

Competition pervades our society. The age-old way of "proving" who is better at something is to decide it with a contest. We shower glory on winners, winners at anything and at any level.

Fishing tournaments are here to stay. The father of walleye competition, the Masters Walleye Circuit (MWC), brought together the best fishing and product-making talent, moved them from town to town, and provided the common grounds to shake out what works where, and to design better walleye fishing tackle and equipment.

There are concerned bystanders who fear the competitive fishing process organizes and glorifies the gang rape of waters. Actually, the reverse is probably true. Yes, it accelerates our learning curve and gives new methods for catching more fish to anyone who taps into the loop. But often with increased proficiency comes increased control and stewardship. Contestants on the MWC circuit are asked to contribute to a voluntary conservation fund, which practically all of them do. At each tournament stop, local natural resources officials are presented with a check earmarked for walleye study and work.

Yes, the tournament anglers catch a lot of fish. Weigh-ins sometimes appall the locals. "If they didn't come here, think of all the fish that would still be out there," one spectator was heard saying at an MWC event.

But if we were to examine his boat, we would undoubtedly see the refinements—the fruits of the touring pro's efforts—reflected in his boat and his gear.

New skunk-breakers filter their way to the public through all the how-to media outlets, and the next year, boats everywhere are trying new ways of catching walleyes.

You see, you can't hide from knowledge. To close our eyes to advancing fishing skills, better boats and finer equipment would be a form of censorship foreign to North American thinking. Tomorrow's walleye fishing will be made or lost through the conscience of tomorrow's more proficient walleye fishermen.

What's in store, then, for our main character? The answer could be many things. Whatever happens, the future of walleye fishing would appear to be in all of our hands. If we continue to keep all the fish we catch, walleye numbers—and size—will drop. But if we—all of us—practice catch-and-release, the future of walleye fishing looks very bright indeed!

Index

banana-shaped heads, 246
detecting bites, 249-250
hook size, 253
line weight, 253
round-ball heads, 246
swimming heads, 246
wedge-shaped heads, 246

K

Kavajecz, Keith, 72, 109-112, 237, 283
Kiedrowski, Gary, 164

L

Lake Erie, 29, 30, 32, 60, 139, 161, 162, 189, 263
Lake Huron, 30, 32
Lake Michigan, 32, 283
Lake Oahe, 25, 30, 33, 186, 280
Lake of the Woods, 32, 162, 227, 286
Lake Okoboji, 288
Lake Oneida, 60
Lake Sakakawea, 29, 32, 153, 164, 263
Lake Sharpe, 186
Lake St. Clair, 32
Lake Winnebago, 283
Lakes, 27-36, 137, 139, 144, 167-184, 210
    eutrophic, 171, 181-183
    eutrophication, 171
    mesotrophic, 171, 176-181
    oligotrophic, 171-176
Lateral lines, 50, 52, 161, 208, 211
Leader, 258
Leeches, 148, 230, 232, 233-234, 253
Light conditions, 46, 47-49
Lindner, Al, 78, 254-255
Lindner, Ron, 78, 254-255
Line weight, 253, 258, 263
Live bait, 150, 229-235, 254-260, 273, 288
Log book, 159
Loran-C, 109, 119-120, 129-134
    accuracy, 131-132
    display, 130-131
    ethical issues, 132-134
    installing, 119-120

line-of-position, 130
master stations, 129
secondary stations, 129
time difference, 130
waypoint, 130
L-serine profile, 55-56
Lures, 235-239, 263

M

Maggots, 231
Manual battery charger, 77, 81
Masters Walleye Circuit (MWC), 7, 8, 13, 95
McClelland, Mike, 16-18, 20, 74-75, 128, 139, 148-150, 157, 162, 167, 177, 190, 199, 207, 211-213, 214, 236, 241, 248, 251-252, 256-258, 287, 294
Meline, Alan, 173, 227
Mesotrophic lakes, 171, 176-181
Mille Lacs Lake, 32, 159, 242, 266
Minnows, 159, 192, 211, 231, 254
Missouri River, 29, 32, 39, 189, 261, 262, 263, 278
Mitzel, Bill, 278
Mortality rate, 60
Motion-sensitive cells, 50-51
Mud flats, 190

N

Near-field displacement, 52
Nelson, Dan, 16, 20, 25, 32, 153, 164, 229, 262-263, 288, 291, 295
Neustrom, Tom, 96, 152, 156, 178, 212, 243, 251
Night running lights, 86
Nightcrawler, 148, 231, 235, 254

O

Oligotrophic lakes, 171-176
Outboard motors, 22
Oxygen content, 157

P

Paddles, 77, 86
Palmer, Don, 280